LONG LOAN

This book is issued for 3 weeks with automatic
newal for up to 12 weeks unless it is recalled
another user.

the book is   called within the initial loan
period it mu   re   ned with in that period.
t is recalle   riod   ust

SOMERSET
AND ALL THE MAUGHAMS

ROBIN MAUGHAM

. . . All well-known writers in swarms do it,
Somerset and all the Maughams do it. . . .

NOËL COWARD

LONGMANS · HEINEMANN

LONDON

Longmans, Green & Co Ltd
48 Grosvenor Street, London W1
and associated companies, branches and representatives
throughout the world

William Heinemann Ltd
London Melbourne Toronto
Cape Town Auckland

© 1966 Robin Maugham
First published 1966

Made and printed in Great Britain by
William Clowes and Sons, Limited, London and Beccles

For
NOËL

CONTENTS

Part I

Part II

LIST OF ILLUSTRATIONS

ACKNOWLEDGEMENTS

In the research and writing of this book, many people helped me. Of these, my first thanks are to Mrs M. A. J. Langford and Mr Stephen Goard, both members of the Society of Genealogists, who made many interesting discoveries about my family and guided my own researches. Other scholars I especially wish to thank include Mr Patrick Montague-Smith, Dr P. H. Reaney, Professor A. H. Smith, Dr Melville Richards, Mr Philip H. Blake, Mr C. Roy Hudleston, and the anonymous researchers at the Office de Documentation of the Bibliothèque Nationale in Paris. I also acknowledge my grateful thanks to Miss Harriet Scofield, Mrs Carmen Jordan, and Major John W. Parker, in Ohio; the librarian at Falmouth in Cornwall, and the librarians at St Servan and Le Mans in France. Others who encouraged me include Monsieur P. Messinesi, Mr A. D. Macleod Robinson, Mr R. F. V. Heuston, my American kinsman Ralph S. Maugham, Canon C. E. Waynforth, the Rev. Paul A. B. Cory, the Rev. A. G. W. Dixon, Mr A. E. Windass, and the Rev. A. J. Sowden; Mr S. Pywell, Mr J. G. Westmoreland, Mr J. G. Brogden, the late Miss Dorothy Yarde, Mr N. F. Burt, the Rev. J. P. P. Newell, Mr H. M. P. Davies, Mr J. R. Smith, Dr P. T. Northover, and Dr and Mrs John Nesfield. Such a list of names may seem coldly formal, but I could never have written this book without their patient and generous kindness to myself and my research assistant, Derek Peel.

The text of the book in itself records the help that Derek Peel gave me, and I can only add my personal gratitude to him. Lastly I wish to thank my friends Miss G. B. Stern and Noël Coward for allowing me to read their long correspondence with my uncle Willie; and I would also like to thank Alan Searle, my uncle's devoted companion and friend for so many years, whose sympathetic interest inspired me throughout my long task.

R. M.

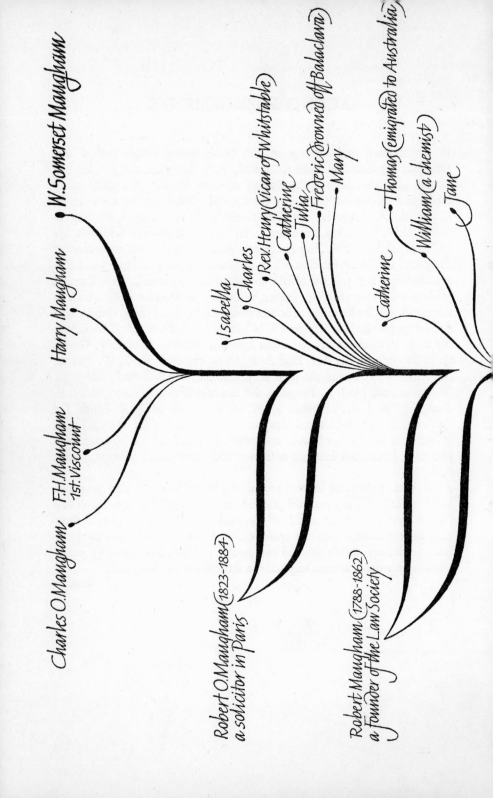

William Mangham (born 1751) a clerk in London

Agnes
Isabella
Margaret
Edward
Elizabeth
John
Thomas

Robert Mangham (1732–1815) a glazier in Appleby

Susanna
William Tutt
William Farrington (a hatter)
John
Lucy (who emigrated to Ohio)
Thomas Marmaduke (a cabinet maker)
George (a farmer)
Theophilus (a sailor)
Robert (a grocer)
Charles
Francis (a bookbinder)

Rev. William Mangham (1726–1814) Vicar of Moulton

Isobel

② ①

Charles
John
Elenor
Sarah
Christopher

William Mangham (c.1680–1771) a Farmer in Brough, Westmorland

Part One

Part One

THE VILLAGE SCHOOLMASTER

MY father, Frederic Herbert Maugham, was fifty when I was born; my uncle, William Somerset Maugham, was forty-two years older than I was. This disparity in age seemed to increase rather than to decrease as I grew up. The two old men loomed over my early years like a couple of ogres. Sometimes the ogres were benevolent, sometimes they most definitely were not, but without any doubt both of them were powerful, important, and immensely successful. My father reached the top of his profession as a lawyer and became Lord Chancellor of England; my uncle was one of the highest paid and most celebrated authors of the first half of the twentieth century.

As a child I often heard my parents and my three elder sisters talk about Uncle Willie. I knew that he was famous because he wrote stories and plays; I vaguely sensed that he was mysterious; and I had dim memories of an attractive man with a skin the colour of parchment visiting the nursery.

He probably only came to look at me because of my mother. Although in a fit of exasperation my uncle Willie once told her that she was the kind of Englishwoman whose idea of bliss was to eat cold mutton in a howling draught – he had spent a wind-swept week-end at her cottage in Littlestone – my uncle was devoted to her. My mother was one of the very few women about whom he never said anything unkind or bitter. And so fond of her was he that when I was seven or eight he asked her to bring me to lunch with him at the Savoy.

I was thrilled at the prospect of going to a place that sounded rather like a palace.

'What happens at the Savoy?' I asked my French governess.

'The Savoy!' Mademoiselle Vogne cried. 'Will he then take you *there*?'

'Why shouldn't he?' I asked.

'Because the Savoy is a *mauvais lieu*,' Mademoiselle Vogne from

Dijon replied. 'It is a wicked place where wicked men take wicked women.'

'What do they do there?'

Mademoiselle Vogne sighed. I now realise that it was a sigh of envy.

'They eat oysters,' she replied, 'and they drink champagne.'

Well, that was it. The words struck home. I realised that with my mother present I hadn't a hope of drinking any champagne, but I was firmly determined to eat oysters.

The great day came. I was dressed in my best suit. In the taxi my mother pinched my cheeks because she said I looked sallow. We walked in through the revolving doors of the hotel, and there we saw a man – even sallower than I was – waiting to greet us. He led the way to a table in the restaurant. The head waiter handed a vast menu-card to each of us. I looked at it hastily but I could see no mention of oysters. Then I noticed – right at the bottom of the list of *hors d'œuvres* – the magic word 'Oysters'. And beside the word was written 'Special Supplement'.

'Now, Robin, what would you like?' my uncle Willie asked after my mother had ordered. '*Hors d'œuvres* to start with?'

'Thank you,' I said nervously.

So Uncle Willie began to read out the list.

'Smoked salmon or potted shrimps?'

I made no reply, but I looked at him hopefully. Patiently my uncle, who had begun to stammer slightly, read out the list to the very end. I remained dumb.

'Oysters?' he suggested at last in despair.

'Yes, please,' I cried. 'Yes, *please*.'

Uncle Willie took out his monocle, fixed it into position, and stared at me in gloomy silence. Then he spoke.

'You would be unlike the rer-rest of the younger members of your family,' he remarked sadly, 'if you did not prefer the most expensive.'

Suddenly he smiled at me, and I knew that I'd got my oysters.

*

Later in my life, on the rare occasions when my father and my uncle Willie were in the same room together, I used to look at the pair of them and wonder where they sprang from. Where did their roots lie?

I knew, of course, that their father had been a solicitor in Paris, and

I knew that their grandfather had been one of the founders of the Law Society in England. But what then? Whence did *that* bad-tempered old man come? Who were *his* parents. No one knew.

'Where do the Maughams come from?' I asked my father one day at lunch.

'From the north of England,' he answered. 'We must be quite an old family. You may have seen our coat-of-arms on my bookplate and the family crest on my silver.'

I had indeed. My mother had shown them to me when I was a child and I had been most impressed. My father was always very proud of his coat-of-arms and crest. I am glad that he died without discovering they were both completely bogus.*

'Our crest looks rather distinguished,' my father continued. 'In fact, it has been suggested that we are descended from John of Gaunt.'

'Can't we find out?'

'How would you suggest finding out?'

My mother had been throwing scraps of food to the chaffinches on the bird-table on the terrace outside the dining-room. She now came back and sat down opposite my father.

'Why don't you go to a genealogist?' my mother suggested.

My father put his monocle up to his eye and stared at her mournfully across the mahogany table.

'My dear Nellie,' he said, 'genealogists are most expensive. It might take a considerable time, and no income could stand it.'

When my father became a Judge his income had dropped to a tenth of what it had been when he was the leading Chancery barrister. But even when he was making forty thousand pounds a year he had worried about money, and the phrase 'no income could stand it' was frequently heard by my mother and the four children. If we wanted a theatre ticket, a wrist-watch, or a genealogist, and my father said 'no income could stand it', we knew we were done for.

My mother sighed.

'Genealogists aren't all that expensive,' she said.

'My dear Nellie, you know nothing whatever about such matters,' my father replied. 'Genealogists cost a fortune. If Robin is so anxious to find out about the family, why doesn't he try to interest my brother

* See Appendix I.

Willie in the affair? We all know that *Willie* has plenty of money to throw away.'

So the next time I was asked to stay with my uncle at his villa on the French Riviera, I brought up the matter.

'So I thought you might like to employ a genealogist,' I concluded hopefully.

Willie, as I called Somerset Maugham from the time I was seventeen, was sitting in a heavily-padded wickerwork chair on the terrace outside the drawing-room with a glass of champagne in his hand. He stared at me in silence.

'What makes you think so?' he asked after a pause.

'Don't you *want* to find out about the family?' I asked.

Willie never used two words when he could use only one.

'No,' he replied.

'Don't you want to know where you come from?'

'Ner-no,' Willie said, using his stammer as he sometimes could to give balance to a sentence. 'I der-don't care a tinker's cuss.'

So there was no hope of getting my uncle to finance the project, and I abandoned it, for I hadn't the spare time to attempt it myself. Before the war I was reading for the Bar; during the war I was a soldier; and after the war – when my head-wound made it impossible for me to be a barrister – I was trying to learn how to write: I was both poor and struggling.

However, in June 1952, *The Genealogists' Magazine* unexpectedly came out with a fascinating and scholarly article entitled: 'Two Royal Descents of Viscount Maugham, Lord Chancellor 1938–1939, and Mr W. Somerset Maugham', which traced back the descent of the two brothers to King Edward the First of England and his wife Eleanor of Castile.* Copies of the magazine were sent to my father and my uncle. My father was extremely impressed. He turned triumphantly to my sister Kate, who was sitting at the end of the table.

'I hope you appreciate that they have traced us back to a King of England – just as I told you,' he said.

'Why don't we try to find a genealogist to explore further?' Kate asked.

My father fumbled for his monocle.

'Because no . . .'

* See p. 93 (Chapter 7).

'No income could stand it,' Kate chimed in, completing the sentence for him.

My uncle Willie's reaction, as usual, was quite different. He was amused by the article. It tickled him to think that royal blood flowed in his veins.

'I'm *terribly* impressed,' he said with a sarcastic smile. 'But I suppose you've noticed that almost all the descents are in the female line. And I think we should keep it dark that we're descended from those Edwards. As you know, King Edward the Second was a notorious pervert, and I wouldn't like my blameless reputation to be sullied. Didn't the Maughams have *any* reputable ancestors?'

'Don't you think we might find a genealogist who could search into the *male* line of the family?' I asked.

'I der-don't see why not,' Willie said. 'And now that four of your novels have been bought for the films you must be rolling in money; you can easily afford to pay for it.'

'That wasn't quite my idea,' I said.

'I didn't think it was,' Willie replied.

But though I was no longer 'poverty stricken' – to use one of Willie's favourite terms – I was too intent on forming my own life to spare the time to explore the shadows of my ancestry. Some years before the war a remote cousin had died and left me a shabby old chintz-covered box containing a bundle of papers and a charming water-colour drawing of 'The Rev. William Maugham of Moulton, Lincolnshire, and his Clerk' with the date '*c.* 1795'. I had been too busy, then, with Bar exams, to do more than glance at the papers. I had stored the box in a corner of my study. But I had had the picture framed and hung near my desk because I was amused by its robust Rowlandson quality of caricature. I was fascinated by the obvious, though not very flattering, resemblance between this eighteenth-century clergyman and his sophisticated twentieth-century namesake. I once even thought of giving the picture to Willie when I next stayed with him at the Villa Mauresque. But I don't think he would have appreciated the gift. He once said to me, 'I der-don't like the clergy.'

It was the chance remark of a guest at lunch that really made me dig back into the story of 'Somerset and all the Maughams' – to use Noël Coward's phrase. An old friend, Derek Peel, glanced at the picture of the priest and remarked: '*Who* was the Reverend William Maugham?'

'I've no idea,' I replied.

'You don't know if he was your direct ancestor or merely a vague kinsman?'

'No.'

'Wouldn't it be interesting to find out?'

'Very,' I replied, wishing that I wasn't in the middle of a film-script.

At that moment I remembered that Derek Peel was an enthusiast in historical research and an expert at it.

'I suppose you wouldn't care to look through the papers, would you?' I asked.

'I'd like to,' Derek replied, so I took out the chintz-covered box of papers and he went off with it under his arm.

I was still asleep when he telephoned me early next morning.

'This is fascinating material,' he said. 'Give me a while to follow it up. You've got the bones of a good story here.'

And so the search began.

*

From the bundle of papers I had inherited we knew that the Reverend William had several links with Stamford in Lincolnshire. He had married a local girl, and their descendants had spread all over the country. We did not expect our visit to yield any more tangible reminder of the parson and his family than a faded entry or two in the parish register, but we decided to go up to Lincolnshire on the trail of our first clue – the Reverend William Maugham of Moulton, *circa* 1795.

*

My worries about the film-script that I had sent off the previous day grew less hectic after we had left the London express at Peterborough and changed into a slow, old-fashioned train that chuffed peacefully between the fields and rich pastureland of Lincolnshire. Stamford is a lovely market-town in the Welland Valley, with a river running quietly between grassy meadows. Graceful church-spires rise above grey stone houses that seem to have been dug out of the earth rather than imposed on it by builders. Though the town reminded me of Cambridge in miniature, I felt that I was in a different world – a world in which I was delighted that my kinsmen should have been born, and this feeling was intensified by the first person we met. The porter on the platform must have been six-foot-four tall. His creased face was harsh yet benign. I told him we were going to stay at the George Hotel and asked if he could get us a taxi.

'There's no need for a taxi,' he said firmly. 'It's quite near. You walk there, and I'll bring your bags on a trolley.'

I bowed to a will stronger than my own, the porter disappeared, and we strolled slowly along the lane that led to the George. By the time we reached the hotel we discovered that the huge porter had put our luggage in the front hall and was striding happily away through the back yard without waiting for any tip, so I had to run after him.

I wonder if the Reverend William Maugham ever visited the George Hotel, for it was famous in his day as a stopping-place for coaches on their way between London and York. Had he any curiosity – any sense of history? Did he realise that the George was built on the site of one of the ancient 'hospitals' of the Knights of St John of Jerusalem? I knew this because I had read about it before I went in to dinner. The food, served by Italian waiters, was as good as any we had eaten outside London. I thought of the Reverend William, with a great tankard of ale set on the board in front of him, tucking in to four hefty slices of roast beef. I suppose this is how the English always picture their Georgian ancestors at table. But I fear that William could seldom have afforded such luxuries – especially after his marriage, for I had gathered from the papers in the chintz box that he had been poor throughout his life. 'Positively poverty-stricken', as Willie would have put it.

That first afternoon in Stamford we strolled through the grey streets of the town and paused to peer into the windows of an antique shop, and there on a shelf we saw a glazed pottery christening-mug with the name 'Margreat Maughan' on it and the date 1849, so I went in and bought it. (I have since learned that Maughan is a quite common variation of the spelling of the surname.) Later, moving towards the heart of the town, we wandered into the little graveyard around the church of St George which is closely linked with the earlier Knights of the Order of the Garter. Most of the upright tombstones had been moved back against the walls, and we glanced at them casually, not believing that we should be so fortunate as to make two discoveries on our first day. But there, close to the east end of the church, was a stone. I had to kneel down to decipher some of the lettering, and I read: 'Sacred to the memory of Thomas Marmaduke Maugham, who departed this life on Sep. 16, 1839. Aged 71. And of Frances his wife, who died April 11, 1838. Aged 74.'

Margreat and Marmaduke in one afternoon – I was certainly being drawn closer into the Maugham story.

*

That night, before going to bed, I spread out some maps and I read chapters of two books on the county[1] to prepare myself for the quest next day – to the village of Moulton, near Spalding, twenty miles or so to the north-east. It was there that the Reverend William Maugham had lived for half a century as Master of the Free Grammar School, until his death in 1814.

We set off early, with a surprising driver. He had been a stone-mason for many years, but he had given up the work because the dust was ruining his health. He had helped to restore churches all over the county, and he knew every one of them intimately. He pointed out each new spire that rose beyond the wide fields, and told us its story, with a craftsman's quiet appreciation. And he was – fortunately for us – the kind of man who appears to know everything about the countryside he inhabits. The district through which we drove is called Holland, and the name is appropriate, for the landscape is as flat as the fields about the Zuider Zee, with acres of tulips and daffodils and an occasional house with a Dutch look about it – a touch of Vermeer against the vast Fenland sky.

Waiting for us at the door of the mellow church of All Saints was the vicar of Moulton, the Reverend Paul Cory. He was a tall, lean man with a vigorous voice and a tang of the Navy about him. He was obviously good-natured, efficient, and sincere. Had my uncle Willie met him, his literary imagination might have seized on the vicar's handsome external appearance, adapted his character, and transplanted him into the South Seas, where the priest would have ended up floating face downward in a lagoon, or playing a trumpet in a dance-hall in Fiji.

As we gazed up at the graceful fourteenth-century perpendicular tower of All Saints, with its crocketed spire, I tried to transpose the vicar to the water-front of Papeete, complete with a guitar. But I gave up the effort and followed him peaceably into the church to see the beautiful stone font which is carved like the trunk of a tree with the figures of Adam and Eve and the Serpent.

'That font was made in 1713,' said Mr Cory, 'so it must have been used at the christening of several of your family.'

Suddenly I had a vision of half a dozen diminutive uncle Willies, bellowing with rage, being dipped, fully-clad and complete with monocles, into the font. I banished this disturbing image and followed the vicar into the vestry where he showed us a cupboard with some fine oak panelling.

'These panels', he said, 'are all that remains of the three-decker pulpit from which William Maugham preached his sermons.'

We told him that we had found the tombstone of a Maugham in Stamford.

'You're welcome to look around here for more,' said Mr Cory, 'though I'm afraid you'll be disappointed. I've had a look myself.'

We searched the floor for a stone with the name Maugham on it, but the lettering on the stones had been worn by generations of worshippers and many of the old brasses had been removed. In the churchyard also we searched, but in vain. Then Mr Cory led us across the village green, to School Cottage, and into the true story.

The Reverend William, who we discovered later was in fact William Somerset Maugham's great-great-great uncle, was the headmaster of the Free Grammar School in Moulton from 1764 until his death fifty years later. The school was founded in 1560 by John Harrox, 'an industrious yeoman' who by 'patient work and honest saving' had 'attained to considerable work'. A local vicar's description[2] of Harrox continues:

Having no children he determined to leave his money in the way most conducive to God's glory ... He willed that subject to certain provisos, one free grammar school should be erected and kept for ever in the Mansion House in which he was then dwelling; and that the yearly profits of certain specified lands should be employed for ever for the founding and maintenance of such a school ... The will was completed just in time, for the very next day ... John Harrox died.

Harrox was buried 'before the stool where he did sit in the Church of Moulton'. He had enjoyed the reputation of being 'a very honest, godly man, and in no way nasty or base'. But it seems that the first governor of his school did not expect to find such virtues in the teachers he employed, for in an early regulation, dating from 1599, there was a warning that 'if the school-master proved a profane person or a heretic, or a drunkard, or a swearer, or a quarreller, or gamester, he was to be privately admonished, and subsequently expelled if he remained un-reformed'.

By 1764, when William Maugham came to live in Moulton, the once prosperous and scholarly grammar school was in such a bad way that the previous headmaster, John Chapman, had been directed by the governors to advertise in the London and provincial newspapers for pupils who would be 'well and carefully taught the learned languages free of all charge except 4d. entrance'.³ The headmaster's house 'being old and naturally decayed so as not to be fit for use' had to be pulled down the following year, and a new house was built for the sum of £286 which was raised by selling a 'parcel of Oak, Ash and Wych Timber' from the lands bequeathed by the godly John Harrox. Even as late as 1777, when there were over sixty pupils under his care, the Reverend William's income was so small that he was given permission to supplement it by assisting the vicar of the parish in his duties. The Bishop of Lincoln confirmed this on June 11, 1782, when poor William was appointed a curate of All Saints Church and assigned 'all the Rights, Profits and appurtenances thereto belonging'. The appointment was subject to the 'condition of keeping a proper assistant' at the school. But as William grew old he must have forgotten this condition – or perhaps he found proper assistants hard to come by – because in 1807 we find a complaint recorded that 'the master's grandson, a lad not fourteen years old, is the principal teacher at the school'.

Though the Reverend William delegated his professional tasks to his thirteen-year-old grandson, he certainly did not neglect his duties to the vicar of the church. 'Judging from the signatures in our church registers,' said Mr Cory as we strolled across the green to the old School House, 'it looks as though Maugham did *most* of the work.'

Mr Cory then introduced us to Mr and Mrs W. B. Tingle, who lived in School Cottage. Mr Tingle, a staunch churchwarden, had been a pupil and then a master at Moulton school which was closed in 1939⁴ and partly torn down in 1953. While we sat over morning coffee he showed me photographs of a building that the Reverend William had put up in 1792. Mr Tingle had watched with grief as the walls tumbled down before the bulldozer.

'But I saved the key-stone from the rubble,' he said. 'I've got it in the garden. Come and look at it.'

We went to the edge of his rockery and there surrounded by flowers was the key-stone with 'W.M. 1792' engraved on it. Here was the Reverend William's only remaining memorial. Mr Tingle leaned down, shook the stone free of clinging earth, and then gave it to me as a present. I carried it gratefully back to the car as if I were already holding all my ancestry in my hands. When our driver saw it with his stone mason's eye, he said, 'That's Ketton Stone, that is – from Ketton near Stamford.'

Mr Cory next led us down a lane near the church and into his elegant vicarage. I had written to him a week before, and, with great kindness, he had tried to gather together the story of the Maughams in Moulton. He brought in a vigorous old gentleman to meet us, Mr J. G. Westmoreland, the thirty-first and last headmaster of the school that my kinsman – the Reverend William – had ruled for so long. Mr Westmoreland talked of Moulton village as if it were all his world, for he loved it with that intense devotion to his patch of earth that we sometimes tend to imagine to be a purely English eccentricity, but which is shared by all races in the world that have built a cluster of huts in mud or stone or brick. As he talked, it was hard to believe that his school had been closed for nearly a quarter of a century, for he made its history come to life, so that one could almost hear the school-bell and the shouts of boys released from their classrooms into the spring sunshine.

When we returned to Stamford, I carried the old key-stone into my hotel and washed it in the bath, and as the dust and lichen drifted away, the initials W.M. became beautifully clear. It was an odd sensation, holding the stone and drying it, trying to imagine what sort of man this Reverend William Maugham might have been, and wondering why the name William had survived and become so famous in my uncle Willie, who cared so little for his inheritance. The vicar of Moulton, Mr and Mrs Tingle, Mr Westmoreland, and others with whom I had spoken that day had all referred to my uncle as 'Somerset' with a warm possessive note in their voice, as if they never doubted that he was one of them. But I somehow don't think that Willie would have returned the compliment, so I never told him the story and I never showed him the stone.

*

The papers in the chintz-covered box told us that the Reverend William Maugham was eighty-eight years old when he died in 1814, so he must have been born about 1726. But when we began to fit the story of his life together some of the pieces in the puzzle were missing. He certainly fathered a large tribe of Lincolnshire Maughams. But what of his own background? One trail led to Louth, some thirty miles north-east of Lincoln, where we had learned of a will made by a farmer, John Maugham, in 1703 – twenty-three years before William was born. But we could find no later wills in the county that might help to identify William's parents, and so we had to abandon this line of research. There was, however, another trail. The bundle of papers revealed that William had studied for the priesthood at Magdalene College, Cambridge, and when Derek Peel checked this in the *Alumni Cantabrigiensis* he found also the remark 'Wisbech School'. By this time we were reading books with such edifying titles as *The North-amptonshire and Rutland Clergy*,[5] and there we found the entry 'Maugham, William, of Magdalene College, Cambridge. Usher at Wisbech School'. And as Wisbech, known as the 'capital of the Fens', is only about thirteen miles from the village of Moulton we decided to search there for the next part of our story.

We drove between bright tulip fields and orchards to Wisbech and wandered through the lovely streets of the town where King John slept for a night during his last, fatal march. As we crossed the fine early-Georgian bridge and walked along the bank of the river Nene towards the grammar school that had been founded in the reign of Edward VI, I tried to imagine William's life as a young man in Wisbech. He was well into his teens when George II led his army to victory at Dettingen; he was old enough to have fought at Culloden. But I saw him rather as a peaceful scholar who paused before entering the church, and made his decision for the simple reason that an ordinary school-master could not hope for much of a career without the authority of holy orders. But perhaps I wrong him: perhaps William was aflame with religious ardour and yearned for priesthood. What is proved by the records is that at the late age of twenty-five William decided to go up to Cambridge University. On December 14, 1751, he said good-bye to his friends at the grammar school and travelled the thirty-five miles to Magdalene College.[6] Four years of instruction in holy orders lay ahead of him.

William was ordained on September 21, 1755. On the same day, the Bishop of Ely appointed him curate at Wisbech St Mary, a little Fenland village only a mile or two from the great town he knew so well. He remained there – so it seemed from the records – until he was made rector of Pilton, a village in the small county of Rutland, eight miles south-west of Stamford. We could follow William's journey as we drove slowly through Wisbech St Mary and over the long straight road that led back to Stamford.

*

When we came back to the George Hotel we were warmly welcomed by the hall-porter.

'How did you get on with your research, sir?' he asked.

I was startled by the question because I naturally assumed that no one in Stamford knew or cared about the purpose of my visit. I stared at him in surprise. I had taken the hall-porter's uniform and his good service for granted, though I did suspect that other talents lurked behind his bony high-domed forehead and his quiet scholarly voice.

'I'm a member of the Society of Genealogists,' the hall-porter explained calmly. 'If I can assist you in your researches in my spare time, I should be delighted.'

England is a land of surprises – usually pleasant. The hall-porter's name was Stephen Goard, and I was lucky to have met him, for during the next few months he gave me valuable help in the quest for my ancestry. One of Mr Goard's first discoveries concerned the years of William Maugham's betrothal and marriage to a Miss Susanna Reid, who was the daughter of the Reverend Farringdon Reid, the Master of Stamford School. As I have said, it seemed from the records that William remained at Wisbech St Mary until he was appointed rector of Pilton in the summer of 1762.[7] But as William and Susanna were married only twelve months or so after he was appointed to Pilton, it appeared that their courtship must in those days have been considered quite unseemly in its haste. Moreover, it must have been very tiring for poor William to ride sixteen miles over rough roads each time he visited his betrothed.

Mr. Goard found the answer.

'I have a notion,' Mr Goard had said in his precise scholarly voice, 'I have a notion that William must have been connected with Stamford in some way, in order to have become acquainted with the Reverend Farringdon Reid and his daughter.'

He therefore searched the records of all the churches in Stamford and finally discovered that William was curate of St Martin's [8] – just above the George Hotel – from February 1759 until June 1764. So William had come to Stamford three and a half years before he was given the living of Pilton – which made his courtship with Susanna quite respectable and tranquil after all. [9]

*

Our last visit in Stamford was to the ancient grammar school. After seeing the flourishing establishment of today with its fine buildings and pupils in smart blue blazers and straw boater-hats, it was difficult to imagine what the school was like in the days of the Reverend Farringdon Reid. The present headmaster, Mr Basil Deed, told me that in the last few years a quarter of a million pounds had been spent on new buildings and playing fields. When the school was founded its income was nine pounds a year. There are now over six hundred pupils; in 1731 when Reid was appointed headmaster at the age of twenty-four there were less than a dozen. The boys assembled in a small early thirteenth-century building now known as the Old School which is used as the school chapel. 'Reid and his usher both taught in the Old School with their desks divided only by an oak table, the headmaster at the east end and the usher at the west, both facing south. The boys' benches had boards between them rather in the manner of church pews, so that nothing lower than the boys' shoulders was visible to the master ... There was no fire in the room.' [10] It sounds cold and grim.

Mr Deed pointed to a carved head above the lintel of the west door. It had been worn by the winds to a skull of stone.

'It may once have been the head of St Paul,' he said. 'But now it's known as the "Old Man". And every new boy has to kiss it.'

I remembered other rituals for new boys at the preparatory school to which I was sent at the age of nine, and I shuddered.

*

It may well have been at Farringdon Reid's instigation that his son-in-law William took up his appointment at the Free Grammar School at Moulton. He was only thirty-eight years old when he became its eighteenth headmaster. But evidently he was weary of moving from one parish to another, and he settled down in the village, to breed a large family, and to govern several generations of schoolboys, over a period of fifty years. It cannot have been a very exciting or rewarding existence.

The water-colour portrait of the Reverend William on the wall of my study was gradually becoming more alive to me. His appearance gives the impression of a robust, strong-willed man, used to being obeyed within the bounds of the tiny world in which he had chosen to live. I possess a whole bundle of his sermons which suggest that he was extremely well-read in the holy scriptures, narrow-minded, and devoid of any sense of humour. The sermons are all beautifully and patiently written in long-hand on pages cut to the size of a postcard and bound together with cotton. The handwriting is firm and clear with nicely-rounded vowels. The span of history that the sermons cover is remarkable – from Wolfe's victory at Quebec in 1759 to Nelson's victory at Trafalgar in 1805. It is amusing to see that some of the more conventional sermons on subjects such as faith or charity bear six or seven dates. The Reverend William saved himself toil by using the same sermons over and over again at discreet intervals. But however overworked he might be, a British victory on land or sea meant a brand new sermon – and no doubt about it.

Here, from the pulpit in Stamford, is the Reverend William celebrating Wolfe's victory at Quebec.[11]

We are here assembled then, by the command of our Sovereign, to celebrate the Praises of Almighty God, for the Signal blessing he has been pleased to give this Nation, in a series of successes over its enemies in different parts of the World, in the course of this War. But more especially for the late defeat of the French Army in Canada, and the reduction of the strong City and Fortress of Quebec to His Majesty's arms. And also for granting us the late seasonable and plentiful Harvest . . .

I like the abrupt transition from the great victory to the Harvest with a capital H. Countrymen like William well knew the importance of the Harvest, for soldiers may win victories but even soldiers must eat.

In the present war indeed [William continued] there were at first but small hopes that we should ever be able to bring things to this happy conclusion. Not that we were under any apprehensions about the justness of our Cause; but from the mighty Powers we had to contend with there was some room to doubt that we should not be able to make the glorious figures which the Event has produced. But we see that the battle is not always to the strong, and that true valour when exerted in a righteous cause, and properly supported by wise counsels, and unanimity of the subjects, which are the sinews of war, will face any dangers and flourish under the severest apprehensions . . .

At that point when he was writing his sermon, I believe that William may have paused as his mind was invaded by an apprehension of a different nature. The King had appointed November 29 as a day of national thanksgiving, and William knew well that there were those in his flock who might be tempted to take the proclamation as an excuse to celebrate the victory too freely – and there was an inn only too near the church. As some of the dark-red bucolic faces of his parishioners slid across his mind, William could see them leaving church and heading intently towards the George. And drink led to ribaldry or even worse. 'Solemn thanksgiving', the royal proclamation had said, and solemn it would certainly be in the town of Stamford if the Reverend William had his way. So he took up his pen again with a frown and wrote his concluding sentence.

Let us in the midst of our joy beware of perverting it from the use for which it is appointed, by unseasonable or profane mirth; but with hearts piously and seriously disposed, let us, both now and ever, in this life, so faithfully serve the Lord, (who hath given the King his heart's desire, and hath not denied him the request of his lips) that we fail not finally to attain his heavenly promises.

*

Thirty-nine years later, Nelson's victory at the Nile [12] in 1798 inspired William to his finest sermon, which he delivered, again on November 29, in the morning at Moulton and in the evening at the neighbouring village of Weston. The beginning has an oddly modern ring to it.

There certainly never was in any of our memories, such dreadful wars as this in which we are at present engaged; and it is also certain that we never before had to contend with such fierce and obstinate men, whose professed determination is to captivate this country; to plunder it of its property; to

William Somerset Maugham, C.H., C.Lit.

The Reverend William Maugham
and his Clerk, of Moulton, Lincolnshire, c. 1795

W. Somerset Maugham,
a cartoon by Ronald Searle

destroy its laws and Constitution; and reduce its inhabitants to beggary, and make them slaves to their own arbitrary pleasure: which, if they could effect, according to their malicious intention, would be a melancholy sight indeed. They threaten us indeed with all this Mischief, but hitherto have performed none of their boasted Exploits, and, if it pleases God, I hope never will . . .

William then treated the villages of Moulton – and of Weston – to a splendid parade of scriptural learning.

To what end or use did the madness of Nebuchadnezzar serve, in commanding the three brethren to be put to an extraordinarily cruel death but to set the Glory of God in a clearer light, by miraculously preserving them from that fiery trial. So likewise concerning the great men in Darius's Court, in relation to Daniel, what did they procure by their malicious persecution of him, but greater favours and higher honours to him from the King, and the utter ruin of themselves and their families . . . The insolence also of Pharaoh, and his monstrous obstinacy towards the Israelites, had the same kind of conclusion; for his outrageous behaviour to that injured People procured for him such a remarkable overthrow as nothing less than a miracle could effect. So likewise the wonderful defeat of Sennacherib's numerous Army is another instance of the glory which is due to God, for defeating the ruinous projects of ambitious men.

I like the phrase 'the ruinous projects of ambitious men'. It has a Churchillian ring to it.

*

I am afraid that William was not at his best when he came to compose his sermon to celebrate the Battle of Trafalgar,[13] in 1805. But he was in his eightieth year, and perhaps one British victory was beginning to seem rather like another.

It is a glorious victory indeed, and will be held in remembrance to the latest period of our history. But as it is a transaction of so late a date, it does not require me to repeat the account of it. Everyone here has heard the particulars attending it, and understand it as well as I do, and all I shall say about it is, to consider it as a mark of the Providence of God, set before us in terms or language so easy as to be comprehended, that it seems to want no proof that it is His doing.

Old William was tired, so let the rest of them get on with it.

*

There is no trace of my uncle Willie's neat diamond-cut prose and stark realism in the whole bunch of his great-great-great uncle's sermons, and though the physical resemblance between the two William Maughams is almost ludicrous, and though in their tenacity and vigour and toughness their characters were similar, the outlook of the two men was very different, and I don't think they would have liked each other. The Reverend William, for instance, was a keen upholder of established society.

'People of every community are obliged by all the laws, both of God and their own Country, to pray for all who are entrusted with Power and to live in due obedience to them', he wrote in a sermon he delivered at Moulton and at Weston in October 1801 on the occasion of the forty-first anniversary of King George III's accession. 'Upon the whole then we are to conclude that we ought to pray for, to fear, to respect and honour, Kings, Princes and Magistrates, and to submit to the Laws of our Country which they have appointed; not only because they govern by God's authority, but out of good will to men, because we are protected in our lives, in our freedom, in our Professions, and everything that is valuable to us, by the Power and Authority which is entrusted to their Dispensation.'

The Reverend William believed enthusiastically in the Establishment. In his heart, William Somerset Maugham did not; secretly he despised the members of the ruling classes that he met. During his years of triumph Willie had many friends in the government who were rich, powerful, and well-connected, but he never felt that he belonged to their society. And behind the soberly-dressed, cynical, famous man of letters there still lurked the compassionate young man who had written *Liza of Lambeth*.

Next, the Reverend William believed that suffering ennobled the soul. 'By adversity men are usually made better, and are generally more approved,' he wrote.[14] 'Whilst their sufferings serve to exercise their patiences – to testify to their fortitude, and to prove to all men what love they bear to the truth, and how much they are willing to bear for God's sake.'

Willie believed the opposite. 'I knew that suffering did not ennoble; it degraded,' he wrote in *The Summing Up*. 'It made men selfish, mean, petty, and suspicious. It absorbed them in small things. It did not make them more than men; it made them less than men.'

But the most important difference between the two relatives was that the Reverend William believed in God, 'who is, not only able, but willing to save us, if we fulfil his will',[15] and Willie did not.

'I cannot believe in a God who is angry with me because I do not believe in him,' Willie wrote.[16] 'I cannot believe in a God who is less tolerant than I. I cannot believe in a God who has neither humour nor common sense.'

These sentiments would have outraged the Reverend William, and the parson's simple approach to life would have exasperated William Somerset Maugham. In fact, I am afraid that my uncle would have liked his namesake no better than he liked my father.

*

One last glimpse of the venerable old parson and village school-master is revealed in a torn, faded note that must have been copied from a local newspaper. The report reads:

Decr. 5th. 1805. At Moulton, near Spalding the Anniversary of the Parish Choir, established 55 years, was held. The Revd. Wm. Maugham, in his 80th year, preached an excellent sermon. The Choir afterwards sang 'God save the King' in full chorus. They then, attended by the principal inhabitants of the Village, retired to the Carpenter's Arms to dine, when the 55th rump of Beef was served up.

*

The following notice appeared in the *Lincoln, Rutland and Stamford Mercury*, on Friday, June 10, 1814:

On Monday the 30th ult. aged 88, universally respected, the Rev. W. Maugham, upwards of 51 years Master of the free Grammar School at Moulton in this county, and Rector of Pilton in Rutland.

His remains were interred in the parish church of Moulton on Monday last; the funeral service was performed by the Rev. Maurice Johnson, D.D., and the pall borne by clergymen.

*

The Reverend William and his wife had at least nine children – all of whom except the eldest, Susanna, were baptised in the lovely 'Adam and Eve' font in Moulton church. In his will, made in 1802, William had provided equally for his surviving children, but later he added a codicil stating that as he then had 'a little more to dispose of' and as his fourth son, George, had 'contributed very much to ye Acquisition of it, and has yet had no Recompence for his Care', he should be rewarded, 'besides his share with ye rest, a reasonable Allowance'.

The Reverend William's son George, who was a farmer, and his son Robert, who was a grocer, seem to have been the only two children who still remained in Moulton in 1814. The others had moved further afield. Francis had become a bookbinder in Spalding; Thomas Marmaduke (whose grave we had found) had become a cabinet-maker in Stamford; William Farringdon, the eldest, had become a hatter in London. Evidently they must have been settled in their own lives, for they did not require their father's belongings, and his chattels were put up for public auction on July 8 and 9. The printed catalogue of the 'House Furniture, Books, Brewing Vessels, Farming Utensils, etc.', which is among the family papers, lists 258 separate items, ranging from 'Two beef pots', an 'Italian iron', and a 'Pair of snuffers in the kitchen' to a 'Quilting frame' and 'Hose stretcher' in the 'Blue Garret'. There was a 'wig block and stand' in the 'Middle Chamber', 'Harvey's Meditations', and 'Caesar's Commentaries' were among the volumes in the 'Best Parlour', and in the cellar were 'Glass bottles by the dozen'.

I am intrigued by the references to 'Brewing Vessels' and 'Glass bottles by the dozen'.

THE CAPTAIN OF THE FORECASTLE

MOST of the Reverend William's children seem to have led rather dull, conventional lives – with the splendid exception of Theophilus, the fifth son. Maybe it was the pious-sounding name that made the boy rebel against the genteel background of his family. Perhaps he felt stifled by the prim atmosphere of the little village in Lincolnshire and longed for an opportunity to escape. He may even have been moved by the staunch patriotism of his father's sermons. But Moulton Grammar School with its musty books and tedious spelling lessons was not for Theophilus, and so he ran away and joined the British navy, in which he served during the French Revolutionary wars.

I think Willie Maugham would have liked Theophilus. He must have been wayward, feckless, and brave. He comes vividly alive from a sheaf of letters I found next to his father's sermons in the old chintz-covered box.

Theophilus was born on September 18, 1772, so he was twenty years old when France declared war against England on February 1, 1793. He had joined the navy several years before then, but the first mention of him that we could discover in the ships' musters at the Public Record Office is in September 1793, when he appears on the roll of the sloop *Thorn*, with the rating of able-bodied seaman and the significant remark, 'Not Prest'. This shows that he had 'entered volunteerly', as the record puts it, and had received a bounty for doing so. Six months later, however, he was in the *Victorious*, a third-rate warship commanded by Sir John Orde. And this time he was shown as 'Prest at Sandwich'.

One can only guess what happened to Theophilus during those intervening six months. Most probably his first enthusiasm had been sapped by the coarse, vicious life at sea. Perhaps he had been disgusted by the bullying and flogging and the unnatural confinement of hundreds of men and boys for months on end. The only hope of shore-leave in those days was to 'run' the ship in port – to desert, in fact.

Perhaps Theophilus was hiding in some cheap lodging-house or tavern in Sandwich when he was caught by one of the ruthless press-gangs, who enforced their peculiar form of 'recruiting' with cudgels and cut-lasses. But all these brutalities were common in their time, and Theophilus never reveals his misdeeds or his punishments in his letters to his family – only his ardent hope of his ship getting to grips with the enemy and earning some prize money. His letters, however, do reveal that Theophilus had not acquired his father's scholarship or command of the English language, for his grammar and spelling are delightfully bad. The first letter in my possession, dated April 2, 1794, was written to his eldest brother William Farringdon Maugham. Theophilus was then twenty-one. The letter has many pleasant echoes of the kind of phrases I read as a troop leader in a yeomanry tank regiment, when I had to censor the men's letters home from the Western Desert.

I hope you are well as I'm at Present time. I received the things which You was kind enuff to Send me on the 1st of the Month which was yeasterday, which I return You Greate many thanks for . . . I Belive we shall Sail in about 10 days time, But Whear I Cant tell. But I Hope into the North Sea for the Ships on that Staision is sending in [Capital] prizes everyday.

Since I left the *Thorn* She has taken 4 or 5 ships laden with Weet and the people expect to Shear £500 a man for them. I hope it will Be my luck to Catch something yet . . . and then I hope to make you Amends for What You have done for me.

I hope my Brothers and Sisters is all well and I wish I could Se them all once more. I dowt if aver we all Gett togeather again as we was wen you and I was at Moulton . . .

I Cant But return you thank for all favers and Believe me to Be Your Loven Brother

Theophilus Maugham

*

No doubt Theophilus soon got his wish to 'catch something', but unfortunately we have to wait until 1798 – when France and England had been at war five years – before we come to his next letter. By then he was serving in H.M.S. *Ethalion*. If there were previous letters, they have been lost, and lost with them is the reason why Theophilus changed his name to 'Thomas Reid'. Reid was his mother's maiden name. Perhaps the young sailor had grown tired of being teased by his mates for having such a sonorous name as Theophilus Maugham. As

before, he is listed in the musters of the *Ethalion* as 'Prest'. He had
been caught once again by a press-gang. But more curious is the note
in the muster, 'Born Jamaica'. It sounds as if for some reason he had
deliberately decided to give a false name and place of birth to avoid
being identified as Theophilus Maugham of Moulton. So Thomas
Reid he became, and henceforth all his letters to his family are signed
with his new name. But I shall continue to call him Theophilus.

The *Ethalion*, a fifth-rate warship of thirty-eight guns, commanded
by a gentleman with the odd name of Captain George Countess, was
built at Harwich early in 1797, only a few months before Theophilus
involuntarily joined her company of two hundred and eighty-four
men. He was then, as before, an able-bodied seaman, earning about
twenty-two shillings a month or ninepence a day, but he seems to have
taken more kindly to his new ship, for he soon gained promotion. On
New Year's Day 1798 his rating is given as 'Quarter Gunner', and
three months later he became 'Captain of the Forecastle', an imposing
title which was given in those days to the leader of the gang of sailors
responsible for the maintenance of cables and anchors on the fore part
of the ship. Theophilus mentions his promotion in a letter to his
mother and father which he wrote from Spithead on March 3, 1798.

Honored Pariants,

We expect to go to Sea Now every day. We hear that the Spanish fleet is
out and that they have taken the Warrior 74 Gun ship. She went with us to
Lisbon and we Left Hir thire, with the Floora frigget. I suppose We shall go
to be a repeting Ship to Lord Bridport[1] as We expect him to hoist his flagg
On board the royal George[2] to go in pursute of them. I hope he will for if
We Fall in with them, I think We shall Give a Good account of them as We
have got a very fine fleet of 3 and 2 Deck'd Ships.

I have hardley time to write as we are very Busey getting redy for sea.
My hands is very dirty wich you must excuse the Letter Bein so . . .

The Capt of our forecastle run a way a day or two a go and I have got his
Birth wich entitles me to 5 shares of prize money if we shud take aney
thing . . .

I Can't say aney more at present But My Love to you and all relations and
Belive Me to Be

                                              Your dutifull Son
                                              Thos Reid.

*

Two months later, in May 1798, Theophilus was at Plymouth and the *Ethalion* was in dock for repair because 'when We Saild from Spithead We Got our Ship a Ground on the Needles point Going round the Island of White and damaged our Bottom.' But Theophilus had some good news to tell his 'Honored Frinds', as he called his parents in his letter.

The time we was Lying in Guarnsey road thire was a Ship came in from Cadis. We boarded her and she proved to have falce papers on board. We made a prize of her and sent her in to portsmouth. We hear she is worth 80,000 £. I hope it is true . . .

Then follows a curious passage in the letter. Theophilus was very worried because he had not heard from his eldest brother William.

I wrote 2 Letters to him the Last Time we was in port But never recd aney answer. I Cant tell what is the reason of it. If he is afronted with me for my misconduct I am very sorrow for it. I know I feel the pain my self which I think will make me more Carefull if please God I should live to Gett on Shore a Gain . . .

What had Theophilus done to offend his brother William? What was his misconduct while on shore? The letter does not tell, and I am afraid that we shall never know.

*

That summer of 1798, on the pretext of aiding the Irish Catholics to expel the English and to establish a republic, France made an attempt to invade Ireland. On August 6, a small force of a thousand French troops under General Humbert set sail from Rochefort aboard four frigates and landed at Killala Bay in County Mayo on the north-west coast a fortnight later. They met the first English troops sent against them at Castlebar but ran away so fast that the encounter became known as 'the race of Castlebar'. On September 8 the French were compelled to surrender at Ballinamuck. A week later a larger French squadron, this time consisting of one ship of the line and eight frigates, commanded by Commodore Bompart sailed out of Brest to relieve General Humbert with a force estimated as between three and five thousand troops. The *Ethalion*, with her bottom repaired, was sent off in pursuit. After watching the enemy for over three exhausting weeks – and once being nearly obliged to fight a lone battle – the *Ethalion* eventually joined a superior force commanded by Sir John Borlase Warren. The next day, on October 12, the combined force overtook and destroyed the French squadron near Tory Island – forty miles north-west of Londonderry. By that time, the tough young 'Captain of the Forecastle' had received a letter from his eldest brother William Farringdon Maugham – presumably forgiving his misconduct, for Theophilus begins his letter describing the chase and the action by thanking William for his letter 'which gave me great Pleasure you may be shure as it is so very Long since I heard from you'. His splendid letter continues:

You ask me for a Lettle account of the Late Cruse. The hardships has Bein so much I Can Scarse relate them. We was a cruising of Brest and had very hard Gales of Wind indeed and on the 19th of Sept. we fell in with the french fleet. There was 8 frigates 1 84-gun Ship[3] and A Schoner all with troops to invade Irland. We had with us 1 more Frigate and a Brigg. We could do nothing with them so we sent the other frigate home to Alarm the Coast of England and the Brigg with us dog'd the french fleet. Thay the Cowards wanted to go in under [their] forts. But they woold Not Lett them come to Anchor. Thay fired at them and made a signell for them to proceed on thire Passage wich thay did with the Devil to Them but how ever they Chased us But Could not catch us. Our Frigate Sails very fast. Thay then steard a way to the Westward and took such a round about way that we could not fall in with aney of our Crusers which we hopt to do. Every day we was at our quarters from the 17th of Sept. untill the day of the Action which was the 12 day of October and Never had our hammoks down thay bein a part of our Bullworks you know. You may be Shure we was very tired and our Boons was sore with Laying on the decks between our Guns. Thay try'd to suround us in the night time but thay Could Not for we kept a good Look out for them the time we was doging them . . .

I find the description of his 'sore Boons' from 'laying on the decks' between the guns so vivid that I longed for his account of the action itself. But by the time Theophilus came to describe the battle and the *Ethalion*'s own victory over a more powerful French frigate, the *Bellona*, he had written a letter far longer than any other he had sent home. He was tired of the strain of composition, and so he dismissed the engagement in a few lines.

We fell in with Sir John Bolace Warren Squdren on the 11th and on the 12 had at it, begun Action at 7 in the morning and kept it up till Noon when we left off and drank a pint of Grogg a man and then we came up with the Le Bellone a 40 Gun frigate with 600 men on Board and we had but 270. We engag'd her 1 houre and 54 minutes when she struck [her colours in surrender], the rest of the fleet Bein in action at small distance and we Boarded hir. We had But One Man Kild and 4 Wounded. I cant say aney more at present But will a nother time. So no more from

Your aff. Brother,
Thos. Reid.

*

In a letter to his father and mother Theophilus adds that 'thire was a Great Slauter on Board the Bellone. We hove men over Board after we Board'd hir and a Great Number Was haveing thire thyes and Legg's Cutt of . . . Thay will Not tell how manay thay had Keeld on Board But we shall know by and by.' And Theophilus makes light of his own injury.

I went on Board the Bellone with Mr Sayer But haveing Bad Weather and her Masts and riggin Bein Shattred so much with our Shot she rold away at hir masts and I had My Leg hurt in Clearing a way the rack so that I was oblig'd to be sent on Board our own Ship to the Surgeon. Its all most well Now . . . It hase Bein a very hard fight and I have had my Shear of it But I don't Care No more a Bout it then to eat my meet, as Long as I have good Officers and that We have at Present thank God.

The *Ethalion* had most of her rigging shot away during her battle with the *Bellona*, but by December 19 Theophilus was able to report from Plymouth that they had 'got everything New', and a month later the ship was 'all ready to go out of the harbour'. There was some 'tallk of goin to the Cape of Good Hope', but Theophilus could not 'say for truth'. He was more concerned about the parrot he had given his family as a present when he visited Moulton at Christmas. 'I am Glad the pariot is such a favourite with you all. You must keep her warm this wenter time and she will finds her tounge a gain in the Spring of the year.' By that stage of the letter Theophilus had once again become exhausted by the effort of composition and he could think of nothing to say, and so he ends – as so many sailors and soldiers have done before and since – with the familiar excuse that he has a more important task than to write to his family. 'You must excuse this Letter,' Theophilus wrote, 'as I have got a very Bad pen and I am in a hurray.'

The *Ethalion* put to sea again at the end of January, and Theophilus took the 'Opitunity' to write a brief note to his father and sent it home by the master of the prize crew they had put aboard a Spanish ship they had caught trying to bring in supplies to France from the West Indies. On April 10, when the *Ethalion* was safely back in Plymouth Sound, Theophilus wrote to his father.

We arrived on Sunday Last at this plase after a very Long and Teadeius Cruse of 10 weeks. We have had the hardest Gales of wind that I ever saw. We fell in with prize to a Jarsey Privrteer in Distress. We took the People out of her and in Less than an hour the Vesel Sunk and Last Sunday week it Blowing a very Seveare Gale of wind we saw a wreck to windward. We Could Nor Cary aney Sail, the Sea run So Very High we got a Boat Out with a Great deal of truble, and Mr Pymm our 1st Leut. got a Vollenteer to Venter with him to see if he Could Save aney Lives which with a very Great deal of truble Got 6 Men out of her and Got safe on Board with them. But the danger Bein so very Great that he woold Not go a gain. Then our Guner he Asked for Vollenteers, and me and five more venterd and saved 9 More men which was all their was in her. She had lost all her Masts in a squall of wind and everything that was on deck. . .

We took a french privrteer of 18 Gun's and 120 Men and sent her in then we fell in with H.M. Ship Naid just as She Was taken a french Ship of 20 Gun's and 130 Men Which we come in for. It has Bein a very Good Cruse . . .

I dont know weather we shall stay hear or go to Portsmouth for their is No room hear for our Prizinor's. We have 150 on board.

The letter concludes with his usual phrase – 'I cant say aney more at present.'

*

For the next five months there is a gap in the letters, and there is little hope of filling it in with complete certainty, because the logs of the *Ethalion* which are kept at the Public Record Office only go up to April 9, 1799. However, the next letter that the Reverend William Maugham received from his son came from the 'Meddeteraian Streats'. In it Theophilus describes how he had seen 'the french and Spanish fleet at an Anchor' off Cartagena and how they had 'taken 13 sail of Spaniards all Load with suplys for the Spanish soldiers on the Island of Mojorca'. He then relates a sinister incident that occurred on board:

A short time after we arrived in this Sea we happend a very Bad misfortune. The Capt. haveing Being Oblig'd to Punish[4] a man. Its usial to have the

Soldiers on Gard. After the Punishment the Gaurde went to return their Arm's in the Chest. By Accident the Chest took fire it haveing a Great deal of [ammunition] in it and had Like to Burnt the ship. But By the Activity of the Officres and men the flames was extinguish'd. But we had 13 Poor Soldeirs Blowd up in Such a Shoking manner you Never heard of.

It sounds as if some sailor on board wanted to take revenge on the soldiers for assisting at the flogging.

The letter continues:

We had 7 Woman Spaniards on Board that Could Not Specke a word of English and was prizinors that we took on Board of a Spanish Brigg. Poor Woman to see how thay assisted in striping and Oiling the Poor Men, all of them totall Blind and as Black as Negro's.

Theophilus seems to have had a compassion for the frailty of mankind quite rare for those brutal days. The letter concludes:

We had 50 men a way at the same time in the Prizes that we had taken and this 13 made us Muster very thin at our gun's. We Whent in to Minorca and sent them to the hospital, got our men out of the Prizes and Whent to sea a gain . . . I cant say aney more at present . . .

*

Unfortunately there is no letter from Theophilus to describe the *Ethalion*'s most lucrative encounter of all, but one can turn to the files of *The Times* for October 29, 1799:

We have the pleasure to state in our Paper of this day the capture of a most valuable Spanish prize from the Havannah. By letters received yesterday from Plymouth, we learn that the *Ethalion* frigate, Capt. Young, has taken and brought into that port the *Thetis* of 36 guns, which they took after an action of about two hours, on the 16th instant . . . She was from Vera Cruz to Old Spain, and had a cargo of cocoa and sugar, together with ONE MILLION AND A HALF DOLLARS.

The galleon was captured off the north-western tip of Spain, near Corunna, after a long chase and 'a running fight, in which the Spaniards had ten men wounded, one of whom is since dead'. There were no casualties on the *Ethalion*, who guarded her prize while the frigates *Naiad* and *Alcmeme* pursued a second Spanish galleon, the *Santa Brigida*, which they took the next day with the assistance of the *Triton*. This second ship was found to have three million dollars on board, and she also was brought safely back to Plymouth. The total gain to the British – and loss to the enemy – was almost one million pounds sterling. As their share of the prize money, the seamen of the *Ethalion* earned sixteen years' wages in one afternoon.[5]

Theophilus was so busy in Plymouth that he did not have time to mention the landing of the great prize until he was back at sea again. This letter – his last from the *Ethalion* – was written at sea off Brest on December 13, 1799.

I Could Not find time to write . . . for all the time we was in the harbour I was on Shore a Gaurd over the Money. I make No doubt But you heard by the Papers what a Show we made in Landing of it. It was the Grandist Sight that ever was sean in this place. The streets was so throng that we was oblig'd to Asist the solders to get the waggons throu the town to the garrison whear we Lodg'd it first.

I hope when this Cruse is out we shall refitt and if we do I shall try to come to London on Libbrty if not home. I Cant say aney more at present . . .

This final letter from Theophilus ends with his usual and typical postscript: 'Excuse the writing my pen is Bad and I have No pen knife.'

Twelve days later, on Christmas Day 1799, the *Ethalion* was wrecked off the coast south of Brest near the Pointe de Penmarch. The report in *The Times* said that 'the loss of the ship was owing to their being deceived by the tides'. Fortunately, the *Sylph* and the *Nimrod* were close at hand, and every person on board was rescued before the *Ethalion* broke in two and sank.

Theophilus may have suffered some bad injury in the shipwreck or he may soon afterwards have fallen victim to the scourge of typhus, which was rife in the navy in those days. I cannot find out. But there are no more letters from him – only a copy of his will, written on July 1, 1800, five months after he joined the *Immortalité*. The will, which is witnessed by the ship's captain, is still in the name of Thomas Reid, and on this solemn occasion Theophilus seems to have had the help of some educated person.

First, I recommend my Soul to God that gave it, and my Body I commit to Earth or Sea as it shall please God to order; and as for and concerning all my worldly Estate, I give, bequeath and dispose thereof; That is to say to my Father, the Revd Wm Maugham residing at Morton (Moulton) Lincolnshire to receive of and from Theophilus Thompson Tutt, Tavistock Street,

Covent Garden, London, the Sum of three hundred Pounds sterling, now remaining in Hands, or whatever Sum or Sums he may hereafter receive for me, and all Wages and Sums of Money, Lands, Tenements, Goods, Chattels and Estate whatsoever, as shall be any ways due, owing, or belonging unto me at the Time of my Decease, I do give, devise and bequeath the same unto my Father, the Revd Wm Maugham . . .

His father, aged seventy-four, was left everything. Theophilus was only twenty-seven years old. A fortnight later his service in the navy ended. All that can be discovered is that he was 'Discharged Dead'.

*

I wonder what the Reverend William and Mrs Maugham thought of their son Theophilus. His behaviour must have distressed them at times, but his letters were certainly treasured. Each one looks as if it had been read many times. And I do know that at least one present that Theophilus gave his parents was cherished by them for in the chintz-covered box I discovered a faded little cutting from a newspaper. Its date is probably around 1863.[6] The report reads:

SINGULAR DISCOVERY. The servant in the employ of the Rev. Johnson, head master of the Moulton Grammar School, this week in digging in the garden discovered a small brick vault, which contained a miniature leaden coffin enclosed in two wooden cases. The coffin contained a few blue and yellow feathers . . . It has been ascertained that it was the tomb of a favourite parrot, which belonged to the Rev. Wm. Maugham, a former master of this school, and was interred with all solemnity by some of the members of the family upwards of 50 years ago.

The 'pariot' would have been their last living memory of their feckless son.

GERALD HAXTON

ONE of the unexpected results of my stay in Stamford was a report in the *Lincolnshire Free Press* for May 15, 1962. 'Earl finds family link with Moulton', said the headline – promoting me to a nobler rank. News of my visit was also mentioned in the *Daily Express*, and as a result I received three letters, all of them from women who traced a connection with the Maugham family. The first, which came from Mrs Cecilia Maturin, an old lady living in Belfast, both delighted and troubled me. Her story did not reach back to Lincolnshire, as I had hoped, but to Whitburn in County Durham, where her maternal grandmother, Jane Maugham, had been born about 1812.

I believe my great-grandfather's name was Edward Maugham [Mrs Maturin wrote]. A very pompous and proud person, I have been told. One of his sons by his first marriage was a doctor of note and lived in style at Newcastle-upon-Tyne, drove a carriage and pair with carriage dogs (Dalmatians) following. My great-grandmother was his second wife; a Mosley heiress. Unfortunately, when my grandmother, Jane Maugham, was eighteen years old she greatly displeased her parents by marrying the son of a farmer on the nearby estate ... She was never forgiven, and was boycotted by the family. What a pity!

I felt there could only be a slender link between the Reverend William Maugham's humble brood – a farmer, a grocer, a hatter in Covent Garden, a bookbinder, a cabinet-maker – and the ostentatiously fashionable son of a proud pompous country gentleman in Durham. However, I wrote to Mrs Maturin hoping that her memory might yield some clue to a common ancestry. She then confessed that she 'got into a grey mist' when she tried to delve further back into the past, but she made a wonderfully kind gesture. One day a parcel arrived from Belfast. Inside were two beautiful early Georgian silver goblets with a note from Mrs Maturin: 'These were the property of the Maughams of the past, and were used at the christening of my grandmother. I should like to return them to the old homeland and the

Maugham of the present. Will you accept them?' I can see the two goblets on my bookcase as I write.

The second letter was from Miss Olivia Sykes, Sister-in-Charge of the White Hart Hospital, Harrogate.

'My grandmother came from Lincolnshire,' she wrote. 'Her maiden name was Susannah Vickers Maugham. She died in August 1916, aged 73 years. Her father was Theophilus Maugham . . .'

Could he be the young sailor, I wondered? But no. The dates didn't fit. The search was difficult because the Christian name Theophilus – oddly enough – was common in those days. But at last we identified him as Theophilus Maugham of Spalding, a grandson of the Reverend William through his sixth son Robert, the grocer. This Theophilus is mentioned in the registers of Spalding. He married a Miss Lucy Vickers, and the first of his three daughters, Susannah, was born on September 8, 1842. He was successively in his life a footman, a beershop keeper, and a general labourer. He died on October 6, 1886 – not so surprisingly – from 'chronic bronchitis and exhaustion'. Miss Sykes added this postscript: 'My mother says that in her mother's day the name Maugham was often pronounced "Moffam".'

The third letter came from an elderly lady living in Wimbledon, Mrs Gertrude Mabel Crooks.

My maternal grandmother was Mary Ann, daughter of a Miss Maugham of Moulton and William Smith of Whaplode.[1] Miss Maugham – my great-grandmother – had a brother Thomas who was a butler to a wealthy family near-by . . .

At that stage of the letter I paused. Grocers, beershop keepers, butlers – I did not seem much closer to tracing my ancestry back to John of Gaunt. The letter continued:

Miss Maugham was a lady's maid or sewing maid with the same family, and Grandma Mary Ann was brought up in the nursery with the children of the family.

Now here was a problem.[2] We finally supposed, however, that this Miss Maugham was Susan, a daughter of the Stamford cabinet-maker. She was born in 1803 and she had a younger brother named Thomas who 'choked whilst eating' – a death I was always afraid would befall my uncle Willie, for he ate with the speed of a boa-constrictor – and died in the Spalding Union Workhouse.

Mrs Crooks ended by telling me that she possessed a book in which

Part of the old school buildings at Moulton, Lincolnshire

The *Ethalion* (second from left) on which Theophilus Maugham served

Gerald Haxton

the family name was spelled 'Moffam'. And this was an odd coincidence, after the previous letter.

'Grandma *always* pronounced it "Moffam",' Mrs Crooks concluded.

'Somerset Moffam' has a pleasant ring.

*

So here were three women who had kinship with my own small branch of the family – a branch so small, now, that Willie and I were the last male survivors. Then something strange happened. On Tuesday, October 2, 1962, I was in a remote part of the country reading *The Times* at breakfast and I happened to glance down the 'Deaths' column, when I read: 'MAUGHAM – on Sunday, September 23, 1962, in his 89th year at St Francis Hospital, Dulwich, Willie MAUGHAM.' I was appalled. At that time my uncle Willie *was* in his eighty-ninth year. But surely *someone* would have let me know. And what in heaven's name was Willie doing in Dulwich? Tokyo or Hamburg, yes. Dulwich, no. I then read further: 'Beloved father of Louise, Gwendoline, Elvina and Henry.' That settled the matter. For *my* Willie had, at most, one offspring, my close friend, his daughter Liza.

By this time in my search for old Maughams I seemed to have gathered together quite a number of part-time assistants. I had become more than ever resolved to find out the truth about my family once and for all. Dimly I could hear my father's mournful voice saying, 'No income could stand it', but we pressed on with our researches. For once our task was easy. We traced Willie Maugham of Dulwich in direct descent from the Reverend William, through his son Thomas Marmaduke, the cabinet-maker, and his son, another Theophilus, who was also a cabinet-maker but became the landlord of the Rose and Crown in Huntingdon where he died of gout at the early age of forty-four, leaving a widow and ten children. I then wrote to the family in Dulwich, and a few days later received an answer from the late Mr Willie Maugham's son-in-law.[3] After telling me of Mr Willie Maugham's career as a 'sanitary and hot water engineer', his son-in-law concluded: 'To my knowledge father had never met Mr W. Somerset Maugham, but I know he took a very keen interest in his activities, and I must say, from photographs I have seen, *there was a striking family resemblance.*'

*

The threads of inheritance, usually unimportant in the pattern of history, are fascinating to members of a family who share the same name and bear the same-shaped eyes and foreheads, the same eccentricities of speech and movement. And it was the 'striking family resemblance' of some American Maughams whom my uncle met when he was staying in New York in 1910 that convinced him in the belief that 'a man hasn't a hope of changing his essential nature'. Willie told me the story of that first meeting in detail, for it had an important influence on his life. But in order to explain the story in its proper context and Willie's reason for telling it to me I must delve back into the past.

*

While he was serving in a Red Cross ambulance unit during the early months of the first World War, my uncle Willie Maugham met a young American called Gerald Haxton who was in his early twenties. Willie was then forty. Gerald, like Theophilus the sailor, was wayward, feckless, and brave, and Willie was immediately attracted to him. Shortly after the war, Gerald became Willie's secretary and companion on his travels. They were together for nearly twenty-five years. But the relationship was not an easy one. My uncle's work was always more important to him than any human relationship. He never allowed his emotions to interfere with the strict discipline he had imposed on himself in order to write as he desired. Gerald had little interest in literature; he was mainly interested in Willie's books and plays because they brought in money. He was an energetic, pleasing young man when they first met. From the days when he had been a schoolboy he had grown used to being admired. He was already a bit spoilt. He had begun to drink heavily and he became wild and violent in his cups. His reputation was notorious and his behaviour was reckless. In the winter of 1915 when Gerald was in London he was arrested on a charge of gross indecency. The case came up before Mr Justice Humphreys on December 7, 1915, and he was acquitted by the jury. But the Judge was convinced that Gerald was guilty of the offence and made no secret of it. A few years later Gerald was declared an undesirable alien. He was never allowed to return to England again. This was one of the factors that decided Willie to live abroad. In 1928 Willie bought the Villa Mauresque on Cap Ferrat, which is a promontory that stretches into the

Mediterranean between Monte Carlo and Villefranche. Gerald always pretended that the reason he never accompanied Willie on his trips to London was because he loathed the place. But the cigarettes he smoked still came from Bond Street, his suits from his old tailor in Savile Row, and his shirts from Jermyn Street.

In 1937 when I was a Judge's Marshal I travelled on circuit with Sir Travers Humphreys.

'That secretary of your uncle's is a rum fellow,' Sir Travers said over his port. 'He's a bad lot, I can tell you that. A bad lot. I can't see what your uncle sees in him. I can't see it.'

But by that time I could see it, for by then I had known Gerald for five years.

I first met Gerald in Vienna when I was seventeen. As soon as I had passed the exams that let me into Cambridge I was frantic to leave school where I was frustrated and unhappy. 'Houses' at Eton differ widely. I was in a 'hearty' house full of tough games-playing extroverts whom I was too lonely and wretched to attempt to understand. I now realise that it was all my own fault. I was – in those days – determined to be an aesthete. I played Beethoven at the school concerts, grew my hair long, and edited a school magazine. My ambition was to be a pianist, and at last I managed to persuade my parents to let me go to Vienna for a year to study under an Austrian teacher. (I learned several things in Vienna at the age of seventeen but, alas, the piano was not amongst them.) A room was booked for me at the *Koenig von Ungarn* in the centre of the town, and I was about to leave England, when one morning at breakfast in the large, gloomy family house in Cadogan Square I could see from the violently trembling copy of *The Times* in my father's hands that something had gone wrong.

'Such a meeting would be highly unsuitable,' my father was saying.

'Then Robin needn't meet him if you don't want him to,' my mother replied.

'But the man's staying *in the same hotel*,' my father answered reproachfully.

Gradually I found out what had occurred. Willie had calmly written a letter to my father saying that he was delighted to hear that I was going to Vienna because his secretary Gerald Haxton was already in Vienna and staying at the *Koenig von Ungarn* and that he would be able to look after me.

'I will not *have him* stay in the same hotel,' my father declared.

'You can hardly force Gerald Haxton to move out,' said my mother.

'Then *Robin* must change his hotel,' replied my father.

So cables were sent off and I was despatched to a different hotel in Vienna with severe instructions never to meet the infamous Gerald Haxton. But, of course, I did. I met him the first night I went to the opera, and I was extremely disappointed, for he didn't look wicked at all: he was a smart, dapper, lean man of forty with a cheerful laugh and an innocent smile. I felt I had been grossly deceived by all that I had heard about him, and I was almost reluctant to accept his invitation to show me round Vienna. But a week later when Gerald got blind drunk in a *Weinstube* I began to appreciate that he wasn't quite as innocent as he seemed. However, by then I had been impressed by his sophisticated man-of-the-world pose. I was grateful for his flowing hospitality, and – let me confess it – I was flattered by his interest in me. So I found a taxi, managed to pull Gerald into the back, and dropped him at the *Koenig von Ungarn* – and I accepted his slurred invitation to lunch with him the following day.

Gerald was almost always full of charm and full of liquor during the ten years that followed. His stability was not improved when he dived headlong into a swimming-pool that had not been filled with water. But Willie always forgave Gerald's transgressions, for in many ways he was a wonderful companion for him. Willie was shy and reticent; he was frequently depressed and silent. Gerald, an excellent host unless drunk, was ebulliently, irrepressibly friendly. When the two men travelled around the world together, it was Gerald who made the contacts that Willie needed for his stories.

My interest has been in men and the lives they led [Willie wrote in *The Summing Up*].[4] I am shy of making acquaintance with strangers, but I was fortunate enough to have on my journeys a companion who had an inestimable social gift. He had an amiability of disposition that enabled him in a very short time to make friends with people in ships, clubs, bar-rooms, and hotels, so that through him I was able to get into easy contact with an immense number of persons whom otherwise I should have known only from a distance.

Gerald helped Willie find the raw material he needed for his work, his boisterous spirits could lift Willie from his occasional fits of gloom, his diligence saved Willie from all the minor irritations of travel, and

his resourcefulness, at least on one occasion when they were out sailing,
saved Willie's life – for had Gerald lost his head when the 'great mass
of water . . . caught the boat and turned it over' Willie would have
been drowned.[5]

The Second World War parted the two friends. When Willie
returned to England, Gerald stayed on in France for a while to rescue
some of the more valuable pictures from the Villa Mauresque. Then he
flew to Lisbon and eventually to New York where he met Willie again
and they travelled together to Hollywood. But in December 1941
Willie moved to South Carolina where Nelson Doubleday, his
American publisher, had built him an eight-roomed comfortable house,
called Parker's Ferry, on his plantation twelve miles from Yemassee in
desolate yet oddly beautiful country. Willie enjoyed the peace and
simplicity of his life there; he liked the placid routine. But the place
was far too quiet for Gerald, who soon became restive. He was only
just fifty; he was bright and virile, and he felt the war was a challenge
to him to prove himself in his own right. He had grown tired of being
tolerated by Willie's friends as a useful adjunct to Willie's existence.
He wanted to succeed – personally and publicly – on his own, so he
took a clerical war-job. During the next two years in Washington,
divorced from Willie's care and sobering influence, Gerald literally
worked and drank himself to death.

On June 26, 1944, Willie wrote to me to say that Gerald was very ill.
He had had an attack of pleurisy in Washington and had then developed
tuberculosis of the lungs. He looked pitifully wasted. Willie was taking
him to a sanatorium in the Adirondacks where the fine air might save
him. Gerald, Willie wrote, had been very good, patient, and cheerful,
but he had not been told how dangerously ill he was. Gerald would be
an invalid for the rest of his life. There was only a small chance of
saving him.

In November 1944 Gerald died in the Doctor's Hospital in New
York, and Willie, stricken with grief, travelled down to South Carolina,
buried himself in his remote little house in the wilds of Yemassee and
went – I can think of no other phrase to describe his condition – into
a decline. He refused to leave Parker's Ferry and he refused to meet
anyone – even his closest friends. It was then that Ellen and Nelson
Doubleday suggested that I should come out to stay with him.

By then I had been wounded in the head in the Western Desert and

invalided out of the army with a fifty per cent disability pension. I was
ill and jittery. The calm of Yemassee might restore my nerves; my
presence might help to drag Willie from his decline. I was keen to go.
And thanks to the kindness of Brendan Bracken in the Ministry of
Information and of Victor Weybright, his American opposite number
in London, I managed to get a passage on a ship to Halifax.

I found Willie overwhelmed with misery.

'With the pills they've given me, I sometimes manage to sleep or
doze for as much as six hours a night,' he said. 'But I think of him every
single minute that I'm awake. I try to forget him all the eighteen hours
of the day. You can't imagine what it was like – hour after hour –
listening to that terrible cough that seemed to tear him to pieces.'

Suddenly Willie lowered himself on to the sofa and buried his face
in his hands. He began to cry with long racking sobs.

'You'll never know how great a grief this has been to me,' he said
when he had controlled himself and could speak again. 'The best years
of my life – those we spent wandering about the world – are inextricably connected with him. And in one way or another – however in-
directly – all I've written during the last twenty years has something
to do with him – if only that he typed my manuscripts for me.'

Willie seemed inconsolable. But at least my arrival forced him to
make a slight effort to recover. He took me up to dine with Ellen and
Nelson Doubleday and their family in what we both called 'the big
house', and their friendliness and splendid if erratic hospitality did
much to restore both of us. As the sunlit days passed by Willie began to
look less forlorn, and soon he began to manage a shaky smile. But it was
not until New Year's Eve that I realised that Willie had managed to
steer himself round the corner towards recovery.

There was a large party up at the big house on New Year's Eve, and
Willie and I were invited. A minute or so before midnight someone
gaily suggested that we should all sing *Auld Lang Syne*. Immediately
Willie's face froze with dismay – not because he was afraid that the
hackneyed tune would remind him of Gerald: by now he could cope
with that misery. I could see from his hectic glances to right and to left
that the reason for his consternation was more superficial and immediate. From childhood Willie had had a morbid dread of physical
contact with strangers, and he was now suddenly confronted with the
prospect of his hands being crossed and then clasped in the sticky palms

of two unknown females who had come in late and who were now standing on either side of him. Into his eyes came the frantic look of a hunted animal. I was wondering how Willie would get out of his predicament when he spoke.

'When on New Year's Eve,' Willie said, 'I hear people singing that song in which they ask themselves the question "should old acquaintance be forgot", I can only ter-tell you that my own answer is in the affirmative.'

That did the trick. Hands that had been crossed and outstretched to clasp Willie's fell down in limp despondency. Mouths that had been opened to chant merrily closed with a snap. And Willie had saved himself. At that instant he caught me looking at him and gave me a broad wink, and I knew that for a while at least he was back to his old form again.

But I wasn't. I was very nervous and overwrought, and I couldn't rid myself of the stammer that had begun after my head wound. Callers to Parker's Ferry would turn in embarrassment from one stammering Maugham to another. I was worn out, and at times I felt suicidally depressed as I thought of the friends in my regiment, officers and men, who had been killed or maimed in the desert. I had been for several months in various hospitals for head injuries. I suffered so badly from complete amnesia or 'black-outs' that each time I was allowed out of hospital I was given a label reading: 'If I am found suffering from a loss of memory please take me back to St. Luke's.' And now in the wilds of Yemassee I came to the conclusion that I was close to going mad. One day I asked Willie if he thought that a psychiatrist could help my condition.

'No,' said Willie firmly. 'Certainly not.'

'Why not?'

'Because he could do you no good. Your injury has exaggerated your defects, that's all. And you can't change your essential nature. All you can do is to try to make the best of your limitations.'

Willie looked at my doubtful face.

'I can ser-see you don't believe a word I'm saying. I can see that you think I'm being wilfully obtuse,' he said. 'So I'll tell you a story to show my point.'

Willie wandered over to the side-table and began to mix a dry Martini.

'Years ago,' he said, 'long before the first World War, I was quite fer-famous because I'd had four plays running in London at the same time, and I came to New York for the rehearsals of one of them. I was staying at the Ritz-Carlton, I remember. And one afternoon they rang up from the desk to say that there was a Mr Maugham waiting down-stairs to see me.

'"There's a mistake," I said. "I'm Mr Maugham."

'"We know," the desk-clerk replied. "But there's still a Mr Maugham waiting here to see you."

'"Then please send him up," I said.'

Willie finished stirring the martini, poured out two glasses and lit himself a cigarette.

'Presently a young man was shown into the room,' Willie continued. 'And this was Mr Maugham. He had dark curly hair and brown eyes and a sallow complexion. He was obviously sensitive, rather Bohemian and very highly strung. There was a striking family likeness.'

Willie paused for dramatic effect – as he always did when telling a story.

'But the oddest thing of all about it,' he said, 'was that the young man spoke with a pronounced stammer.'

Willie handed me my glass.

'And he told me that the Maughams came over to America a century ago,' Willie continued. 'But the essential characteristics had obviously still persisted in the young man.'

Willie took a sip of his drink.

'We're the product of our genes and chromosomes,' he concluded. 'And there's nothing whatever we can do about it. And that's the reason why I tell you that a psychiatrist couldn't help you. No one can. Because we can't change the essential natures we're born with. We can't alter the essential product that we are. All we can do is to try and supplement our own deficiencies. Meeting that young man in the Ritz-Carlton made me certain of it. There's no point in trying to change. One hasn't a hope.'

*

Who was the young American with curly dark brown hair and a stammer, I wondered? I discovered his name, wholly by chance, almost twenty years later. I noticed that there were three or four

Maughams in the Manhattan telephone directory, so I selected one of them at random. The name was Mr Ralph S. Maugham – then a complete stranger – and I wrote to him. He answered my letter from Spain. He had recently retired from being an executive in American Airlines and he was on holiday in Torremolinos. He was planning to come to England anyway, he said, and he might be able to help me. He suggested that we should meet in London when he arrived. A few weeks later he rang me up and asked me to lunch with him and his wife at the Westbury Hotel.

As soon as I walked into the Westbury I recognised him. The resemblance to my father and to my uncle – particularly in the colour and setting of his eyes and the shape of his forehead – was extraordinary. He was about sixty-five. He had no stammer but some of his movements reminded me at once of Willie. With Ralph Maugham was his charming wife Olivia, and I soon began to feel I had known them both for years. Over an excellent lunch Ralph told me about his family. His grandfather had emigrated from England to America in about 1850, and he believed that his ancestors had come originally from County Durham.*

Ralph Maugham, I now realised, had not even the faintest *trace* of a stammer, but it was still possible that he might have stammered as a young man.

'Did you ever meet my uncle, Somerset Maugham?' I asked.

'Only once,' Ralph Maugham replied. 'It must have been about 1910. I was only fourteen at the time, but the scene is quite clear to me still ... One of Somerset's plays was being produced in New York, and my father was determined to meet him to see if there was any family relationship. We were living in Tenafly then – it's a village fourteen miles up the Hudson – and Somerset very kindly took the trolley-car from the Jersey side. It must have been a hell of a trip, but he was a good sport about it. He and my father had a long talk, but apparently they were both very vague about their family backgrounds, and I don't think they made much progress. But I can remember peeking into the room where they were talking, and thinking that Somerset was a very handsome gentleman.'

* I discovered later that the Maughams had flourished both in Durham and Northumberland. The account of our researches into Ralph Maugham's family will be found in Appendix II.

As we settled down to our coffee I reflected how strange it was that Willie who boasted that he didn't care a tinker's cuss where he came from should have bothered to make that trip. Then I realised that there was still another question that I must put to my American cousin.

'Did you by any chance have a relation who stammered?' I asked.

'Oh, yes,' Ralph Maugham said promptly. 'That was my brother Monte, six years my senior. He was Joseph Beaumont Maugham. He was called Joseph Beaumont after his grandfather. Monte's dead now ... He was away when Somerset came out to see my father in Tenafly. But I remember that Monte did once call on Somerset at the Ritz-Carlton. Poor Monte, he stammered very badly.'

THE EMIGRANTS

SOON after I started to write this book Willie Somerset Maugham handed over to me several letters he had received from Americans who claimed kinship with him. By now I felt certain that I was related to Ralph Maugham, and I hoped to find more cousins. But, as it turned out, I found the most romantic of all my family's links with America in yet another small bundle of letters from the chintz-covered box.

A grand-daughter of the Reverend William Maugham of Moulton was venturesome enough to emigrate to Ohio in 1839. She was Lucy Eleanor Maugham, born in 1801. She was the daughter of Frances and Thomas Marmaduke Maugham, the cabinet-maker in Stamford, whose tombstone I had found the first evening of my quest in Lincolnshire. Little is known about her early years, but she cannot have been very happy or comfortable, for her father – to use one of Willie's favourite phrases – was 'positively poverty-stricken'. Lucy Eleanor Maugham may have decided that she would fare better on a farm, where there was at least a supply of meat and eggs and milk. We cannot tell. We only know that she left Stamford and went to live with her uncle George Maugham at Moulton, earning her keep as a dairy-maid on his farm. And it was in Moulton that she met and fell in love with Emanuel Andrew, a young farmer from the neighbouring village of Whaplode. She married him in 1833.

Six years later young Emanuel Andrew took the decision that was to change their lives. He made up his mind to follow the example of his brother Robert and to emigrate with his wife and his young children to America. It was the second year of Queen Victoria's reign, and thousands of families, many of them friends or neighbours, were leaving the cramped Old World to seek their fortunes in the New. It must have been a brave adventure, especially with small children. Their eldest son Emanuel, known as 'Manny',[1] was not yet five years old; the next child, Bob, was only three. The first steamships had begun to ply regularly across the Atlantic in the previous year – taking about ten or twelve days. But Emanuel Andrew's family went by sailing ship because the fare was cheaper. They endured a voyage of forty-eight days.

The story of their hopes and misfortunes in the New World is told in the little bundle of letters written to their uncle George Maugham in Moulton and his son George Richardson Maugham. In a way, it is the story of the whole of that pioneering epoch.

The first letter, dated April 11, 1839, was written by Emanuel from New York.

Dear Uncle,

Here we are all well after a most tempestuous passage of seven weeks. We left London on the 9th February at 6 o'clock in the morning and arrived at New York on Good Friday [March 29] at 10 o'clock at night. Our whole passage was one continued blow hard, so that we had a most miserable time of it . . .

New York, which fifty years previously had been a small town of thirty thousand people, was now a city with a population of a third of a million. The new age of the steamboat and the railway had given the city almost a monopoly of transportation to the West. Emanuel's enthusiasm for New York is tempered by loyalty to Old England. His letter continues:

New York is a most beautiful place but nothing equal to London in size. However it has one advantage – it is wonderfully clean. Most of the houses are painted so that they present a very different aspect to the houses of London. There is another thing that gives the city a rather curious appearance, namely the discrepancies in the sizes of the buildings. Here you see an Hotel equal to a Palace and the next house a boarded building not so good as your barn. These wooden tenements were in all probability built by the first Dutch inhabitants who I am told take a pride in transmitting them to their posterity in all their original simplicity, and cannot be prevailed on to sell them on any account . . .

Emanuel then told his uncle about the cost of living in the New World:

It is a mistaken notion about things being so much dearer *here* than with you. Everything is much the same price as in England except woollen cloths. They are excessively dear – twice your price. Silks are a great deal better and cheaper than in England . . . Excellent veal can be bought here for 4d a pound

and finer fish than I ever saw for 1½d a pound. There are waggon-loads of
live tortoises in the markets; I am not aware what they do with them.
Potatoes from England are the very worst that ever I eat. I don't believe your
pigs would eat them ...

But there were some dark clouds on the horizon. The country was
going through a severe financial and political crisis. In Washington, the
unpopular President, Martin Van Buren – 'the careful Dutchman from
New York', as he was called – was trying to clear up the muddle
resulting from the financial policy of his predecessor. General Andrew
Jackson had tried to check the fever of paper-money speculation in
1836 by ordering the Treasury to accept only gold and silver in payment for the Western lands it was selling at the rate of thousands of
acres a day. This had produced a panic as alarming as the bursting of the
South Sea Bubble. And there was the threat of war with England, due
in part to what was known as the 'Aroostook disturbance'.[2] Aroostook
was the name of the disputed territory lying between the American
state of Maine and the British province of New Brunswick.

But in spite of the commercial unrest and the threat of war, Lucy and
Emanuel were determined to make their way to Ohio and to buy a
farm there. They were looking forward to their journey up the Hudson
'by one of the magnificent steamers' as far as Troy, and thence by
canal boat along the Erie Canal, through the Mohawk Valley and the
orchards south of Lake Ontario. At Buffalo they would change on to a
'walk-in-the-water' as the paddle-steamers were called and cross Lake
Erie to Cleveland where Emanuel's brother Robert was to meet them.
'The whole expense of 750 miles will not cost more than it did from
Spalding to London,' said Emanuel. 'And we shall enjoy ten times the
comfort.'

*

It must have been some time in June 1839 that Emanuel and Lucy
Andrew took possession of their farm within the 'Township of Boston'
in Summit County, Ohio – a settlement on the Cuyahoga river, some
twenty miles south of Cleveland. Several weeks passed before Emanuel
Andrew's next letter[3] home to Uncle George Maugham in Moulton.

Dear Uncle,
    I delayed writing to you before now because I wished to get settled before
I sent word to you and have now to inform you that I have bought myself

a farm containing 30 acres of very good land 25 of which is cleared and fit for cultivation. I broke up $1\frac{1}{2}$ acres and sowed wheat which looks well and shall sow about 3 acres more wheat in the Spring, on some Indian Corn Land which was cleared too late to sow this fall of the year . . .

I gave 600 Dollars for my farm, 400 of which I paid Down, and am to pay the other 200 on the first Day of June next. This is about 4 £, 3s. an Acre. This may appear very little when compared with the price in England. The land is as good as land needs to be and will produce anything . . . I have no time to give you a particular account of everything . . . but will just say that I would not return to England to live if I could have 50 acres of land for nothing . . .

After this proud declaration of faith in the New World comes the first indication of their worry about money.

Now Uncle you possess the means, will you assist me with 60 £, for after the expenses of the Voyage and journey up the country of more than 700 miles, and the keeping of my family for more than a year before I shall get anything off my farm and the payment of 84 £ on the place I shall have nothing left to complete the purchase next June . . .

But uncles who possess the means are, alas, sometimes loth to part with a single penny, and so Emanuel asked his wife Lucy to add a postscript to the letter to soften her uncle's heart. Lucy's spelling and grammar, as one sees at once, were no better than that of her late seafaring uncle, Theophilus, and her sentences are rather confused. Lucy wrote:

My dear Uncle,
I writ to say me and my children are well and to say that I have got a home of our one which I shuld never had in england. Now dear Uncle if you will, please assist with what we ask you and I think you will do. You at least ort to give me something for the years I was with you. I think of you as my Father . . .

I do not know if Lucy's plea was successful, but the next letter from the Andrew family which was written by Emanuel and taken back to England by a neighbour in May 1840 begins fairly cheerfully. 'All of us enjoy very good health, except at times that I have the Rheumatism . . .'
Emanuel's uncertain health was the danger that loomed over their whole enterprise. The death of Lucy Eleanor's father, Thomas Marmaduke Maugham, is later mentioned briefly; but the main part of the letter is concerned with Emanuel's need for ready cash.

Money is very scarce just now owing to the banks being in a very unsettled state – consequently every thing is very low ... I have as much Oak lying on 4 acres of land as would make 1,000 £ if sold at Moulton and I must *burn* it all to get it out of the way ...

His clearing of the wood reminded Emanuel of the garden he intended to make. And in the list of seeds and roots for which he asks there may be a hint of homesickness for his old country.

If it is not too much trouble I wish you to get a tin something like a yeast tin and fill it with the following roots well dried. When you get this will be just the time. Snowdrops – Blue, White and Yellow Crocuses – Hyacinths, Daffodils, all sorts of Tulips – Laburnum seeds ... Holly berrys, Red and White Raspberry seeds ... Mountain ash berrys – 10 Apricot stones – Golden drop plum stones if ripe – a root of yellow aconites – a few Blue bells ...

Crocuses and bluebells must have swept Emanuel's mind back to the village of Moulton and to Lucy Eleanor's sister, Susan Maugham, in particular, who had also been employed on Uncle George's farm. And the letter continues:

What has become of Susan? She would do well here, for women *helps*, as they call charwomen and servant girls here, are the scarcest thing in this country. They are not to be had for money. A Tavern Keeper's wife offered 16 s to 20 s a *week* for a cook, and could not get one.

Slavery was, of course, prohibited in Ohio, and people were prepared to pay wages for a white servant which were high in comparison to the low price of food. Such was the demand for 'helps' even in those days in America that it was not considered odd for a landowner to be also in private service.

Emanuel's financial problems were shared by almost the whole country. He, however, was more concerned with his private worries than with the problems of the Federal Government, and the only person to whom he could turn was his uncle. His next letter is dated December 16, 1841:

I will now explain our own affairs as well as I can ... In November my brother Robert borrowed all my remaining money except 4 pounds to take him to England promising to return early in the spring and to lett me have sufficient money to pay the remainder of the purchase money and to buy implements etc. for the farm ...

Robert appears to have been an amiable but most unreliable character. His jaunt in England had left Emanuel almost destitute of ready
money.

I have nothing that will fetch cash except at a most awful sacrifice. Now I
want you to send me if you possibly can a ten pound bank of England note
immediately you receive this letter and ten pounds more by Mr Dolby when
he returns. I do not ask you to give us the money, for if we live and have our
health you shall have it again . . .

Emanuel has, in fact, followed what might be described as the classic
pattern of borrowing: he has explained why he needs money; he has
stated the precise sum that he requires; and he has promised to repay the
loan. But he now makes a mistake.

'Times are good with you,' Emanuel continues. 'And you can spare
Twenty pounds without knowing that you have lent it.' Such a
remark is bound to irritate a man who is asked for a loan, for most of
us would prefer to be thought poor but generous rather than rich and
stingy. However, Emanuel makes some amends by telling his uncle
that he has had to work two and a half days as a labourer 'on the road'
to pay his taxes, and in the final paragraph of his letter Emanuel makes
a comparison – probably quite innocently – between his own behaviour
and that of his brother Robert and his neighbours.

You are under a great mistake about the good manners of the Americans.
99 out of every 100 chew large quantities of Tobacco and 3 of them in half
an hour would spit enough on a floor to require a pair of boots to get across
it. My Brother will Chew, smoke, and spit as much as any of them, and also
drink as much wiskey. This damned, infernal liquor is only 1s 6d a gallon
retail, and as low as 10d if you take a whole barrel. And most part of the
English as well as the Yankees drink it to excess. For my part I hate the smell
of the cursed stuff.

*

Emanuel got his loan – as his next letter, written a year later on January
3, 1843, shows. 'The order you sent came to hand at a real seasonable
time. In fact it saved us from almost ruination.'

'Almost ruination' is precisely the right note to sound. So far, the
loan technique is excellent. His uncle in the peace and security of
Moulton village must have felt a glow of self-satisfaction at the noble
action he had performed at such little personal inconvenience. But

W. Somerset Maugham and Robin Maugham in the living-room of the cottage at Parker's Ferry, 1945

Cragg House, Brough, near Appleby, Westmorland

The swimming pool at the Villa Mauresque

Emanuel spoils it all by continuing in the very next line, 'And if you would send another order for the same sum it would set us quite out of harm's way.' He has lost the sympathy of his audience by such an *immediate* request for another loan. He should have waited for at least three further pages of the letter. As it is, the news that Lucy Eleanor has had yet 'another child, a girl, born on the first day of last July' must have dropped into unsympathetic ears. And the information that Emanuel was so short of ready cash that he had difficulty in raising the price of the postage to send the letter to England may have been met with utter disbelief – as even Emanuel in his innocence and artlessness seems to have realised.

This is another real foul day, snowing away wet snow as fast as it can. And as we have contrived to raise a Quarter of a Dollar (1s), I will now finish the letter and send it off. I almost fancy I see you laugh at the idea of a man that owns 30 acres of Freehold land and has plenty of stock on it being hard set to raise an English shilling in metal, but the Post Office will take nothing but specie . . .

Emanuel was good and hard-working, but his letters to his uncle approached the old man in the wrong way, and he did not receive a second money-order; he did not even get an answer to his letter.

His worst fear now faced Emanuel. His health was fading and he realised that his physical strength, which alone made it possible for his family to live from day to day, would soon be sapped. But he still resolutely planned for the future.

I have got the land ploughed for 5½ acres of wheat and I shall try hard to get it sown this week. I got a great many logs sawn last winter and am going to put up a New building 24 feet long, 14 feet wide and the posts 12 feet high for a chaff house, 2 Cow Stalls, and a hay loft over the whole. Also a waggon hovel at the end 10 feet wide . . . 3 more days framing will finish it . . .

But the problem of erecting the new farm buildings remained. Emanuel could not put them up by himself; his sons were still too young to help him, and he had no ready cash to spare. The solution to his problem lay in that 'damned, infernal liquor – that cursed stuff – wiskey'. It was an understood custom in the district that if you offered your neighbours enough hard liquor to drink they would work for you for nothing.

I shall then get 2 gallons of wiskey and invite 20 men, and they will put it up in about 2 hours. Thus far it will have cost me nothing but hard labor. To get the nails is a more difficult matter. They are a cash article, and we spent very near our last shilling to-day for a barrel of salt . . . Our animals eat about 3 lbs a week . . .

*

Perhaps Emanuel was not the stuff of which successful pioneers are made. He seems to have been a frailer, gentler person than many of his fellow immigrants who were, I suppose, better equipped to withstand transplantation from the ancient earth of Europe to the virgin soil of America. Yet his letters must be typical of those written 'home' by many other small farmers in Ohio during that period. The wonder is that the settlers survived, and stayed, and that their descendants flourished.

The story of Emanuel's attempt to create a prosperous new life for his family in Summit County, Ohio, ends with the last letter in the bundle that I found in the chintz box. The letter tells of Emanuel's death on March 10, 1845, and it is written by one of Lucy's neighbours on Lucy's behalf – presumably because she was too distressed to write it herself.

Dear Uncle,

After two years nearly of pain and sickness death has at length released Emanuel from his sorrow and sufferings . . . My Dear Husband died on the tenth day of March in the evening, worn completely out, in a deep consumption. It was his wish that his lungs might be examined after his death, consequently two Doctors attended the day after he died and opened his chest, and on examination found his lungs completely destroyed by his disease, not a sound portion left. And it does seem strange how any one can live so long under so fatal a complaint.

It was his wish to be buried on his own farm, on a spot he had selected and staked out some time before his death. He was buried on the twelfth in the afternoon, attended by a few neighbours, amid deep snow. An Episcopal minister attended, and after an appropriate address in the house, finally conveyed him to the grave he had chosen, and concluded by reading the English burial service. This was a day of deep distress to me . . .

Lucy's plight must have seemed almost hopeless and the future was bleak – as she herself pointed out:

I am surrounded with a large family of small children, a Widow, in a strange country, amid strangers and a thousand difficulties. All these harrow up my feelings and make me exceedingly distressed and unhappy...

Then follows a tribute to the American settlers in the district which I think is all the more moving for being so obviously spontaneous and heartfelt.

My neighbours have been exceedingly kind to me in every thing except money – and that few of them have any more than myself. Whatever faults the Americans have otherwise, they are certainly exceedingly kind to the sick and distressed, to those who are unable to succour themselves. During my Husband's illness, they paid us all possible attention and brought us a hundred comforts we could not possibly have got but for their kindness ...

After her husband's death, Lucy may have considered the possibility of selling the farm and returning to England with her family. But I believe it was the unexpected kindness bestowed on her by her equally impoverished neighbours in the time of distress that made her decide to stay on. She was calmly determined to bring up her children in the New World to which she now felt bound 'by ties that seem indissoluble'. And she never returned to England.*

* For the later history of Lucy Eleanor Andrew and her descendants, see Appendix III.

EARLY MAUGHAMS

IT's odd how often mere legend proves to be fact. With the help of my researchers I had established the existence of a whole line of Maughams in Lincolnshire; yet I was interested by a family legend that the Maughams had even earlier roots in the Lake District. On one of the few occasions in his life that my father spoke to me with affection – we had dined together at the Garrick Club – he told me that he believed that one of our ancestors was a 'statesman', a small working landowner, living on the borders of Cumberland and Westmorland. He also said that he seemed to recollect that his grandfather had been educated at the famous old grammar school at Appleby in Westmorland. I had also to take into consideration the Maughams in the neighbouring counties of Durham and Northumberland – including the forebears of Mrs Maturin and those of my American namesake, Ralph S. Maugham. Whence, precisely, did the Reverend William Maugham spring? Where was he born and who were his parents?

A few weeks after my visit to Stamford the answer came from Mr Stephen Goard, the energetic genealogist who was the hall-porter at the George Hotel. He had made a brief visit to Westmorland and had discovered in the registers of the parish of Brough, only a few miles from Appleby, the baptism of the Reverend William Maugham, born on July 10, 1726, to William Maugham of Cragg House. He had also discovered a reference to the baptism of old William's younger brother Robert, on May 9, 1732. Mr Goard's search had been prompted by this entry which he found in the *Lincoln, Rutland and Stamford Mercury* for December 22, 1815:

Died. On the 5th inst. at Appleby, Westmorland, in his 84th year, Mr Robert Maugham, brother to the late Rev. William Maugham, Master of the Moulton Free Grammar School in this County.

Two more pieces of the jig-saw had fallen into place. William Maugham of Cragg House was obviously the 'statesman' my father had spoken about. And I soon realised that he was, in fact, the great-great-great-grandfather of my father and my uncle Willie. Eight of this William's children are mentioned in the printed registers of

Brough, together with two wives – Ann, who died in 1717, and Sarah, who died more than eighty years later in 1800. His own burial on November 24, 1771, at the age of ninety-one was also mentioned, so he must have been born about 1680 – though no record of his birth has so far been discovered. But Cragg House, where he had lived, was still standing. Mr Goard had visited the present tenant farmer, Mr J. G. Brogden, who had assured him that I should be welcome to call on him at Cragg House whenever I came up to Westmorland.

Our quest, which continued throughout the summer of 1962, was often frustrated when patient searches through the records of other parishes in the Lake District yielded an assortment of Maughams who, oddly enough, seemed to have no established connection with my branch of the family. But sometimes we were rewarded by finding a marriage or a will that concerned the descendants of William Maugham of Cragg House. And, early in October, armed with a bundle of notes and documents, Derek Peel and I made the long train journey from London to Carlisle, where a car was waiting to drive us to Appleby.

In the reign of the first Queen Elizabeth, an anonymous visitor[1] to the Lake District had written:

Appleby is memorable for antiquity and situation onely. It standeth in a pleasant site, encompassed for the most part by the Eden, but so slenderly inhabited and the buildings so simple, that were it not for its antiquity it deserved to be accounted the Chief town of the Shire and to have sessions and assizes kept in the Castle, which is the Common gaole for malefactours, it would be little better than a village. For all the beauty of it lieth in the one broad street, from N to S, with an easie ascent of the Hill. In the nether end is the Church and thereby a Schoole which Robert Langton and Miles Spencer, Doctors of the law, founded; the Maister whereof is Reginald Bainbridge, a right learned man who governeth the same with great commendation.

Three and a half centuries do not seem to have changed Appleby much, and this description might have been written yesterday, for the lovely little town is still only 'slenderly inhabited'. In fact, the only changes seem to be that the 'Common gaole' is no longer in the Castle at the top of the 'one broad street'; that in the Tufton Arms Hotel where we stayed you can have a better dinner, I suppose, than any sixteenth-century traveller could have enjoyed; and that the present 'Maister of the Schoole' is named Mr A. E. Windass – though I found

him as 'right learned' as ever his Elizabethan predecessor could have
been, and I have no doubt that he also 'governeth' his pupils with
'great commendation', for I saw two canes in the corner of his study
when I visited him on my first morning.

It is almost certain that the Reverend William Maugham was
educated at 'The Free Grammar School of Queen Elizabeth' before he
became an usher at Wisbech – perhaps through the patronage of the
headmaster of the time, when there was something like a 'closed shop'
in the teaching profession. In those days, Appleby School was only a
small building, close to the ancient church of St Lawrence on the west
side of a little street with the curious name of Low Wiend. An eighteenth-century part of the school still exists, a block of three cottages
facing the pleasant green known as King George's Playing Field. But
the older buildings were pulled down in 1887 when the school moved
to its present site beyond the river Eden.

To keep my appointment with Mr Windass, the headmaster, I
drove across the river and up a hill called Battlebarrow[2] – now part
of the busy A.66 highway carrying traffic between Glasgow and
London – and found a rather dull grey stone school with no hint that it
had much of a past or a future. So it was a pleasant surprise when the
headmaster showed me the vast modern blocks that had been cleverly
added behind the Victorian façade, with workshops, laboratories, and a
theatre to seat five hundred boys and girls.

'Though the school was given its Charter by the first Queen
Elizabeth in 1574,' Mr Windass told us, 'it had actually existed on its
former site by St Lawrence's Church since the fourteenth century.
When Appleby was sacked and burned by the invading Scots in 1388,
the old school was one of the few buildings that survived the fire.'

As I left he handed me three small ruled exercise-books.

'I'm afraid these are the only records I've been able to find that relate
to the time when your forbears were at Appleby,' he said. 'You're
welcome to borrow them to see if the name Maugham is mentioned.
But you may be disappointed because they're in no way complete
registers of the school.'

I searched in vain. Two of the books contained copies of the ancient
decrees and deeds associated with the school and lists of benefactors.
The third was more interesting: it was an 'Account of Money Received
for the Use of Appleby School by me, Ri: Yates, since Feb^{ry} 20th 1724:

All rec^d by the Boys before that Period being squandered by the Head Scholars.'

Richard Yates was one of Appleby's greatest headmasters. During his rule of almost sixty years from 1723 until his death in 1781 he formed the school's unusually excellent library – with many volumes dating from the fifteenth century. His accounts, patiently kept until almost the day he died, list the title and price of every book he bought for the boys, and every penny he received. Many of the departing scholars gave as much as half a guinea, but the Reverend William Maugham is not among them. As one of the large brood of a modest farmer, I presume he could not afford to compete with the sons of the landed gentry, such as members of the Lowther family, kinsmen of the Earls of Lonsdale.

I discovered that the school's scholars included – surprisingly enough – two of the sons of a Virginian planter who had himself been educated at Appleby. They were Lawrence and Augustine Washington, the elder half-brothers of the first President of the United States of America. Had their father not died before the children by what he described as his 'second venture' were old enough to leave home, George Washington might have followed his half-brothers to Appleby, and the history of America might have taken a different course. It was amusing to read the two entries in the handwriting of Mr Yates, the headmaster: '1732. Dec. 4. Lawrence Washington ... 10s. 6d.,' and '1741. Dec. 3. Augustine Washington ... 10s. 6d.' Lawrence, of course, would have left the school before the Reverend William Maugham arrived. But William would certainly have known Augustine. I wonder if he ever invited him home for Sunday tea at Cragg House.

*

Later that day in Appleby I met the Vicar, the Reverend A. G. W. Dixon, a friendly man with the build of a rugger player, whom I had noticed in the Tufton Arms the previous evening moving happily between groups of his parishioners, gripping a silver tankard of beer. He seemed to know everyone in Appleby; they all waved at him and smiled as we stood chatting on the steps of the hotel. Mr Dixon had been forewarned of my visit and he had made several discoveries in the parish registers, mainly concerning the Robert Maugham who was born at Brough in 1732. His most important find was the baptism of

Robert's eldest son, William. This was the link that had been troubling me since the researches began. For this William Maugham was undoubtedly the father of my great-grandfather, Robert Maugham, who was educated at Appleby Grammar School. But more of that later.

There are two principal churches in Appleby – St Lawrence's, the lovely parish church dating from the twelfth century and situated at the 'nether end' of the broad street, and St Michael's Bongate, below the castle at the far end of the town, which was rebuilt in the seventeenth century and unhappily restored in Victorian times. All references to my family in Appleby have so far been found in St Michael's, but the same registers may have served the two churches, when there was, as now, only one vicar to officiate in both.[3]

'Bongate was a Scandinavian settlement about a thousand years ago,' Mr Dixon explained as he drove me across the river Eden and out along the Brough road. 'Later, in the reign of King John, it was the place where the "bondmen" lived who attended upon the lord of the castle.'

There is even a Scandinavian tombstone, dating from the eleventh century, set in the north wall of St Michael's Church where my great-great-great-grandfather was buried in the reign of George III. And it was fascinating to sit in the vestry of the church as the vicar turned over the thick yellow parchment pages of the registers to show me his findings. The first entry was the banns of marriage on September 10, 1758, between Robert Maugham, 'bachelor of St Lawrence, Appleby', and Agnes Stephenson, 'spinster of Warcop'.

'I expect they were actually married at St Columba's in Warcop,' Mr Dixon said. 'It's only five miles from here on the way to Brough.'

We also found a reference to the burial of Agnes, on September 2, 1801, aged sixty-six, and to Robert's own burial on December 7, 1815, aged eighty-three. His occupation was given as 'glazier'. And then there were the baptisms of several of their children, beginning with that of their eldest son, William, on July 10, 1759. I was interested to notice that the family name was spelled with an n – 'Maughan'.

Later that afternoon we went over to Warcop, hoping to meet the vicar of St Columba's Church, but he was out, so we drove on to keep an appointment with the Reverend A. J. Sowden, vicar of St Michael's Church at Brough. The very landscape seemed to be subdued by history as we followed the straight Roman road into the village and turned south past the ruins of the fortress of Verterae – as the Romans called Brough – and then along a rough lane that dipped down to the vicarage. Mist was already creeping up the valley as Mr Sowden led us across the graveyard towards his church – another splendid example of mediaeval building in which Westmorland abounds – with a pronounced slope in the floor of the nave so that the congregation must look up towards the altar.

The vicar showed us a replica of the famous 'Brough Stone' which was discovered in 1879. It is a memorial to young 'Hermes of Kommagene' who may have served as an auxiliary with the Roman legions and who was buried there at Brough about seventeen hundred years ago, long before it became a Christian burial ground. The inscription is so beautiful that I cannot resist quoting the English translation.[4] The allusion to the Cimmerians may be poetic or may refer to the strange, unknown people who inhabited Scotland.

Should any traveller chance to see sixteen-year-old Hermes of Kommagene, foredoomed by fate to the grave, let him speak as follows: 'My greetings to you, boy, fast though you passed your mortal life; for you were flying to the land of the Cimmerian-speaking folk.' And you won't be wrong, for he was a good chaste-living boy.

*

The country of my ancestors, which had been fought over and ravaged by Romans, Scandinavians, Normans, and Scots, seemed very peaceful in the pale autumn light as I sat at tea in the vicarage looking out of the long windows at the garden and the wide landscape beyond.

'I've dug out some old registers for you to look at,' the vicar said. 'But I don't suppose you'll find anything that isn't already in the printed volumes.'

But he was wrong. I found the entries for the Reverend William Maugham and his brother Robert, the glazier – both born at Cragg House, as I had supposed. But then there came a surprise: all their half brothers and sisters – the children of their father's first marriage – were described as 'ye son' or 'ye daughter' of 'William Maugham of Old Park'. So where and what was Old Park? The place sounded quite grand, but the vicar had never heard of it.

'Ask Mr Brogden when you get to Cragg House,' he said. 'Perhaps he knows.'

So we drove on from the vicarage at Brough, up into the desolate fell land, with the evening mist lying like a blanket over the stillness of the wild countryside, muffling even the sound of the traffic on the busy main road less than a mile away. I followed the one-inch Ordnance Survey map as carefully as if I had been back in my tank in the Western Desert. But luckily Derek and I were in the safe hands of a local man, Mr Wiser, who had been engaged to drive us during the weekend. He steered us safely through a wilderness intersected by rough, uncemented stone walls. The fells seemed to be inhabited only by sheep heavy with wool. Then we bumped along a narrow cart-track, opened and shut three gates, and at last saw the first sign of human life we had seen for a long while – Cragg House, a plain stone farm building standing firm and solid on open ground that sloped gently towards the valley. Smoke was idling through the chimney, and a man with a bucket in his hand was opening the gate that led into the farmyard. Except for the incongruous sight of a television aerial, we might have been back in the early eighteenth century, with my great-great-great-great-grandfather, William Maugham, coming home from the fields in time for his evening meal.

Mr Brogden closed the gate and came forward to welcome us.

'So you've come to see your old family home,' he said. 'I don't suppose it's changed much from the outside.'

He led us into the house to meet his wife and family. In the pleasant little sitting-room his two younger daughters were sprawling in front of the fire watching television, the newest excitement in their lives, for the set had been bought only two days previously and specially adapted to the diesel engine that generated the electric light for the farm. Mrs Brogden showed us round the house, which was strongly but strangely built. There were no passages and the walls were almost three feet thick in places. The rooms led one into the other through low doorways and were set on different levels. The farmhouse was certainly of a great age and was built long before William Maugham came there with his second wife, Sarah. This must have been sometime *after* 1722, when the house was shown in the Brough parish registers as occupied by one John Holme, and *before* 1726, when the Reverend William was born there. I tried to imagine the elder William sitting at the head of the table, surrounded by his five sons and three daughters. Charles, the eldest of William's five children by his first marriage, was born in 1708 so he was already grown up when Robert, the youngest son, was born in 1732. No doubt he and his next brother, John, did most of the work on the farm, while their sisters Elenor and Sarah helped their step-mother in running the house and looking after her own young family.

When Mrs Brogden had finished showing us round the house, her husband led us to the farmyard to look at his flock of geese and the fine herd of dairy Shorthorns that he had brought in for the night from his pastureland of one hundred and forty acres. We stood gazing across the valley in the fading light, and I remembered the question I had to put.

'Have you ever heard of Old Park?' I asked.

'Why, yes,' Mr Brogden answered. 'It's right over there, across Argill Beck. You can just see it between the trees. It's another farm, like this, only smaller – with no more than forty acres. But the house itself has been empty for years.'

So after we had said goodbye to the kind Brogdens and taken our leave of Cragg House we drove to Old Park. It was no more than two thousand yards across the valley as the crow flies. But it took us over twenty minutes to approach the property, bumping along the rough winding roads and cart-tracks. The last track seemed to end in a field some distance from the house, and there we left the car and stumbled over thick wet loam in the gathering darkness. We crossed a narrow footbridge spanning a stream that gurgled over smooth boulders, and climbed up the steep grassy slope that led to the farmhouse. Across the valley we could see the cheerful lights of Cragg House, where Mrs Brogden was no doubt preparing supper for her family. But Old Park seemed oddly and almost disquietingly lifeless. The panes were still in the windows, but the door hung open, and inside on the ground floor and upstairs the floors of the derelict rooms were littered with straw, for they had been used as shelters for the flocks of sheep. Paper hung limply down from the damp-streaked walls. The house looked very forlorn. I asked Mr Wiser how long he thought the farm had been unoccupied.

'It's hard to tell,' he said. 'Perhaps since the war, or even before. People don't like living out in the wilds nowadays. There's been a steady stream of people moving from Westmorland down to the big towns in the south. You'll find many abandoned farmhouses like this in these parts. When the families move away to the towns, their farms are bought up by business men from the south who run whole stretches of land as ranches for beef cattle on the American pattern. But they don't need the farmhouses because they can't get the farm-workers to live in them, so they go to ruin.'

As we were leaving Old Park, I noticed some rough carving above the stone doorway within the triangle of the pediment. In the flame of my cigarette lighter I picked out the letters G.N.H. and the date 1717. This inscription meant nothing at first, until I realised that 1717 was the year in which William Maugham's first wife, Ann, died leaving him with five young children – the eldest, Charles, being only a boy of nine, and the youngest, Christopher, an infant a few months old. It seemed reasonable to suppose, therefore, that William sold the house to G.N.H. and moved away – perhaps to his own parents, where his children could be properly cared for. And then, when William married again, a few years later, what more natural than his wish to return to the land he knew so well? So sometime between 1722 and 1726 William was able to take over Cragg House – the farm he had always seen just across the valley. This theory may seem a little too easy, but at least it makes sense.

When we reached the car at the end of the dark, soggy field I turned back. The valley was now obscured by mist, but on the far side I could still see the lights of Cragg House, and it occurred to me how distant in more senses than one was that small stone farmhouse, set in the desolate fells, from the trim lawns and neat terraces of the Villa Mauresque, Cap Ferrat, where my uncle Willie lived with a staff of ten servants, surrounded by the paintings and furniture, the statues and porcelain that his success had enabled him to buy.

*

Early on Sunday morning I searched the graveyards of both the churches in Appleby, hoping to find a Maugham tombstone – as I had in Stamford in Lincolnshire. But I was disappointed. The red sand-stone used in these parts is so soft that many of the inscriptions on the unsheltered memorials have been wholly obliterated. Maughams there may have been – Robert the glazier, for instance, and Agnes his wife – but I could not find them. However, I noticed several instances of one name, Harrison, which is important to my story, for it was to a

Catherine Harrison that Robert's eldest son, William, was married in the 1780s before he in his turn moved away from his ancestral home to seek a new life in the south.

At noon Mr Wiser arrived in his car to drive us over to lunch with Lord Lonsdale at Askham Hall – one of the many manor houses on his huge estate that was once fortified against the marauding Scots but has now been put to a more amiable use. I have to thank James Lonsdale not only for a most enjoyable day but for giving me access to his formidable collection of manorial rolls and other documents which might have yielded some information on the Maughams. The fact that the family name is not once mentioned confirmed my belief that we Maughams come from very humble stock indeed.

One of the many pleasant surprises of the day was meeting James Lonsdale's mother, Muriel Viscountess Lowther, who turned out to be an energetic member of the Cumberland and Westmorland Antiquarian and Archaeological Society. I told her that I had managed to trace my family back to 1680.[5]

'If you were here as early as that,' she said, 'I expect you were *always* here. You may even have Scandinavian roots – like so many other families in this part of the country.'

*

The exciting idea that my ancestors might have been stalwart Vikings led me and my friends on a long, frustrating chase. We were not helped by the fact that the old books we consulted each stated with fine assurance that the Maughams came from entirely different places. The Maughams appeared to spring from Cornwall, from Monmouthshire, from Ireland, and even from St Malo in Brittany. But later, when we sought the opinion of some of the scholars of today who study the sources of personal names and place names we found that they were far less ready to commit themselves than their Victorian predecessors, and none would give any definite ruling.

Our hopes were raised at one stage by finding two place names in Cumberland which seemed to be connected with my family – *Pow Maughan*, a stream that flows into the river Eden, and *Maughonby*, a hamlet about six miles to the north-east of Penrith. Some scholar had traced these names through their several variants and had reached back to the Old Welsh personal name of *Merchiaun*, and this in turn was

linked with the Old Breton name *Merchion* and compared to the Latin
Marcianus. So perhaps the Maughams were Welsh – with Breton and
Roman connections? We wrote to Professor A. H. Smith, the Honorary Director of the English Place-Name Society. He answered that he
was 'not sure if "Maugham" did, in fact, originate as a place-name',
and he then referred us to Dr Melville Richards, the Reader in Celtic
Studies at the University of Liverpool. Dr Richards replied at some
length and quoted several instances of similar Celtic personal and place
names, but admitted that he doubted whether the Maugham family
had 'any connection with Wales, at least as far as the name goes'.

I next tried to examine the theory that our Maugham ancestors came
from Ireland. Both my father and my uncle Willie had told me at some
time or other that the experts said we were originally Irish. Here,
too, there was a possible Scandinavian link, because in the tenth century Norwegian raiders came over to the Lake District from Ireland.
Evidence of their occupation is still seen in many of the place names in
Cumberland and Westmorland, and some of these names can be linked
with Ireland, with which the Norwegians maintained close contact
for a number of years. But though I made all kinds of searches I could
still find nothing definite.

My American namesake and friend, Ralph S. Maugham, then
produced a completely different suggestion. He wrote to say that he
had always believed that 'the first Maugham was a groom to the Duke
of Normandy and came over to England in 1066'. I was delighted by
this theory but could find no foundation for it, and I was still groping
around in the dark when I was given a suggestion that, on examination,
seemed to make the best sense of all. I received a letter from a genealogist saying that he had found 'what looked like an early form' of my
name – *de Malgham*, or *de Malghum* – in Yorkshire, in the thirteenth
and fourteenth centuries. 'If you have not yet written to Dr P. H.
Reaney,' he added, 'it might be worth your while to do so, to ask him
the derivation of your name and thereby possibly get a hint of where to
look for it.' So we wrote to Dr Reaney, the distinguished etymologist,
whose *Dictionary of British Surnames*[6] was published a few years ago.
He replied with scholarly care, answering each possible theory, and he
led us to the remarkable conclusion that – by circumstantial evidence,
if not by actual proof – the Maughams probably came from the West
Riding of Yorkshire, even as far back as Saxon times. The extraordinary

fact is that the family from whom we may be descended – variously named *Malham*, or *Malgham*, or *Malghum* – once flourished around the villages of Malham and Kirkby Malham, which are only thirty-five miles south of Brough in Westmorland, and the fells where we know that William Maugham lived until his death in 1771. Still more conclusive is the definite fact that the family named *Malham*, *Malgham*, or *Malghum* sometimes pronounced their name 'Mawm'. And we have since found further evidence, all of which seems to point to our taking our name from this little Saxon settlement in a beautiful corner of the West Riding. (An account of our researches into the matter and our conclusions will be found in Appendix IV at the end of this book.) I have little doubt that if we searched long enough in the West Riding we should find the parents of William Maugham of Cragg House. Most likely his father was called Charles, for that is the name he gave to his eldest son, but I have yet to find a Charles Maugham who married in the 1670s.

*

If my ancestors were anything like the later generations of my family, they must have been rather short and dark, and they must have lived to a great age. But I must stick to the story as far as I know it – beginning with my great-great-great-great-grandfather William of Cragg House. As it is, the story covers a long enough span of history, for William was born when King Charles II was still on the throne.

I suppose that William's life as a farmer must have been simple in the extreme, and I suspect that he kept himself to himself – as the saying goes – for these small yeomen or 'statesmen' of the Lakeland were a sturdy and independent lot who wanted no truck with the outside world and developed their own ways and characteristics. But William must have had some learning to have encouraged the education of his children. And isn't it true that in such native strength and individuality – in men whose forbears were too humble to receive mention even in the local records during the early seventeenth century – lay the seed that eventually flourished in some of the most famous men of scholarship and the arts? William Maugham of Cragg House could not have dreamed that his descendants, five generations later, would include a Lord Chancellor of England and the most celebrated novelist of his time. Yet they in turn owed much of their vigour to the yeoman farmer who wrought his living on the bleak fells of Westmorland.

*

I do not know what became of William Maugham's sons and daughters by his first marriage; nor have I tried to find out, for they do not concern my story. My interest is in his children by his 'second venture' – the Reverend William, of Moulton, and – more particularly – his younger brother Robert, for he was Willie's and my direct ancestor.

Robert Maugham, as I have said, was baptised at St Michael's Church at Brough on May 9, 1732, and since he became a glazier we may suppose that he began his apprenticeship in 1746 or 1747, at the age of fourteen or fifteen, and perhaps lived above his master's workshop near the church of St Lawrence in Appleby. He was twenty-six when he married Agnes Stephenson of Warcop. By then he was probably earning a good enough living to move into a cottage of his own, for a skilled glazier could always be assured of work in the churches and in the mansions of the local gentry. Anyhow, Robert and Agnes were living somewhere on the hill called Battlebarrow when their first child William was born in the summer of 1759. Seven more children followed at appropriate intervals – Agnes, Isabella, Margaret, Edward, Elizabeth, John and Thomas. Those that survived were all grown up when their mother died in 1801. One can suppose that, in accordance with the custom of those days, Robert Maugham did his best to provide marriage dowries for his daughters and to give his sons a useful start in the world. This may account for the fact that at his own death in 1815 he was able to leave his children only ten shillings each.

*

I have a copy of Robert Maugham's will, made in 1814, and much of it is illegible to my unpractised eye, but it does give us the only glimpse into the man's life in his old age. In his will he directed that 'all my stock of Glass & Lead & all my Tools thereto belonging' and 'all my Wearing Apparel' be sold to settle 'my just debts and ffuneral Expenses'. After the token bequests to his children he made arrangements for his housekeeper, Margaret Garth, to be provided for. She was to receive 'ffeather Bed & Bolster which she usually slept upon & also the other Bed Cloathes thereto belonging and also the Bedstead

Robert Maugham of the
Law Society

The portrait of Robert
Maugham which hangs in
the Law Society's Hall

Anne Alicia Snell, the maternal grandmother of W. Somerset Maugham

General Sir Henry Somerset from whom the name 'Somerset' came into the Maugham family

and Hangings thereto belonging'. I must confess that I am interested in the phrase 'which she *usually* slept upon', for it surely implies that there were occasions when Margaret did *not* sleep in that particular 'ffeather Bed'. Can this have been the reason why the children were only left ten shillings each while Margaret Garth was given 'the large table in my Kitchen, the Stand Table in the garret, and the Iron Oven' together with various utensils? One can't help wondering. But whatever their relationship, Robert evidently trusted his housekeeper Margaret, for the next sentence of his will reads: 'She has many things of her own in the house which I hope no body will hinder her of taking because I am certain she will claim nothing but her own. . . '.

Robert's will also gives us the clue to the migration of Maughams away from the simple pattern of farming and craftsmanship, which had been their lot for generations, in the search of a more ambitious and refined mode of living in the south of England. With only one exception – Elizabeth, who had gone to live with her husband in the town of Barnard Castle – Robert Maugham mentions all his children as being 'of London'. This was, of course, part of a general trend. People were moving away from the country towards the towns. But there may have been special reasons that drew my own particular family to London at the end of the eighteenth century, and in support of this theory I offer two suggestions. The first is based on a guess. One of the witnesses to Robert Maugham the glazier's will was named Thomas Thompson. It's not an uncommon name, but my guess is that Thomas Thompson was connected with the Reverend Francis Thompson (1665–1735) who was the Vicar of Brough at the time that Robert and his brothers were baptized. (The vicar's second son was the poet and clergyman, William Thompson, one of Appleby School's most famous scholars.) So perhaps Thomas Thompson, the witness to Robert Maugham's will, may have been a man of influence with friends in London who were able to take Robert's sons into their employment. The second – and more likely reason – concerns another eminent pupil of Appleby School, who was a year junior to the Reverend William Maugham. He was John Robinson, the son of "a thriving Appleby tradesman" and a cousin of Wordsworth. The article on him in the *Dictionary of National Biography* traces his long and adventurous career – scholar, attorney, town clerk and mayor, magistrate, deputy lieutenant of the county, and member of Gray's Inn. We are told of his successful marriage to a wealthy heiress with a fine inheritance of property in Westmorland and the political votes that went with it. We read of his election to Parliament under the patronage of Sir James Lowther (who became the first Earl of Londsale) with whom he later quarrelled so bitterly over Britain's policy towards the American Colonies. We learn of his enjoyment of high office and his friendship with George III. But John Robinson is best remembered to-day because of Sheridan's malicious remark in the House of Commons when asked if he could name the man whom he was accusing of political bribery.

'Yes,' Sheridan replied, 'I could name him as soon as I could say Jack Robinson.'

Robinson may not have known the Maughams socially, but he was such a power in his native town that the few inhabitants would certainly have sought his advice and help if their sons had any pretensions of following in his footsteps. So perhaps as one approaches the next stage in the quest for 'Somerset and all the Maughams' one need seek no further than Jack Robinson for the reason why Willie's and my ancestors entered the legal profession when they forsook the dark fells and misty valleys of Westmorland for the alien hubbub of London.

THE BREAKTHROUGH

ON March 9, 1788, Willie's paternal grandfather was born in Chancery
Lane, London, and christened Robert – after his grandfather the glazier
in Appleby. I know this much from the registers of the church of St
Dunstan's in the West, where he was baptized on April 6 – 'Robert, son
of William & Catherine Maugham, born March 9 in Chancery Lane'.[1]
I don't know the precise address of the family at that time, but Robert
later declared that he was born 'in the Liberty of the Rolls',[2] the small
territory that embraces the Public Record Office, and his first memories,
which were to influence his whole life, were of the long narrow street
that his contemporary, Leigh Hunt, described as 'the greatest legal
thoroughfare in England'.

Quite apart from Robert Maugham's distinguished career in the legal
profession, the environment of his childhood makes it reasonable to
assume that his father, William, was also connected in some way with
the law. He may have worked as a clerk for one of the stationers or
booksellers whose shops abounded in Chancery Lane. But after more
than a year of painstaking inquiry in Westmorland and in London all
that we know of this William Maugham – Willie's great-grandfather
– is that he was baptized in Appleby on July 10, 1759; that his wife's
name was Catherine Harrison; and that by her he had at least four
children, all of whom were born in London and christened at St
Dunstan's in the West.[3]

*

Meanwhile, other Maughams of William's generation had come south
to seek their fortune in London. William's brother John was living in
Chancery Lane with his wife Susanna,[4] and not far away, near Covent
Garden, there was William Farringdon Maugham, the eldest son of the
Reverend William of Moulton – William the hatter I shall call him, to
distinguish him from his first cousin, William the clerk of Chancery
Lane – and he must have come to London when he was still in his early

twenties. But to explain *why* he came, I must go back to Moulton for a moment – to the will made by the Reverend William. The will was witnessed by the vicar's brother-in-law, Theophilus Tutt, who had also married a daughter of the Reverend Farringdon Reid of Stamford. Now 'Uncle Tutt', as he was known in the Family, was in business as a 'Trimming Manufacturer' in Tavistock Street, Covent Garden – which in those days was known as 'the great emporium of millinery and mantua-making'. And it was to Tavistock Street that young William Farringdon Maugham came to learn the trade. He first became a tailor and then a hatter. And he was the son of William Somerset Maugham's great-great-great-uncle.

William the hatter lived with his 'Uncle Tutt' for a while at the 'trimming manufactory' at 23, Tavistock Street, and then became his neighbour for some years. I know this because 8, Tavistock Street is the address given on the first letter that his seafaring brother Theophilus wrote to him in April, 1794.[5] William's name does not appear in the London directories as being in business on his own account until 1798, when he is listed as a hatter of 19, King Street, Covent Garden. In a later list he appears as a 'Hat and Cap Manufacturer', but there are no records to show whom among the rank and fashion of the day he numbered as his customers. However, I discovered three letters from William the hatter in the old chintz-covered box. In one of them, written on December 2, 1790, to his brother John, he mentions that his young brother Theophilus the sailor – then only eighteen years old – had called on him the previous day 'for the last time' since his ship was expected to sail from Deptford. He adds that the boy seemed 'in high spirits and good health' – an impression that I'm sure Theophilus always gave until the very end of his short life. Then William makes the only reference to his trade: he apologises to his 'dear brother' for not sending his 'coats etc: much sooner', but his excuse is that he has 'been allmost done up for this 3 or 4 weeks'. 'We shall soon begin to be verry busy', he adds[6] – which makes me think that the 'rag trade' must have suffered just as much from the Christmas rush in the eighteenth century as it does now.

It is sad that William the hatter gives us no picture of his life in Covent Garden, for it must have been a delightful neighbourhood then – in contrast to the seething, lorry-cluttered chaos of today. 'No walk in London, on a fine summer's day,' Leigh Hunt wrote in

The Town, 'is more agreeable than the passage through the flowers here at noon, when the roses and green leaves are newly watered, and blooming faces come to look at them in those cool and shady avenues, while the hot sun is basking in the streets.' He added that 'the ladies who come to purchase, crown all'. And I like to think that it was on such a fine summer day, while enjoying his lunch-time stroll through the flower market, that William the hatter first met Hannah Perry, whom he married in 1797. Their wedding was at St Paul's in Covent Garden. The church had just been rebuilt on the plan of Inigo Jones' lovely building, which had been destroyed by fire two years previously. 'Uncle Tutt' and his wife were probably among the guests: their own wedding had been in St Paul's twenty-six years before, and I expect they came there again for the baptism of William and Hannah's first son, born on October 6, 1798, and christened William Tutt Maugham. But a misfortune spoiled the happiness of the young hatter and his wife. In April 1799, when their child was only six months old, the little boy became so sickly that he was 'sent out to nurse' – as was the custom of the time – and two weeks later he died. On April 29, William the hatter described the episode in a letter to his mother:

I should have wrote last week to you, but my whole attention was taken up with Mrs Maugham, who is almost broken hearted on account of the Death of our poor Dear little Boy, who we were both uncommon fond of & she had fix'd her whole heart & affections on. He was little but growing a nice Boy . . . He was sent out to Nurse a fortnight ago, a little beyond South Lambeth. He went very well & the Wednesday week following he died . . . his mother never had seen him since he went . . . He was buried yesterday at Clapham . . . but it will be a long time before she forgets him & before she gets better, as ever since she has been very low & ill . . .

Half a year later William and Hannah were consoled by the birth of another son, whom they also christened William Tutt Maugham. This time, all was well.[7] And the pattern of William the hatter's life seems to have continued happily until he died on January 6, 1831, at the age of sixty-five. He was buried in St Paul's in Covent Garden. In his will he left everything to his 'Truly beloved wife Hannah'. She lived another seventeen years and was buried in the same churchyard on April 1, 1848, at the age of seventy-five. And William Tutt Maugham? Well, I saw his name in a London directory for 1868, when he was almost seventy and living at 7, South Square, near Gray's Inn. But I admit that I haven't bothered to pursue his career, for by that time the Maughams in London were as plentiful as they had once been in Westmorland, and I was more concerned to follow up the story of my uncle Willie's immediate ancestors.

*

So I must now return to Chancery Lane in the 1790s – to Willie's great-grandfather, William the clerk, his wife Catherine, and their four children, the youngest of whom, Jane, was born on May 27, 1794. But I return to a dismal lack of information. William's name appears several times in the Rate Books for the Liberty of the Rolls[8] between the second half of 1788 – a few months after his first child was born – and the winter of 1797, when he is shown as having moved to a house in Carey Street, which runs westwards from Chancery Lane and is the home of the London Bankruptcy Court. The old joke about 'being in Carey Street' was sadly apt in William's case: he was apparently living beyond his means and had been in arrears with his rates for some time. While he had been living in Chancery Lane, only quite small sums were involved – thirty or thirty-five shillings – and he managed to pay these off within the year. But once he had moved to Carey Street, which even in those days was associated with bailiffs and bankrupts, he was always in debt to the full amount of his rates. And his rates rose from £4 11s. a year in 1799 to £7 3s. in 1802. After 1802 the penurious William is not mentioned at all, so perhaps the bailiffs caught up with him. Or did he flit away from London and hide in the wilds of Westmorland? It may only be a coincidence, but 1802 was the year in which John Robinson died, and with him must have ended whatever patronage he had been able to give to the sons of Appleby, his native town.

From the slender evidence of William the clerk's existence that one can find in the Rate Books, we know that he certainly lived until his elder son, Robert, was about fourteen years old; so William probably instilled into his son the legal and literary history of the small corner of London in which they lived – a rich history to which Robert was to contribute when he grew to manhood. As Robert walked along Chancery Lane as a boy he would have been fascinated by the thought that the Lane had been laid out almost seven hundred years previously, by the English chapter of the Knights Templars – the 'Poor Knights of Christ and of the Temple of Solomon', to give the full title of the crusading warriors who gained influence in almost every kingdom of Christendom. Their jousting ground was close to the present church of St Dunstan's in the West, and they built their first 'temple' near the northeast corner of the Lane on an estate which they sold in the middle of the twelfth century to Robert de Curass, Bishop of Lincoln, when they moved south to what is known to this day as 'The Temple'. Early in the fourteenth century, soon after the Knights Templars had 'decayed through pride' – to use Spenser's polite description of their ruthless suppression on the charge of sacrilege and gross debauchery – their 'bricky towers' beside the Thames were leased to the professors of the Common Law and converted into two 'Inns of Court' – the Inner Temple and the Middle Temple – as hostels for their students. These, together with Lincoln's Inn (named probably after Henry de Lacy, Earl of Lincoln) and Gray's Inn[9] (named after the family of Lord Gray of Wilton) thus formed in this small stretch of London what John Stow, the Elizabethan chronicler, described in the sixteenth century as being 'a whole university, as it were, of students, practisers or pleaders and judges of the laws of this realm'.

Young Robert Maugham grew up in the very heart of this legal university, walking on ground where the queerly-behaved Knights Templars had held their jousting tournaments and where Bishops and Earls had sauntered. But perhaps Robert turned from dreams of the past to contemplation of his own future – unaware that, due partly to his own success, one of his grandsons would join the proud company of Cardinal Wolsey, Sir Thomas More, and Sir Francis Bacon as Lord Chancellor of England, or that another grandson would become a great man of letters. Yet Robert's own pretensions as a writer – and he published more than a dozen books – may well have been encouraged by the famous literary figures who had flourished in the district, side by side and often in conflict with the officers of the law. Shakespeare's patron, the third Earl of Southampton, lived in a fine house now marked by Southampton Buildings; John Donne was once Vicar of St Dunstan's in the West; Izaak Walton had his haberdasher's shop at the foot of Chancery Lane, and his *Compleat Angler* was first published in St Dunstan's Churchyard; Dryden had once lived in Fetter Lane, Oliver Goldsmith in Wine Office Court, and Dr Johnson in Johnson's Court – which must have amused him, for it was named after another. Dr

Johnson had died only five years before Willie's grandfather was born, so it is reasonable to suppose that young Robert Maugham heard stories about him at first hand from the regulars who had gathered in those low-roofed sanded rooms at the Cheshire Cheese tavern to listen to the great man as he sat with his friend Goldsmith, enjoying his beef-steak pudding and his punch.

One Sunday in London when the city was as deserted and quiet as an old print, I walked through all those streets in that legal district, feeling that I belonged to them remotely and that Willie belonged to them to – in spite of his careless assertion that he didn't care a tinker's cuss about his ancestors.

*

The early years of Robert Maugham seem to have puzzled others besides myself. Though he became famous enough to merit an article in the *Dictionary of National Biography*,[10] the customary opening remarks on birth, parentage, and education are omitted altogether – as if he had been some foundling dumped on the pavement of Chancery Lane and left to fend for himself. But we had discovered all the proof we needed of his birth from the record of his baptism in 1788, and I have little doubt that he received at least part of his education at Appleby Grammar School – as my father once told me. During that period the boy probably lived with his grandfather, Robert the glazier. And he probably came back to London at the age of seventeen – because, in the preface of one of his books published in 1825, he speaks of 'nearly twenty years of active practice' in the legal profession.

In 1805 or 1806, soon after he returned to London, Robert Maugham entered the employment of George Barrow, an attorney in Threadneedle Street near the Bank of England. But in spite of Robert's claim, in 1825, to nearly twenty years of *active* practice, he cannot have been more than an ordinary clerk during his first years with his master, occupied in such humble tasks as keeping the ledgers and delivering messages, because he was not formally 'articled' to George Barrow until March 1812. This view is shared by Mr Michael Birks, who saved us a lot of research by writing a splendidly informative article about Robert Maugham in *The Law Society's Gazette* for December 1959. Mr Birks was unable to name the important day when Robert's long apprenticeship was over and he had passed his exams and was 'admitted an attorney'. But we discovered that it was in April 1817. Robert was then twenty-nine years old. Mr Birks wrote:

Maugham's name first appears in the *Law List* for 1819 and for several years he practised on his own. He must have been fairly successful, but his real interests lay elsewhere, and it was those other interests that finally settled the course of his career. Quite early in life he began contributing articles to various magazines, but as they were published anonymously, I have been unable to trace any of them. He also began to take an interest in the affairs of his profession. He was probably a member of the Metropolitan Law Association, set up in 1819, to try to rid the profession of its less desirable elements, for this association later furnished him with a great deal of the material for his *Treatise on the Law of Attornies* which appeared in 1825.

*

What sort of a man was Robert Maugham? My uncle Willie used to relate that as a boy he had met an old solicitor, Albert Dixon, who told him that his grandfather was the ugliest little man he ever saw. It seems strange that while his legal and literary careers are on record so little should be known of his private life. There is only one small note-book of his among my family papers. It is bound in green leather and kept closed by a slim wooden pencil, and Robert used it as a diary when he visited the Continent in 1820. Willie implies that this is the diary he is referring to in *The Summing Up*, published in 1938:

Many years ago when I was destroying the papers of one of his sons, my uncle, who had died, [Willie writes] I came across the diary that my grand-father kept when as a young man at the beginning of the nineteenth century he did what I believe was called the Little Tour, France, Germany, and Switzerland, and I remember that when he described the not very impressive fall of the Rhine at Schaffhausen he offered thanks to God Almighty, be-cause in creating 'this stupendous cataract' he had given 'His miserable creatures occasion to realise their insignificance in comparison with the pro-digious greatness of His works'.

But error has somehow crept in here, for Robert never visited Switzerland in 1820 nor did he go within a hundred miles of Schaff-hausen. So I assumed that either Willie's memory was at fault or he was referring to some other diary. Accuracy, as I was gradually discovering, did not distinguish the writings either of Willie or my father when they came to describe their family. But the Schaffhausen story seemed oddly familiar, and I was not surprised to find the passage in Willie's novel *Of Human Bondage*, published in 1915. It occurs towards the end of the book when Philip is reading 'a yellow packet of letters' which his uncle, the Reverend William Carey, deceased, had written 'when as an Oxford undergraduate he had gone to Germany for the long vacation'. Here is the description:

The letters were formal and a little stilted ... The falls of Schaffhausen made him 'offer reverent thanks to the all-powerful Creator of the universe, whose works were wondrous and beautiful', and he could not help thinking that they who lived in sight of 'this handiwork of their blessed Maker must be moved by the contemplation to lead pure and holy lives'.

Since *Of Human Bondage* is largely autobiographical, one can assume that the diary to which Willie refers in *The Summing Up* twenty years later was in fact written by Willie's own uncle, the Reverend Henry Macdonald Maugham – not by his grandfather.

*

Being a solicitor must have been a lucrative business early in the nineteenth century, for it seems that after only a couple of years in practice Robert Maugham was able to keep up the appearance of a gentleman. He mixed and travelled with the kind of people to whom his grandfather in Appleby would have touched his cap. Even his passport, which I found folded into a flap of his notebook, has a seignorial appearance. It is an imposing document, issued in London, not – as is the custom today – in the name of the British Foreign Secretary, but by the French Ambassador[11] to the Court of St. James. It was signed on September 9, 1820, and Robert Maugham left London the same evening with a companion – perhaps another young solicitor – to whom he refers as 'H' in the diary. 'H', he writes, 'talked nearly all night in French', to a French lady who was travelling in the coach with them to Dover. Robert says that he 'stretched' his 'French faculties to the utmost to collect the substance of the discourse but soon became exhausted'. However, he did manage to remember enough of the language from his schooldays to write part of his diary in extremely bad French – beginning at the moment when the packet-boat *Lady Cockburn*[12] had 'debarqué à Calais à Trois heures' on the afternoon of September 10, and thence to his 'heureux trajet' by cabriolet to Meurice's Hotel, where they dined 'à Table d'Hôte' and drank '**Grave,**

Burgundy & Champaign', in the company of 'a Gentleman of the Army' who joined them and 'passed the evening'.

Robert Maugham does not record the purpose of his journey, but much of it was over the ground that had marked the closing scenes of the Napoleonic Wars. Napoleon was still alive – a prisoner on St Helena, where he died eight months later – and the wars in which he had aspired to become dictator of Europe and conqueror of half the world had ended only five years previously. Robert appears to have shown some interest in the battlefields, but no passionate wish to see 'precisely where it all happened'. He had no particular destination; he was on a round tour from London and back, with a glimpse of four countries on the way. He travelled from Calais through the fields of Flanders to Douai, passing rather dismal towns that had been fought over for centuries. Robert was not impressed. He noted that the 'chaise de Poste' was 'dirty, and awkward in structure' and that the countryside was 'indifferentment cultivé'. He resented the fact that 'at the fortified towns' their passports were 'demanded'. 'Account was taken', he says, 'of our Names, Condition, from whence we came, where going, and the purpose of the Journey.' At Douai, he noticed that 'the trees which generally adorn the roads' had been cut down during the war 'to enable the garrison to observe the approach of the enemy', and at Cambrai he walked around the ramparts that had been 'la scene de l'Anglais Armee de observation apres la Battaile de Waterloo'. His French was rusty, and he does not seem to have been enjoying himself. But at La Capelle there was a fair, and the villagers 's'amusement en dansé' quadrilles and waltzes on the road – which Robert found 'gay and novel'.

At Sedan the troops were having a field day, marching about with bands playing in the Rue de Turenne – which made Robert feel thirsty, so he 'drank tea' and – typically English comment – was 'surprised to find it so good'. At six o'clock the next morning they set forth in starlight, and for the first time in the diary there comes at last a note of excitement. There was a sudden alarm that highwaymen might attack the coach. Robert's comments are delightfully terse and controlled. 'Suspicion of robbery', the entry reads 'Put money in our boots.' One can almost see the firmness of his upper lip. But all was well. There was no attack, and after travelling throughout the day they arrived at the 'miserable village of Florinville' where they put up at 'a poor Inn', had for their supper 'Eggs, Fowl, Fruit and a Bottle of Wine' that would have been considered 'disgusting' by anyone 'less hungry' than Robert and his friend, and then – worst of all – there was 'one Bed only'.

In *The Summing Up*, Willie said he wished he had read his grand-father's essays. 'For I might have learned from them,' he wrote, 'something of the kind of man he was.' I dare say. But I don't believe that Robert Maugham's diary would have helped Willie much in his quest for his grandfather's character. Here, for instance, is one of the longest entries:

Saturday 16th at Luxembourg. Hotel de Cologne.
After the fatigue of 15 hours travelling yesterday we slept till the unusual hour of 7 this morning, Walked thro' the town. Went to Church. First Mass performing. 'Bell, Book and Candle.' The majority of the Congregation of the poorer classes. Some of them came in with their market Baskets, muttered in quick time their Ave Marias & Pater Nosters, crossed themselves, bent the knee to the altar and departed. Others continued in long devotion. Some knelt on chairs, others on the steps of confessionals and others on the pave-ment. The church large. Lofty pillars. No pews. Several confessionals in the side aisles. Pictures. The general aspect imposing, chiefly so by the silence that prevailed – disturbed only by the occasional sounds of the Bells. The raising of the Cross. The Benedite pronounced. The grave & earnest devo-tion of the congregation imparts a solemnity & excites an emotion, even at the moment you internally smile at the singularity of the scene and the minute attention to trifling & irrational ceremonies.

It tells us that Robert was conventional, that he was a Protestant, that he was determinedly observant, that he was capable of emotion, and that he lacked the imagination of his grandson, but it tells us little else – except perhaps that he was rather cold in temperament. And thus it is with the rest of the entries made during his dispassionate tour. Robert never states his own views, and his journey and his terse entries continue as he travelled slowly over the Rhineland in a 'poor chariot' which he describes as 'the best vehicle we have had'. He did at least see 'some pleasing and some pretty faces' on the way but considered that 'the Countenance of both Sexes' was 'confoundedly ugly', for the unfortunate natives had 'lowering and dull aspects and no speculation in the Eye'. But he was delighted when he 'sipped and drank Moselle on its native Banks' and then retired to his 'chamber above the river' where the only sound was the 'silvery tide rippling in murmurs on its bed'.

Gradually as I read through the little green notebook I realised that Robert was seeing the landscape through the eyes of an amateur artist. The first hint after this came with the brief remark 'took sketches', soon after he began his cruise down the Rhine. He now began to make sketches quite often – near Boppard, where 'the sun towards its declension shone up the Glen and illumined the tops of the opposite Hills'; at Andernach, where the sun was shining on the vines that 'cloathe the slopes of the Hills', and at Linz where the 'cloudless lustre of the Sun rendered the whole Country, now considerably extensive as seen thro' the opening glades, eminently enchanting . . . The Sun, the fountain as well of heat and colour as of light, is everything to a landscape.' It is sad that Robert's sketches have been lost, for I suspect that they would have revealed a tender side of his nature which he kept hidden from the world.

Robert left the passage boat at Bonn, took a chaise to Cologne, then a diligence to Brussels, which he dismisses with the succinct comment, 'Hotel de Flandre. Three Englishmen. Little conversation.' From Brussels he returned to Calais and thence to London after a ten-hour crossing in the packet-boat and a twelve-hour ride in the coach. He arrived home at six o'clock on the morning of October 2.

*

Eighteen months later, on April 13, 1822, Robert Maugham was married at the parish church of St Mary, Lewisham, in South London, to Mary Corrock. His wife seems to have been lost in obscurity: neither the marriage, nor the fact that she bore Robert eight children, are mentioned in the article in the *Dictionary of National Biography*, and I know little more about her childhood than the fact that she was born at Margate on September 15, 1793, and that her parents were called Robert and Mary. This was found out from the registers in the Church of St John-the-Baptist in Thanet, only a few miles away from where uncle Willie was to spend a miserable childhood.

Willie never knew her, for she died in September 1874, only eight months after he was born. But my father stayed with her in London in 1870 – when he was four years old and his family had fled from Paris during the Franco-Prussian war. 'My grandmother Mary was a woman of considerable education,' he wrote in his autobiography. 'I still possess the little Pickering edition of the New Testament in Greek in which she used on Sundays to follow the appropriate lessons.'

When Robert and Mary Maugham's first child was born, on December 7, 1823, they were living at 17, Great James Street, just north-west of Gray's Inn. Robert also carried on his practice there, in partnership with a Mr Fothergill. The child – Willie's father and my grandfather – was baptized at St Andrew's, the Wren church near Holborn Circus, and given the names of Robert after his father, and Ormond, after the surname of his maternal grandmother. At that time Willie's grandfather was putting the finishing touches to the first of his major legal works which was published by Longmans in March 1824, under the cumbersome title of *A Treatise on the Principles of the Usury Laws, with Disquisitions on the Arguments adduced against them by Mr Bentham and other Writers, and a Review of the Authorities in their Favour*. During the next ten years or so Robert and Mary Maugham had seven more children – Isabella, Charles, Henry, Catherine, Julia, Frederic, and Mary, and Robert wrote several more books with equally cumbersome titles – among them *A Treatise on the Law of Attornies, Solicitors and Agents: with Notes and Disquisitions*, *A Treatise on the Laws of Literary Property, comprising the Statutes and Cases relating to Books, Manuscripts, Lectures*, and *A Complete Collection of the Statutes and Rules and Orders relating to Attornies*.

As Mr Michael Birks points out in his article in *The Law Society's Gazette*,

With the exception of a collection of statutes and decisions relating to attornies, published some sixty years earlier, Maugham's work was the first attempt to provide attornies with a text-book covering every aspect of their professional activities. Although he wrote many other books, including one on the law of copyright and several students' text-books, the *Treatise on the Law of Attornies* was by far the most important and appeared at an opportune moment.

Strangely enough, it was the preface that was to have the most lasting effect. Robert wrote:

It is indeed most remarkable, that the Attornies of the metropolis, two thousand four hundred of them in regular practice (beside many uncertificated), are destitute of all facilities to cultivate the higher branches of their profession, and therefore it is not surprising that the majority should remain, at least 'unaltered and unimproved', if they do not actually *recede* from the learning of their predecessors.

There is neither opportunity nor incitement afforded to the students or the junior practitioners of the law, to extend their knowledge and cultivate their talents by those means which are afforded in other professions . . . We possess neither college nor hall, library nor society, yet the necessity of every possible assistance in legal studies is surely equal to that of any other science, and none can be more important than the LAW.

Some of Robert's colleagues shared his view, and on June 2, 1825, at a meeting of a number of attornies and solicitors in the hall of Furnival's Inn,[13] 'it was resolved that a society called "The Law Institution" should purchase a piece of land with the view to the erection of a suitable building'.[14] A Committee of twenty-four was appointed, and Robert Maugham, with 'his expert knowledge of professional matters' was chosen as Secretary. He was also made the Institution's Solicitor, and 'the original Trust Deed must have been prepared in his office'. Thus was born what we know today as The Law Society, which ranks after the four Inns of Court as the most important legal association in Britain. It is responsible for the education and examination of all articled clerks and the admission of all Solicitors in England and Wales, and it has a membership of about eighteen thousand. I have a twinge of pride when I think that it was my great-grandfather – the son of a clerk and the grandson of a glazier – who helped to found such a noble and enduring institution.

At first, the committee met at Searle's Coffee House, on the south side of Carey Street. Then, in 1828, after they had raised a capital of £50,000, they secured two adjacent properties, 108 and 109, Chancery Lane – on the west side and within the Liberty of the Rolls, where Robert Maugham had been born forty years previously. In the same year, Robert moved his practice and his family to 19 Chancery Lane. During the next three years the imposing central block of the Law Society as designed by Lewis Vulliamy took shape – 'a Grecian temple wedged into Chancery Lane', as one writer described it – and in July 1832 the institution was opened for the use of members.

Robert Maugham's position as Secretary and Solicitor to the Law Society was confirmed in 1832, when he was given a salary of £400 a year and an apartment for his family in the Hall. The only stipulation was that he should 'attend daily in the committee room from midday until three o'clock'. Otherwise he was free to pursue his own business. In 1833 he entered into partnership with a young attorney, Thomas Kennedy, at 100 Chancery Lane – only a few steps from the Law Society – and in 1844 he became one of the founder members of the Law Assurance Company. But Robert gave most of his time to managing the weekly *Legal Observer*, which he had founded in 1830. He remained its owner and editor for twenty-six years. A Maugham had made good at last.

'It would not be an exaggeration,' says Mr Birks, 'to describe Robert Maugham as "the father of legal journalism".' He continues:

The *Legal Observer* was the first successful legal journal to combine current professional news with reports of cases and articles of practical interest to lawyers. As early as 1761 a quarterly journal on those lines had appeared, but did not last more than a year or so. I suppose the real difficulty was that a specialised journal could not hope to increase its circulation and therefore stood little chance of success until improvements in transport could bring it within reach of readers all over England. So for a long time publishers contented themselves with journals that were, in Maugham's words, mere bundles of essays with no pretence of being topical, or which were little more than lists of court sittings, bankruptcies and the like, but were cheap to produce. By 1830, however, coaching had become the most highly organised industry in the land; few towns were more than twenty-four hours' journey from London, and a weekly journal with a country-wide circulation was now feasible.

For twenty-six years Robert Maugham produced his little weekly newspaper, championing in its columns the policies which he and his colleagues of the Law Society sought to promote through legislation. But as the years passed by and 'its ageing editor gradually ceased to move with the times, the paper eventually acquired a dated look'. In 1856, when he was sixty-eight years old, Robert sold out to a new publication called the *Solicitor's Journal*, which still flourishes. He was consoled by his colleagues with the gift of £600 and what my father described as 'a valuable piece of plate ... designed and beautified according to the approved taste of the mid-Victorian era'. Willie describes the gift as consisting of 'a salver, a tea and coffee service and an epergne, in silver, so massive and ornate that they had been ever since an

Edith Mary Snell, W.
Somerset Maugham's
mother

Rose Snell, the younger
sister of Edith Mary Snell

Terracotta statuette of Robert Ormond Maugham, the father of W. Somerset Maugham

The photograph of W. Somerset Maugham's mother which stood on the table by his bed at the Villa Mauresque

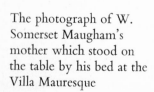

embarrassment to his descendants'.[15] Where are these embarrassing objects now? Sold, I expect, for I have never seen them.

Although he retired from active practice in 1856, Robert Maugham continued as Secretary of the Law Society, and there he collapsed and died on July 16, 1862. But in a way his presence endures to this day, for on a wall of the Hall is the big oil portrait[16] that my great-grandmother Mary gave to the Society. Willie suspected that the artist had grossly flattered his grandfather whom Albert Dixon – the old solicitor Willie knew as a boy – had described as the ugliest little man he ever saw. 'The painter', Willie wrote, 'has given him very fine dark eyes under black eyebrows, and there is a faintly ironic twinkle in them; a firm jaw, a straight nose and pouting red lips. His dark hair is windswept as becomingly as that of Miss Anita Loos. He is holding a quill and there is a pile of books, doubtless his own, by his side. Notwithstanding his black coat, he does not look so respectable as I should have expected, but slightly mischievous' – and slightly sinister, I am bound to add.

Robert Maugham's energetic talents as a lawyer and as a writer were to flourish in two of his grandsons, and his suppressed talent as an artist was to reappear in three of his great-granddaughters – my sister Honor, and my cousins Daphne and Clarisse. Though we know much about his achievements we know little about his character and personality – whether he was a good husband or a good father. We have only one glimpse of his private life in a story that old Albert Dixon told Willie. When he was a young articled clerk, Dixon had been invited to dine with Willie's grandfather in Chancery Lane. Willie has put the story into *The Summing Up*:

My grandfather carved the beef, and then a servant handed him a dish of potatoes baked in their skins. There are few things better to eat than a potato in its skin, with plenty of butter, pepper and salt, but apparently my grandfather did not think so. He rose in his chair at the head of the table and took the potatoes out of the dish one by one and threw them at each picture on the walls. Then without a word he sat down again and went on with his dinner.

When Willie asked the old solicitor what effect Robert's behaviour had on the rest of the company, he replied that 'no one took any notice' – which seems to suggest that Robert was habitually bad-tempered, unless he was so dotty by then that he always insisted on being served with baked potatoes just for the pleasure of hurling them at pictures.

Those of his guests who had read their host's book, *Outlines of Character*,[17] must have been very shocked, for in his chapter entitled 'The Gentleman' Robert had plainly stated that 'the quality in which the perfect gentleman ... is most eminent is *refined taste*'. And the essay had continued: 'His attainments, including all the elegant exercises of the age, consist more of the ornamental, than the positively useful. He has too many refined avocations, to be *eminent* either in music, or the other fine arts. He is something, and avowedly but little, of an amateur. He possesses very polished manners, a mingling of ease, grace and dignity.' And it is clear from Robert's essay on 'The Man of Genius' that he had tried to model himself on the noble character that he outlined in his description of 'The Sublime Genius':

He is distinguished by a proud and lofty bearing; by a spirit, sometimes, of imperious command; yet, with an aspect very different from that bold confidence, and rude audacity, which is displayed by some who possess more of talent than feeling, and who have neither the taste of the man of learning, nor the sensibility of the man of genius. A being of this order is excited by whatever is vast, elevated and profound.

But, as we know to our cost, no man is perfect. And if a genius – 'a being of this order' – is also excited by a baked potato we should not complain.

*

When I decided to use Noël Coward's phrase *Somerset and all the Maughams* as the title of this book, I did not realise how many Maughams there were going to be. Willie and myself were the last two males in our branch of the family; so now there is only one left. But two or three generations ago there were countless Maughams, spreading not merely over the counties of England, but planting our name in America, in New Zealand, and, perhaps, by now, in Timbuktu.

Some months before he died Willie discovered that we also had cousins in Australia. He gave me a letter he had received from Mrs Wilma Foster, a lady living in Mentone, near Melbourne, whose grandfather had emigrated in the 1880s. He was Thomas Maugham who settled in Brisbane, where he became well known as a chemist and 'a poor people's consultant'.[18] I eventually discovered that he was born in Lambeth, in South London, on August 16, 1844, and that his father was William Maugham, who described himself in the birth certificate as a 'lecturer on chemistry'. And this William was none other than the young brother of Robert Maugham, Willie's grandfather, the secretary of the Law Society.

I had always believed that Willie's grandfather was the first 'professional' member of our family. But evidently his brother William (born April 11, 1792) must also have been professionally qualified to become a lecturer in chemistry; and I should imagine, fairly prosperous too at one time, for he had his own business as a 'consultant chemist' in Westminster. I have not tried to pursue his story, but it seems that his prosperity did not last, because towards the end of his life he was admitted a 'brother' or pensioner of the Charterhouse, the beautiful Carthusian monastery in the London borough of Finsbury that had been purchased in 1611 by Thomas Sutton both as a home for impoverished gentlemen and as a school for the sons of poor gentry.[19] He died there on May 30, 1875, at the age of eighty-three.

*

I have sometimes wondered why my great-grandfather Robert did not mention his brother William the 'consulting chemist' in his will. But perhaps they didn't get on with each other any better than my father and Willie did. Robert made his will in 1847, so it bore little relation to his circumstances at his death fifteen years later, in 1862. By that time, three of his family had died – Mary, the youngest daughter, when she was only a child of eleven; Charles, the second son (who had become a solicitor and clerk to the Law Society), at the age of thirty-two; and Frederic, the youngest son, who had lost his life in 1854 during the Crimean war, at the age of only twenty. Most of Robert's estate, including that embarrassing epergne, was left to his widow Mary; but the surviving children were well provided for, because the family had inherited a considerable bequest from a lady named Isabella Sarah Wilks.[20]

By 1862, then, my branch of the Maughams had become respectable and reasonably well-off members of Victorian middle-class society – a bit prim and dull, I suspect, but a typical family of their generation, with a widowed mother attended by two spinster daughters, the third daughter married to a clergyman, one son in the church and another in the law – all safe in their beds and unperturbed by the Queen's enemies. The only one who had ventured out of his sheltered pattern was

Frederic, who, like his cousin Theophilus sixty years before him, had gone to sea and died in the service of his country. Had young Frederic survived the Crimean war, he might have become the guardian of my uncle Willie in 1884, instead of his pompous High Church brother Henry Macdonald Maugham, and Willie's life might in consequence have been very different. But on the morning of November 14, 1854, Frederic was drowned when his ship was wrecked in the Black Sea, half a mile out from the harbour of Balaclava. The Russian town and its port had lately been occupied by the British. On October 25 the Light Brigade had made their gallant and disastrous charge 'into the valley of death' against the Russian field batteries. On November 5, an even bloodier battle was fought at Inkerman; and then a new, more cruel enemy, the winter, menaced the Allies. On the night of November 13, a violent storm arose just as a fleet of British transports had reached Balaclava. With them was the new steamship *Prince*, on which Frederic Maugham was serving as purser.[21] She was carrying a cargo worth half a million pounds – treasure, medical comforts, forage, clothing, and all the other precious supplies needed by the army to fight the winter. During that storm, nearly thirty transports were wrecked or badly damaged; hundreds of men were lost, including Frederic and 143 of his comrades on the *Prince;* and the disaster was magnified by the consequent appalling misery and loss of life suffered by the thousands of British soldiers in the Crimea.

The fate of the *Prince* – and of my great-uncle Frederic – is told in the *Illustrated London News* (December 16, 1854). One of the few survivors, Midshipman Cotgrave, wrote this account:

While lying at anchor in 25 fathoms water, with two anchors down, about half a mile from the shore, the wind blowing a terrific hurricane from the southward and westward, No. 16 Transport fouled us, doing some damage, and we were obliged to cut away all masts. About 9h. a.m. the port cable parted (all hands being on deck at the time): endeavoured to steam ahead; but, on account of some wreck being afoul of the screw, were unable to do so. About five minutes afterwards the starboard cable parted, and the ship drifted in rapidly towards the rocks.

Captain Goodall, who had been on deck from the commencement of the gale, called all hands aft, and, with Captain Baynton, R.N. Transport Agent, pulled off their coats, Captain Goodall, at the same time, saying, 'Now, my lads, I've done the best I can for you; every man must try and save himself.'

About 9.15 a.m. the ship touched the rocks, and, owing to the great force of wind and severe sea setting in at that time, in fifteen minutes after not a vestige of her was to be seen. After thumping about five or six times the ship broke in halves about amidships, and I jumped out of the mizen chains on part of the wreck, and, being about ten minutes in the water, was washed ashore.

I did not see Captain Baynton or Captain Goodall after the ship struck. Every person seemed very cool and collected under such awful circumstances . . .

*

Of the five surviving children of Robert Maugham of the Law Society, I have found little of interest to record of the three daughters – though I have set down such facts as I know in an appendix.* More important, so far as my story is concerned, are Robert's two surviving sons – Robert Ormond Maugham, Willie's father and my grandfather, and his brother Henry Macdonald Maugham, who became Willie's guardian.

I don't think anyone ever said a good word of Henry Macdonald Maugham. Even my father described him as a 'very narrow-minded and a far from intelligent cleric'. But the Anglican Church had many such men in his day, and I have no doubt that he chose such a career because he had neither the brains to follow his father in the law nor the energy to join the adventurers who were helping to build Queen Victoria's empire. The Church offered a nice secure life for a gentleman of modest means, and if one observed the ritual and did not offend the bishop it was possible to get by without giving too much thought for the sick or the needy. Willie wrote of his uncle Henry, when he was vicar of Whitstable, that 'he was incredibly idle and left the work of his parish to his curate and his churchwardens'.[22]

Of course, Henry had to climb the clerical ladder like anyone else, and it was some years before he found himself a comfortable niche. His education indicates a certain indecision. First he studied theology in London at King's College, of which he became an associate in 1848; then he went up to Oriel College, Oxford, and tried his hand at mathematics in which he achieved no more than a third class honours degree. But the pulpit seemed more attractive than a schoolmaster's desk, and Henry returned to theology. He was ordained deacon at

* See Appendix V.

Oxford in 1853, and priest at Winchester in 1855, when he was also appointed curate at St Thomas's Church in Ryde on the Isle of Wight. From then, until he was made vicar of Whitstable in 1871, he moved no less than eight times, probably because the various parish priests he served made him work too hard.

On July 27, 1858, when great-uncle Henry was curate at Chertsey in Surrey, he was married in the parish church to Barbara Sophia von Scheidlin. His father and mother came down from Chancery Lane for the wedding and they signed the register as witnesses. Henry was then twenty-nine and his bride was thirty. Sophie, as she became known in the Maugham family, was the daughter of a German merchant and banker, Georg David Nikolaus von Scheidlin and his wife Christiana Aurelia (*née* Cella).[23] They lived in Nuremberg, but Sophie's 'residence' on the marriage certificate that we found in Somerset House is given as Tettenhall, Staffordshire – a suburb of the industrial town of Wolverhampton. What she was doing up there I cannot imagine: it was hardly the place for her to air the aristocratic pretensions of which, if we may believe what Willie wrote in *The Summing Up*, she was so 'primly arrogant'. (Willie also said she was 'penniless' – but I don't see how this fits in with her father being a banker.) The polite market town of Chertsey with its ruined abbey beside the Thames would have been much more to her liking; but she was not allowed to stay there long because in 1860 Henry moved to the bleak landscape of Kirton-by-Boston, in Lincolnshire, where they lived for seven years.

The Reverend Henry Macdonald Maugham must have been aware that he had relations living in Lincolnshire – descendants of his great-great-uncle, the Reverend William Maugham. And the village of Kirton is only nine miles due north of Moulton. But he doesn't seem to have bothered very much about them. He was probably more attracted to taking the curacy in Kirton because the vicar was too ill to interfere. And there his poor wife Sophie began the long patient task of attending to her husband's every whim and comfort – a routine from which death eventually released her, more than thirty years later.

I have not been to Kirton, but Mr Stephen Goard, the genealogical hall-porter at the George Hotel in Stamford, tells me that it is 'flat, marshy, uninspiring, open to the winds and very cold'. He discovered that the vicar in my great-uncle's time, a Mr Ludlow, became so ill after a few years that he applied to the Bishop of Lincoln to engage a curate, so that he might live elsewhere. The application was supported by four doctors, who found the wretched man had an enlarged liver and spleen and suffered from fevers that left him in a state of depression and nervous tension; and one of the doctors wrote in his report that 'Kirton being a malarious district' Mr Ludlow could not reside there 'without being subject to these attacks'.

Henry Maugham seems to have survived the climate better than his vicar. While Mr Ludlow was taking the waters in Germany, Henry was enjoying his first taste of independence, with the free use of a pleasant house and garden, a stipend and various perks that amounted to a hundred and fifty pounds a year, and two thousand parishioners to swell the collection on Sundays. Mr Ludlow described the church at Kirton as being 'cold and damp', but the dutiful Sophie was always there in the vicarage to see that Henry had his chair by the fire, his slippers, and his boiled egg for tea.

I know that Henry left Kirton at least twice during those seven years. On July 12, 1862, he officiated in London at the wedding of his eldest sister Isabella and the Reverend William Andrew at St Thomas's Church, in the Liberty of the Rolls.[24] I expect the reception afterwards was at the Law Society's Hall.[25] The next occasion was for the wedding of his eldest brother, Robert Ormond Maugham. Otherwise no records survive of Henry's long sojourn in the fenlands of Lincolnshire. We only know that in 1867, perhaps ambitious for promotion, he came south again into the more salubrious climate of Kent, where he and his wife Sophie were to remain to the end of their lives – first for a few months at Sturry, a couple of miles outside Canterbury, then three years at Sandwich, then two more quick changes, at West Farleigh and East Malling, near Maidstone, and finally, in 1871, the long-awaited preferment to a vicarage of his own at Whitstable, with his own curate to do most of the donkey-work.

And so the scene was set for the arrival of his nephew Willie at the vicarage in Whitstable thirteen years later – the unhappy, stammering, little orphan boy who was to weave out of his misery one of the greatest novels in the English language.

*

My uncle Willie never mentioned the fact in his books, but he actually had *two* guardians when his father died in 1884. He was probably so obsessed with the Reverend Henry Macdonald Maugham that he forgot that the second guardian was Albert Dixon, the London solicitor who had told him of old Robert Maugham and the baked potatoes. But my father knew Albert Dixon well. He described him as a 'kindly man who did his best for us'. I have since discovered that the Dixon family played quite an important part in the story of the Maughams.[26]

Albert and an elder brother, William, both became solicitors, and I believe that they were coached by Willie's grandfather, as his father was also. In fact, William Dixon's name appears in the records of the Law Society as the 'attesting witness' when Robert Ormond Maugham was articled, in February 1841. And soon after their five-year apprenticeship was over and they were admitted solicitors they set up in partnership as 'Maugham and Dixon'.[27]

The Maugham-Dixon relationship was evidently profitable for both families. Within a year or two of William Dixon and Robert Ormond Maugham setting up in partnership, at 1 Staple Inn, the two young solicitors were seeking to expand their business, with an office in Paris. By 1848, they were established at No. 12 in the Rue Royale, as successors to a firm of English and French patent agents, founded in 1823 by an Englishman, Thomas Lawson. William Dixon continued in London, where he was joined some years later by his brother Albert; while Willie's father took over the Paris office, and about 1850 he was given the semi-official appointment there of solicitor to the British Embassy.

There was quite a lot of coming and going between London and Paris during the years before the Franco-Prussian war, and their business prospered. The London office was moved at least twice – first to 4 Raymond Buildings in Gray's Inn Road, and about 1861 to 10 Bedford Row. And the Paris office was also moved twice – first to 16 Place de la Madeleine, and in 1863 to 54 Faubourg St Honoré, almost opposite the British Embassy. I should like to think that my grandfather was involved in some splendid cases, but such records as survive in the Public Record Office are disappointingly dull.

Somewhere, sometime, during these early years in Paris, Robert Ormond Maugham met and fell in love with a young English girl who had been born in India and brought up by her widowed mother in France. Her name was Edith Mary Snell. They were married at the British Embassy on October 1, 1863. Robert's brother, the Reverend

Henry Maugham, came over to conduct the wedding. The bride was twenty-three, and very lovely; the bridegroom was almost forty, and like his father, so ugly that their friends called them 'Beauty and the Beast'. They were the parents of my father, of my uncle Willie, and their two brothers, Charles and Harry.

Paris was then a world of elegance far removed from staid, respectable mid-Victorian London, and a whole world apart from the earthy setting in which our ancestors had flourished a few generations before. Who in Westmorland would have supposed that their descendants would 'go foreign'? And who, especially in Paris, would have guessed that such a union, between a beautiful young girl and an ugly middle-aged man could become so happy? Willie used to wonder why such a lovely woman should have been so contented with such an unprepossessing man. But he eventually found a possible reason. He tells the story in *The Summing Up*. Among his mother's devoted friends was Lady Anglesey. One day she said to Mrs Maugham: 'You're so beautiful and there are so many people in love with you, why are you so faithful to that ugly little man you've married?'

Willie's mother smiled.

'Well, you see, in all the years we've been married,' she replied, 'he's never hurt my feelings.'

THE MAUGHAMS IN PARIS

I NEVER dared disagree with my father about anything: as a judge, he believed that his opinions were inviolate – within the family as well as in court. But I have since discovered that some of the 'facts' he stated in his autobiography were shaky – so far as his own ancestry was concerned.

Here is an example of what I mean. My father wrote in his autobiography, *At the End of the Day*, 'My maternal grandfather Major Snell . . . . lost his life in the Indian Mutiny of 1857. I know little about him except that he came from Cheshire and that he married my grandmother, a Miss Brereton . . . ' My father should have written, 'My maternal grandfather Major Snell . . . died in India in 1841. I know little about him except that he came from Cornwall and that he married my grandmother, a Miss Todd . . . '

The story of the Snell-Todd marriage is quite romantic. It begins in the ancient sea-faring town of Falmouth, on the south coast of Cornwall, where Charles Snell was born, in modest circumstances, on May 6, 1791, to Robert Snell, a sailmaker, and his wife Ann. He must have grown up with all the lively noises of the shipyards about him – more lively still after 1793, when the twenty long years of war with France began – and no doubt Robert Snell encouraged his son to follow one of the crafts which Falmouth men had practised from earliest times. But young Charles was more adventurous – and ambitious. In 1806, when he was only fifteen years old, he ran away from Falmouth, enlisted in the service of the East India Company, and was posted to the Madras Native Infantry as a cadet.

A year later, on August 27, 1807, Charles was commissioned ensign, and he was promoted to lieutenant in April 1810. Then followed what appears from the records at the India Office to have been a rather uninspiring, conventional military career, with only one hint of anything 'irregular' in his conduct. This was the birth, about 1819, of Charles Snell, Junior; but there seems to be no trace of who the mother was or when the boy was baptized.[1]

I think uncle Willie would have been delighted at the idea of a black sheep in the family. It seems probable that Charles Snell atoned for his indiscretion by caring for his son until he was old enough to fend for himself, and he may even have set him to work in his own office, for between 1820 and 1835 Captain Snell, as he was then, was busy superintending provincial surveys in various parts of India. Then, in July 1835, he was 'permitted to resign his appointment in the Survey Department', and shortly afterwards he returned to England on leave.[2]

The scene now moves back to Falmouth – to the home-coming of the sailmaker's son, bronzed and resplendent in his uniform, and to Pendennis Castle, high on the headland. It must have been a proud occasion for Charles Snell when he was invited up to dine at the Castle House; it was a romantic occasion too, for it was there that he met a beautiful young girl named Anne Alicia Todd. They fell in love, and after a suitable courtship, they were married in Falmouth on January 7, 1837. Charles, whose promotion to brevet major was gazetted three days later, was forty-five; his bride was only twenty. His wedding gift to her sounds strangely up-to-date; it was a guitar – which has survived and is now with kinsmen in Devonshire, together with a letter written by Mrs Snell saying that it 'must never be sold'.

*

It was this marriage between Charles Snell and Anne Alicia Todd that infused some blue blood into the veins of the Maughams and gave us our link with King Edward I and his Queen, Eleanor, the daughter of King Ferdinand of Castile – a link as slender as a tiny twig of the royal tree.[3] Willie was sardonically amused by this tendril to nobility; but I think my father was secretly reassured to know that he was descended, through his maternal grandmother, from such grand people as Humphrey de Bohun, Earl of Hereford and Essex (died 1322), Hugh de Courtenay, Earl of Devon (died 1377), Sir John Savage (died 1492), Sir Thomas Grenville (died 1512), Sir William Brereton (died 1541), Sir Bernard Drake (died 1586), and Sir Philip Perceval (died 1647); and that he was connected, however slightly, with a whole host of warriors and statesmen – among them Sir Richard Grenville of the *Revenge*, and John Churchill, the great Duke of Marlborough. Moreover, the roots of the royal tree spread back far and wide, to Henry II and thence to

William the Conqueror, Alfred the Great, and all the dynasties of Europe.

I have told the story of the parents of Mrs Snell – Willie's maternal grandmother – in Appendix VI. It is sufficient here to remark that her father, Francis Todd, was a Yorkshire squire of property and wealth who invested and lost his fortune in a Cornish tin mine; and that her mother, Caroline, came of the Brereton family which gave Willie and me so many grand ancestors. They were married in 1808 and had four sons and four daughters, of whom Anne Alicia was their fourth child. The eldest boy, Francis, born in 1810, became a captain in the Duke of Wellington's Regiment, but his army career was cut short by a blow from a cricket ball. The other sons were Robert, Brereton Frederick, and lastly, in 1821, Henry Somerset. I was delighted to have made this discovery, for it was of course from his great-uncle Henry Somerset Todd that Willie Maugham got the name Somerset. And Henry took his name from his godfather, General Sir Henry Somerset (1794–1862),[4] eldest son of Lord Charles Somerset and nephew of the sixth Duke of Beaufort. The General fought with distinction under Wellington in the Peninsular War and at Waterloo; he served at the Cape and in India, and he was described as 'a most able, indefatigable and upright man'.

Willie Maugham never knew why he was called 'Somerset', and by the time I had found the answer it was too late to explain. He was too deaf, and too ill to understand.[5]

*

For some months after the marriage in 1837, Major Charles Snell and his wife lived in Exeter; then he took her back with him to India – a tedious four month long voyage which was made more wretched for Anne Alicia by the circumstances attending the birth of her first child, a daughter 'who just breathed and died'.[6] When they landed in India, Major Snell returned to active duty within the Presidency of Madras, and, according to the India Office Records, he 'assumed command of his corps' on December 27, 1839. He must have been stationed for a while at Trichinopoly, for it was there that his second daughter, Edith Mary, was born, on May 10, 1840. This time, all was well, and the child – Willie's mother and my grandmother – was baptized eight weeks later, on July 4.[7]

Mrs Snell was then only twenty-four. Despite her unhappy experience on the voyage to India, she still enjoyed the vigour of youth. But her husband, Charles, in his fiftieth year, had lost his health in the unwholesome climate. He died on June 3, 1841, at Mandum, near Seringapatam – eight weeks before his third daughter, Rose Ellen Cleveland, was born at Bangalore, on July 29.

The young widow, with her two small girls, must have stayed on in India for at least a couple of years, because the children learned to 'prattle Hindustani much better than English'. My father, who recorded this in his autobiography, remarked that when the Snells came home to England and their Indian nurse took the children out in the streets of Bristol one day, they promptly got lost, because the *ayah* spoke no English at all. My father added that his grandmother brought home 'a quantity of almost worthless Indian furniture and warehoused it at the premises of some well-known agents in Whitehall at a cost of about £50 a year'. Later, 'when urged by her grandsons after many years to get rid of it in order to increase her small income, her reply was to weep. Nothing could be done and the furniture was still in Whitehall when she died', in 1904. Apparently the whole lot was sold for about £5 – a poor return after spending some £3,000 to store it for sixty years.

A few years after Major Snell's death his widow returned to Europe and settled in France, where the children attended a convent school. According to my father she 'had a generous widow's pension from the East India Company, and inherited a substantial amount of money which she spent or lost'. In fact, as I discovered later, her pension was £265 per annum, which I should have thought was hardly sufficient to keep herself and educate her two daughters. She cannot have inherited any substantial legacy from her parents, for Francis Todd's venture in the Cornish tin mines ruined the family fortune, and his widow Caroline, who lived until 1874, was cheated by the trustee who absconded with most of what was left. But my father was correct in saying that Mrs Snell 'then made an income for herself by writing novels and children's books in French'. This talent was shared by her younger daughter, Rose. I obtained a list of their books from the Bibliothèque Nationale in Paris. The titles are charming: Mrs Snell's first was *Notre Dame de Bonsecours, ou l'Orpheline du Monastère*, published in 1858 by Mégard in Rouen; and Rose followed with *La Famille du pêcheur*,

and then *La Fête d'une mère, suivie de: Adèle et Lucie*, published by
J. Lefort in Lille. Mother and daughter each kept to their separate
publishers, and their books ran into several editions – sometimes
re-issued under different titles. Six titles are listed for Rose, and twelve
for her mother, who wrote under the name of Anna Snell. I have been
told by a cousin of hers that Mrs Snell wrote one of her books for a
wager with a 'Romish priest' who bet her one hundred francs that she
could not write a Catholic story of which he would approve. The
result was a pretty tale about a French convent school, published in
1862, which received the approbation of 'no less a prelate than His
Eminence the Prince Cardinal Archbishop of Rouen'. I hope the
doubting priest paid up.

After Edith Mary Snell had married my grandfather, Robert Ormond
Maugham, at the British Embassy in Paris, on October 1, 1863, Mrs
Snell and Rose went to live by the sea, at St Malo. By then, Rose
may already have been suffering from tuberculosis – the disease that
killed both her and her sister and very nearly killed Willie when he
was a young man. Rose died on March 12, 1869, aged twenty-seven;
and we discovered – from a will made by her mother in 1887 – that she
was buried 'in the Cemetery of St Servan', which adjoins St Malo.[8]

Although Mrs Snell continued to live in France after Rose died, she
saw little of Willie's mother, her elder daughter. While Edith Mary and
her husband, Robert Ormond Maugham, were busy making their
own lives in Paris society, with the added responsibility of caring for
their own young family, Mrs Snell resigned herself to an old age that
was to become increasingly embittered by ill-health and loneliness.
Her only real escape from this introspection came in July, 1870.
Napoleon III, the old and ailing Emperor of the French, had foolishly
declared war against Prussia in a vain attempt to deter Bismarck's
ambitions and to retrieve for his own nation the unity and prestige that
had been squandered during years of political strife and mounting unrest among the labouring poor. While many other English residents,
including the Maughams, fled the country as the victorious Prussians
approached Paris, Mrs Snell remained. My father recalled in his autobiography that she 'organised a hospital for the wounded, which was so
successful that when the hospital was ultimately closed she was given a
civic reception and a public vote of thanks'.

There must be some truth in this. But despite exhaustive enquiries in

France and diligent searching through the journals of the time, we have been unable to discover any other account of Mrs Snell's hospital work. All I know for certain is that she lived in St Malo until she made her will there in 1887. By then her elder daughter Edith Mary had died and her four grandsons were all in England. The eldest, Willie's brother, Charles Ormond Maugham, was the only one mentioned in Mrs Snell's will. She wished him to have her 'four large hand-worked tapestry pictures', her prints and books, and her 'house linen, glass and china of every description'. Everything else was to go to a niece, the daughter of her favourite brother, Henry Somerset Todd. Mrs Snell also expressed her 'desire' that her body, together with that of her younger daughter Rose, should be 'brought to England and reburied there'. But her lonely life dragged on for another seventeen years, and at her death in 1904 in Le Mans she was so much in debt that even her one desire could not be granted, and she was buried quietly in the alien soil of France.*

*

When I began to read the recollections of my father and my uncle Willie describing their childhood in Paris, I was struck by a difference between them that I had never noticed before. Whereas my father was concerned with human beings only inasmuch as they related to things, places, and events, Willie was concerned with things, places, and events only inasmuch as they related to human beings. My father mentioned his 'parents', but he never described them. Only the objects in the rooms and the incidents in the streets beyond had any meaning for him. But Willie, in a few brief sentences, made his parents come to life, and each object or incident he described served to illuminate their characters. This essential difference between the two brothers was, I suppose, one of the reasons why my father became a lawyer and Willie became a novelist.

Willie remembers his mother as 'very small, with large brown eyes and hair of a rich reddish gold, exquisite features and lovely skin'; he also remembered 'the string of donkeys' which used to stop outside their front door in Paris 'to provide her with asses' milk', which it was hoped would alleviate her tuberculosis. And he recalled his 'very ugly' father, whose 'romantic mind' had excited him to visit Morocco, Greece, Turkey, and Asia Minor, and to fill his apartment

* See Appendix VII.

with travel books and such exotic souvenirs as 'Tanagra statuettes, Rhodes ware, and Turkish daggers in hilts of richly decorated silver'.[9]

I do not know when Robert Ormond Maugham set off on these adventures. It may have been during his bachelor years soon after he had begun to practise in Paris, or it may have been on his honeymoon after he married Edith Mary Snell in October 1863. At that time, as I mentioned earlier, the office of 'Maugham et Dixon, jurisconsultes anglais', was at 54 Faubourg St Honoré, almost opposite the British Embassy to which my grandfather had been appointed solicitor some ten years before. His apartment was also nearby, on the third floor of 25 Avenue d'Antin,[10], a broad street lined with chestnut trees on the south side of the Champs Elysées and close to the Rond Point – in the elegant heart of the French capital.

Paris in the 1860s was a city of pleasure and frivolity. Robert Ormond Maugham's career was prospering; he and his wife could afford to take their place in the society that revolved around the British Embassy. Their apartment was spacious, with a large drawing-room, and a billiard-room lined with books, and they had a large staff of servants to attend on them. In those days the *beau monde* of Paris lived in a world of its own – in sad contrast to the rest of the country; and though the English and other foreign diplomats may have seen the dangers arising from the new power of Bismarck's Germany and the growing unrest among the French industrial workers, nothing disturbed the whirl of receptions, parties, and dances in which Robert and Edith Maugham began their married life. Nothing, at least, until November 14, 1865, when their first son, Charles Ormond, was born. Their next son, Frederic Herbert – my father – followed on October 20, 1866; and then Henry Neville – my uncle Harry – on June 12, 1868. So for a while, with three little boys to bring up, Edith Maugham had to divide her time between the *salon* and the nursery. But soon the children were big enough to be taken by their nurses to play in the Champs Elysées and to become excited by a new 'game' that their father was playing in the summer of 1870, after Napoleon III had declared war on Prussia.

After describing his first memory of childhood my father wrote in his autobiography:[11]

The next scene I can remember, beyond the indistinct figures of my father, mother, and brothers, and of a servant or two, is of the Franco-

W. Somerset Maugham and his uncle, the Rev. Henry Macdonald
Maugham, outside the old vicarage at Whitstable, c.1885

The Rev. Henry Macdonald Maugham, Vicar of Whitstable, c. 1880

Barbara Sophia von Scheidlin, the first wife of the Rev. Henry Macdonald Maugham

Prussian war of 1870. There was a billiard-room in our Paris apartment, and at some date a large map of France was pinned up in it. It was made interesting by the fact that little flags, coloured red and blue, were stuck on to it and moved from time to time. I can distinctly remember my mother explaining to us . . . that when the flags which represented the German Army reached a certain place on the map we should all leave Paris and go to London. It was to me a wonderfully exciting and welcome idea, though I had already imbibed from our servants, who were all of them French, a very distinct horror and detestation of *les sales Allemands*.

Defeat soon began to seem inevitable. The Maughams, like most of the other English residents, moved out before the Germans invested Paris. Soon after the disaster at Sedan at the beginning of September, when Napoleon III and most of his army surrendered to the enemy, Robert and Edith Maugham and their three small sons said goodbye to their servants, paused to place a Union Jack on the balcony of their apartment, and hurried to the railway station.

For a while during their enforced stay in London the three boys were left in the care of their paternal grandmother Mary, the widow of Robert Maugham of the Law Society, while their parents went to Italy on holiday. My father wrote that he had only the 'vaguest recollection' of landing in England, but that 'the siege of Paris . . . was a memorable incident even as told to a child of four'. During the five months that the French capital held out against the Germans several messages were sent over the Channel by carrier pigeons; and in the spring of 1871, after the Germans had come and gone and Paris was being ravished by the revolution known as the *Commune*, the Maughams received a message from their French servants, 'asking whether Madam desired the usual cleaning to be done and the summer covers to be put on the furniture in the drawing-room'.

During the five months of siege the main peril of the people of Paris had been starvation, and even the lions and tigers in the zoo had been killed and sold for food. But the peril during the *Commune* was the bitter, vindictive hatred of Frenchman for Frenchman. In six weeks of bloody civil war, under the eyes of the victorious Germans, the mob destroyed and burned many of the public buildings and monuments in the city; and in the last week of May 1871, when the government forces regained control, more than 20,000 *Communards* were killed. When the Maughams returned to Paris in August they found the city 'a scene of desolation', with burnt walls and heaps of rubble everywhere; but their own apartment in the Avenue d'Antin was unscathed. They were met at the Gare du Nord by their manservant François – so thin and pale that none of them recognised him at first – and he told them that two German soldiers had actually tried to requisition the apartment, but that 'on being assured that the owner was an Englishman, and having had their attention drawn to the Union Jack on the balcony, they retired'.

*

The Franco-Prussian war marked a considerable change in the fortunes of my family. As sightseers flocked to gape at the torn and gutted buildings, and as the diplomatic community resumed their pattern of entertaining, Paris regained a superficial air of prosperity and gaiety. But Willie's father was faced with the task of raising up his practice again, almost from scratch: many of his old clients never returned, and had it not been for his connection with the British Embassy I daresay he might have been forced to give up the elegant apartment in the Avenue d'Antin and return to London, to rejoin his partner Albert Dixon[12] at 10 Bedford Row. As it was, Robert Ormond Maugham was obliged to work harder than ever to re-establish his position and to keep his growing family. He left home early each morning, and returned late each evening, and he evidently denied himself all leisure for a few years for the sake of his wife and children.

My father and his brothers Charles and Harry remained in Paris for six years, until 1877, when they were sent to school in England. During part of that time they attended a *lycée*, but most of their education was left to English governesses and, for a while, to a tutor whom my father recalled as 'a young man with whiskers who was a curate at the English church in the Rue d'Aguesseau'. The man seemed a fortunate choice as a teacher, in Latin and other subjects, and he inspired confidence in his young pupils; but he was suddenly dismissed when it was discovered, to the 'agreeable surprise' of the boys, that 'though he had been acting as a curate, he had never been ordained and was in short an impostor'. If he had been Willie's tutor, no doubt the young man would have ended up as an unsavoury character in one of his novels; but my father made only the polite comment that the congregation of the English church were 'greatly upset' and that he wondered 'how the much respected incumbent of the important living managed to explain so strange an event'.

When I was last in Paris, searching for the places associated with my family, the Champs Elysées and the surrounding streets were as usual crowded with bars and restaurants and night clubs and with English and American tourists in search of *la vie parisienne*. But Paris was very different during my father's childhood. Then, he recalled, there were 'very few amusements'. No shops or theatres intruded upon the broad avenues of private houses and luxurious apartments; and the only diversions for children were the merry-go-rounds and puppet-shows near the Place de la Concorde, and two large circular buildings near the Rond Point, in one of which was 'a most realistic panorama of the siege of Paris, with real guns and implements of war, and "dead bodies" in real French uniforms'. If it was fine, the Maugham boys were allowed to play with the French children in the Champs Elysées, and sometimes, in warm weather, to swim in the Seine; and when it was wet their governess took them for improving tours in the galleries of the Louvre or the Luxembourg. But most of their pleasures were home-made within their comfortable apartment, in which my father remembered the 'gracious figure' of his mother 'moving about and speaking pleasant words to her boys', and 'watching over their happiness'.

Early in 1874, when my father was seven years old, my uncle Willie was born. Owing to the appalling slaughter during the Franco-Prussian war, it had been decreed that all children born on French soil should take French citizenship and thus be liable, in due time, to serve in the French forces. So it had been arranged that Edith Maugham should have her *accouchement* within the British Embassy, so that her fourth child might be born on British soil. And in the Embassy, on January 25, 1874, William Somerset Maugham came into the world. It is perhaps ironical that though the place of his birth ensured him British citizenship, Willie later chose to spend most of his life in France. It is even more ironical that the unfortunate litigation which arose from Willie's attempt in his confused old age to disinherit his daughter Liza and to adopt his secretary and companion Alan Searle as his heir might never have been necessary if Willie had been subject to French instead of British law.

*

When Willie was born his mother was almost thirty-four years old.

Despite her frailty, due to tuberculosis of the lungs, everyone remarked on her beauty. She also had a great sense of humour, and my father recalled that it was 'hardly an exaggeration to say that she knew almost everyone worth knowing in Paris'. Two of her closest friends were the second secretary at the British Embassy and his wife, who had been married in 1872. He was the Hon. Henry Wodehouse, a brother of the first Earl of Kimberley (after whom the famous mining town in South Africa was named), and his wife was the rich and vivacious Mary Livingstone King, a daughter of the American railroad and banking tycoon, John Pendleton King. 'Minnie', as she was known to all her intimates, remained my grandmother's devoted friend. Her husband died only fourteen months after their marriage, at the age of forty-three; but the widow stayed on in Paris and eventually, in 1880, she married Henry Paget, fourth Marquess of Anglesey. He was a descendant of the flamboyant general who lost a leg at Waterloo and was famous for his crisp response to a mob who were demonstrating in favour of Queen Caroline. The general had no regard for George IV's ugly German consort, who was then on trial for adultery. 'The Queen,' he cried, 'and may all your wives be like her!'

This anecdote reminds me of a story that Willie was fond of telling about the end of Minnie's own disastrous marriage to Lord Anglesey. I have heard Willie tell it many times, and this is how he once wrote it for an American magazine[13]:

One evening the Angleseys were giving a dinner at which the Russian ambassador was to be the guest of honour. The guests arrived and Lady Anglesey greeted them, but Anglesey did not appear. Lady Anglesey thought he was still dressing and she apologised to the ambassador. They waited and still he did not come. At last she sent a footman to his room to tell him that their guests were assembled. The footman came back to say his lordship was not in his room and gave her a letter, addressed to her, which he had found pinned on the pincushion. In it he told her that he was leaving her for good and had started for England with Madame de So-and-So . . . How the dinner proceeded I do not know. It must have been a grim affair. When all the guests had departed and only my mother remained, she tried to console Lady Anglesey, who throughout the evening had put on a bold front.

'He'll come back to you,' she said. 'After all, Madame de So-and-So is as ugly as sin.'

Lady Anglesey gasped. 'If she's ugly, he'll never come back.'

She was right. Lord Anglesey remained with his French mistress for the rest of his life.

My grandmother's other great friend in Paris was Isabella Williams-Freeman,[14] whose husband[15] was also one of the second secretaries at the British Embassy. The Williams-Freemans lived in the Avenue de l'Alma (now the Avenue George V), and, like the Maughams, they had several young children, one of whom was a god-daughter of Edith Maugham and, like Willie, born in the Embassy – in the same room two years later. She was Violet Williams-Freeman, later Mrs Arthur Hammersley. When I first met her she was eighty-seven and living in elegant retirement at Totland Bay on the Isle of Wight. I visited her there one day in 1963, and was enchanted by her vitality and her splendid sense of humour. And I was fascinated by her lively reminiscences of the Paris that she and Willie knew as children. Her house was Victorian, but she had added a circular patio with frescoes by Duncan Grant, and on that summer's day in 1963 it was full of the scent of lilac and lilies-of-the-valley. Beyond was a smooth lawn, dominated by a vast tree, and further still I could see the Solent, an azure glimpse of sea framed by a gap in the box-hedge.

Mrs Hammersley's conversation was of long ago – of Lytton Strachey, Desmond MacCarthy, Virginia Woolf, and all the 'Bloomsbury set' of intellectual painters and writers into which Willie so passionately hoped to be accepted when he was a young man. As we walked out into the garden Mrs Hammersley draped a black lace shawl over the purple cardigan and white lace mantilla she was wearing and we sat in deck chairs beside a white pergola festooned with wistaria.

'Do you like Willie?' I asked after we had settled ourselves comfortably.

She was silent. I looked at her long, intelligent, sensitive face. I noticed the twinkle in her dark round eyes.

'I'm very fond of him,' she said. 'But I don't think I really *like* him.' Suddenly she smiled, and for a moment she looked very young.

'Can you remember much about Willie as a small boy in Paris?' I asked. 'Did he stammer then – while his mother was alive?'

Mrs Hammersley thought for a moment, searching back into her memory.

'No,' she answered. 'I wasn't aware of whether he stammered or not as a child. But I remember that he told us wonderful stories. And he was highly imaginative. When my mother was 'at home' on Sunday afternoons, we children were also allowed to invite our friends to tea. Willie often came, and because he was so imaginative he was allowed to invent the games we should play.

'Willie also joined us sometimes in the Champs Elysées, which was a great meeting place for children. We formed ourselves into clans to play such games as *Les Barres* and *La Tour prend garde*. Willie used to fascinate us by passing off imitation *sous* at the *kiosques* where paper windmills and coloured balloons were sold together with pieces of flat gingerbread pricked out in patterns. And he passed off his false *sous* to the itinerant old woman who had a tin strapped to her from which she used to sell *gaufrettes* powdered with icing sugar. My elder sister was very shocked by Willie's trickery, but my youngest brother and I thought it was very clever that these fierce-looking traders could be gulled by this innocent-looking boy.'

'And do you remember Willie's parents?' I asked.

'But of course,' said Mrs Hammersley. 'Though I was very young at the time I remember them clearly. Mrs Maugham was my god-mother. She was lovely, with russet hair, a straight little nose and a creamy complexion, almost wax-like. Her great brown eyes were always sad. She must have suffered a lot of pain, and was terribly ill sometimes with this dreadful consumption. My mother, who always took me visiting with her in the afternoon, often had tea with Mrs Maugham. Your grandmother would give me a doll dressed like a fisherwoman to play with, which I took with me under the tea-table. I remember it was a big round table spread with a white cloth. I could hear them above me talking in low and earnest tones. It seemed that the whole trend was always of sadness.'

I reminded Mrs Hammersley that my grandparents had been known as 'Beauty and the Beast' by their friends. She smiled happily.

'Oh, yes,' she said. 'Your grandfather was *very* ugly. Almost a monster to look at, with a large very yellow face and very yellow eyes. I think he had cancer of the liver. But he was a loving parent and wonderfully kind to children. He always came to our house on Sunday afternoons. He would take me on his knees and tell me little stories, and he would blow on his hunter fob-watch to make it open. That always delighted me. It was odd. To a child he was terrifyingly ugly.

But somehow there used to come out of him an intense sweetness which transformed him, and I remember a sense of complete safety and happiness. You know, he was a man of great virtue – a man one could tremendously respect. And he adored his wife. My impression of her was that she was a person of intense feeling who had had some kind of unhappy love affair before she married your grandfather.'

Mrs Hammersley died a few months after my visit to her. By a coincidence she died on Willie's ninetieth birthday – January 25, 1964. Only that morning she had written to me. She stamped the letter, but she never posted it. Her solicitors found it and sent it on to me. It was quite a short letter, lively yet muddled, but I was able to make out the first few lines. 'Dear Robin,' she wrote, 'I feel I must write you a line because on every page of every paper which passes through my hands I am faced with photographs of Willie, and dissertations about him – his dignity, benignity, deep loving kindness – until I scarcely feel I ever knew my faithful friend at all. . . . And yet I'm sure I did. . . . '

It was like reading the end of a chapter that began a long time ago.

*

In September 1877, when Willie was nearly four years old, his three elder brothers were sent to boarding school in England, at Dover College, and the gap in age that divided them became wider still. During the next few years, except for the holidays, Willie had his mother and her love all to himself. I suppose that this was one of the most important periods in his long life, for though he was to write only a little about it in his reminiscences, his early boyhood and his mother's illness and her death had a profound effect on his character which endured to his own death. Her love, her protection, her physical beauty, her comfortable apartment, and her elegant pattern of living – all were suddenly torn away from him and replaced soon after by an environment so alien and bleak and so lacking in affection that it scarred his mind for ever. But there were still a few years of happiness before that terrible day came.

At the apartment in the Avenue d'Antin Willie shared a bedroom with his French nurse, but in the mornings he was allowed into the warm seclusion of his mother's room, while she rested in bed after her bath. And in the afternoons, when his nurse brought him back from playing in the Champs Elysées, he was taken in to meet his mother's friends at tea. Sometimes famous people came. Willie once told me that as a child he remembered meeting Georges Clemenceau, who was to become the Prime Minister of France. In those days Clemenceau was the leader of the Extreme Left in the Chamber of Deputies. To have invited him, then, to her *salon*, shows considerable discernment and lack of political bias on my grandmother's part.

I might mention at this point that some of Willie's biographers, perhaps misled by his own devout respect for his mother's charm and talents, have rather exaggerated her position and influence as a hostess in society. Two of the names which have frequently been bandied about as being among her 'intimate friends' are those of Gustave Doré and Prosper Mérimée.[16] But Mérimée had died at Cannes more than two years before Willie was born; and Doré, though his engravings certainly adorned the apartment in the Avenue d'Antin, was too busy making his fortune to have spared much time for the family of the solicitor to the British Embassy. Yet perhaps I do my grandmother an injustice.... Her obituary in *Le Gaulois*[17] spoke of her as a woman 'dont la beauté éblouissante rayonnait naguère dans nos plus élégants salons'; and a writer in *Gil Blas*[18] paid a touching compliment to 'la jeune Mme Maugham, une femme charmante, qui ne comptait que des amis dans la haute société parisienne, où elle occupait une des premières places'. The fact that her name is not mentioned in any of the biographies of Mérimée or Doré or of other contemporary French writers and painters seems to show that her *salon* was social rather than literary or artistic; and the important word *naguère* – 'formerly' – in the notice in *Le Gaulois* also indicates that she had been forced for some years to reduce her social life, probably because of her increasing illness. (This is confirmed by the fact that no mention of her appears, until her death, in any French newspaper, nor even in the *Gazette des Étrangers*.) But though Willie's imagination may have played tricks with his memory as to exactly *who* were his mother's friends, it is certainly true that Edith Maugham occupied a special place in Paris society. She was one of the few foreigners listed in the yearly directory, *La Société et le high life*. And *Galignani's Messenger*,[19] which gave little space to the world of fashion, wrote that she was 'greatly admired and respected for her social graces and domestic virtues'.[20]

This last comment, on Edith Maugham's 'social graces and domestic virtues', is probably the truest assessment of her character. She certainly never sought the limelight, nor, I suspect, could she have afforded to stay in it for long. When she took her sons to the seaside in the holidays, it was not to Nice or Cannes or other expensive resorts on the Riviera, nor to Trouville, where most of the rank and fashion of Paris spent the summer when the celebrations of Bastille Day were over. They went instead to Deauville, then a little fishing village with its *plage de famille*. The recollections of my father and Willie are curiously different on this period of their lives. My father gives no picture of his parents in his autobiography, but he remembered the 'wooden jetty', the 'endless sands' and the 'pony races' in one of which he 'came in a good second on a borrowed animal'. It was typical of him to remark on this event, ' ... I did not think I was justified in using a whip on a strange horse and I believe I ought to have won that race'. He also recalled that his father, who usually came to Deauville by train on Saturdays after a hard week's work in his office, once 'arrived with a machine, afterwards to be known as a bone-shaker', on which the family 'all learnt a surprisingly rapid means of motion'. Willie recalled his mother sitting 'on a campstool on the beach, busy with her embroidery' and keeping an eye on her sons while she chatted 'with the acquaintances she had made with other *estivants*'. And he remembered also the 'shabby little painter, far from young, who used to wander about the beach', mostly in Trouville, 'making little paintings on a panel of the smart ladies in the fashionable dress of the day'. The paintings were offered at only five francs each, but Willie did not think the shabby little man often made a sale because 'the sort of people who spent their summer at Deauville, rather than at Trouville, were not in the habit of throwing money away'.

'I like to think that my mother may have been tempted to get one', Willie added, 'but refrained because she knew my father wouldn't like it.'

The painter was Eugène Boudin, and when Willie saw one of his little pictures eighty years later in a gallery in New York the dealer asked him seven thousand dollars for it.

From these long summer vacations the three elder boys, Charlie, my father, and Harry, returned to their studies at Dover College, and Willie once again had his mother's love all to himself. But as she slowly declined in health he was frequently left to the care of his French nurse with whom he spent still more time when his mother became pregnant again. I cannot put an exact date to this, but it must have been when

Willie was about five years old. In those days doctors believed that childbirth was helpful to women who suffered from consumption. But the child, a boy, was still-born. After this, Edith Maugham spent part of each winter, with Willie and his nurse, at Pau, the popular health resort in the Basses-Pyrénées near the Spanish frontier. But the relief afforded by the mild climate and the pure air was only temporary, and when she returned to Paris the disease took hold of her once more.

Sometime in 1881, when she was once again pregnant, Edith Maugham suddenly realised that she would not live much longer. Willie, who recalled the episode in *The Summing Up*, described how his mother was lying in bed, probably after a haemorrhage, when 'the thought came to her that her sons when they grew up would not know what she was like when she died'. So 'she called her maid, had herself dressed in an evening gown of white satin and went to the photographer's'. It was a brave, defiant gesture, typical of her long fight against her illness and typical of her rather touching vanity in appreciating her own great beauty.

On January 24, 1882, Edith Maugham gave birth at her apartment to her sixth son. The child was quickly baptized, with the names Edward Alan, and died at three o'clock the next afternoon. It was Willie's eighth birthday. Six days later, on January 31, Willie's mother also died. She was forty-one years old.[21]

*

It is a moving story, but the last episodes were strangely distorted by Willie in the opening pages of *Of Human Bondage*. And yet the very distortion was probably due to his passionate, unreasoning, childish love for his mother. He kept a copy of that last photograph of her beside his bed throughout his life. It was his most treasured possession – far more precious than the paintings which he acquired and subsequently sold. And that photograph was beside his bed on the day he died, almost eighty-four years after the death of his mother.

There is something rather sad about the fact that the person who had made Edith Maugham's elegant life financially possible was her ugly little husband who slaved away in his office in the Faubourg St Honoré, hiding what Willie described as his 'romantic mind' behind dusty piles of legal documents and the files of other people's worries, so that he could afford to pay for the servants and the carriages, the summer

holidays at Deauville and the winter cures at Pau. Edith Maugham may
have died before her time, but while she was alive she lived intensely.
For her husband, there was no such adventure in those years after the
Franco-Prussian war. His only real diversion was in building a country
house on the outskirts of Paris. This is Willie's description of it in
The Summing Up.

He took it into his head to build a house to live in during the summer. He
bought a piece of land on the top of a hill at Suresnes. The view was splendid
over the plain, and in the distance was Paris. There was a road down to the
river and by the river lay a little village. It was to be like a villa on the Bos-
phorus, and on the top floor it was surrounded by loggias. I used to go down
with him every Sunday by the Seine on a *bateau-mouche* to see how it was
getting on. When the roof was on, my father began to furnish it by buying a
pair of antique fire-irons. He ordered a great quantity of glass on which he
had engraved a sign against the Evil Eye, which he had found in Morocco
... It was a white house and the shutters were painted red. The garden was
laid out. The rooms were furnished, and then my father died.

The house still exists. For some curious reason it was not sold when
my grandfather died, and it remained unoccupied for a very long time.
My uncle Charles – Willie's eldest brother – who was the head of the
family, seems to have forgotten all about it. When I wrote to his widow,
my aunt Beldy, after beginning this book, she could only recall that she
and Charles went to see the house 'some time before 1914' – a quarter
of a century or so after Robert Ormond Maugham's death. 'I remember
very little about it,' she wrote, 'except that it was like a Swiss châlet,
with the same sort of balconies and roof, etc. But you see, your uncle
Charles thought that as it had been unused for so long he had better
see if there was even a possibility of living in it. But Suresnes was by
then a very unpleasant little "banlieue" – a row of common little shops
and cafés, etc., and then above them this "Swiss châlet". I forget how
one got to it, but I think I remember it was dark and, well, just not
"sympathique" at all, and a horrid place to live in and go up and down
to. Uncle Charles decided then and there to sell it after consultation
with his brothers ... '

Armed with this harsh but – as I discovered – quite accurate description of my grandfather's one venture in architecture, I drove out from
Paris to Suresnes, which lies just west of the Bois de Boulogne, close
to the Seine. I had got hold of an old street plan of Paris and I managed

to find the house in 5 Rue Worth which runs along the side of a steep hill. The street was named after the famous English fashion-designer, Charles Worth, who was couturier to the Empress Eugénie; but whatever romance may have attached to the house in the 1880s had long since vanished. Only the view remained – a splendid panorama over the Seine, the racecourse at Longchamps and over the whole of Paris, now dominated by the Eiffel Tower. The house is very odd indeed – half Swiss châlet and half Japanese, with a projecting roof, stucco walls, and wooden supports for the little balconies, which Willie had grandly described as 'loggias'. But I was sad to see no trace of the 'great quantity of glass' engraved with the unusual sign against the Evil Eye that Robert Ormond Maugham had found in the Sahara.

'My father was a stranger to me when he was alive,' Willie once told me. 'Yet somehow that sign against the Evil Eye seems to have bound us together, for as you know I've used it a great deal.'

*

My grandfather's odd sign is printed on the jacket and stamped on the cover of all Willie's books. It was used by his American publisher as a watermark on each page of paper of his collected works. It was impressively engraved outside the gate that led into the Villa Mauresque – which Willie bought for £7,000 and which was worth half a million at his death. The sign was over the front door of the villa – and on all the matchboxes at the Mauresque until Willie stopped it because he complained that his guests used to pinch them for souvenirs.

Investigations at the British Museum suggest that the sign may possibly be intended to represent an upright sword covered by the arch of the sky. It could be the symbol of a sword piercing through darkness into light. Alternatively, the vertical and horizontal lines within the arch around it may well be the cross of Lorraine. But why should my grandfather have discovered a cross in the depths of Saharan Morocco?

Oddly enough, I think I discovered the answer when I lived with a tribe of Tuareg while I was writing *The Slaves of Timbuktu*. The Tuareg were originally nomadic Libyans. Invasions from Carthage and Rome pressed them back into the interior. Their eyes were not accustomed to the glare of the Sahara, so they wore a veil, the *nicab*, to cover their head and forehead. Then they could not endure the thick sand-storms, so they wore another veil, the *litham*, to protect their nose and the lower part of their face. But there is evidence that the Tuareg were once Christians. Their swords are cross-hilted, the pommels of their camel-saddles take the form of a cross, and the same symbol is much used by their leather-workers and metal-workers. There are several words in the Tamachek language which suggest a Christian origin. Two striking examples are *Mesi*, meaning God, and *andjelous*, meaning angel. The names Samuel and Saul, which are rarely used by the Arabs of Africa, are common among the Tuareg. Roman soldiers and merchants had brought the Gospel to North Africa at the end of the first century when the Tuareg were still in Libya. Arabs who had been converted to Christianity painted the traditional symbol of strength on the walls of their houses and even drew it in the sand. Arabs and Africans – long before Islam – may well have borrowed the sign of the cross from the Christians as a talisman to ward off the evil eye. The Tuareg may have taken the sign with them into the Sahara. And my uncle, Willie Maugham, the agnostic, may have been protected throughout his life by a Christian symbol without knowing it.

*

After I had been to the house in Suresnes and returned to Paris, I called on Monsieur P. Messinesi. His name and address had been given to me by some kind official in the British Embassy who had discovered that my grandfather's firm of solicitors, 'Maugham et Dixon, jurisconsultes anglais', still exists under the name of their successors, 'Bodington & Yturbe', now at 4 Rue d'Anjou, and M. Messinesi is one of the senior partners. I was shown into a waiting-room, because M. Messinesi was engaged with a client, and as I glanced around I noticed a terracotta statuette of a small, rather plump figure, with 'mutton-chop' side whiskers, seated in a low, high-backed chair. I was particularly intrigued by the curious pose, as the figure was cross-legged, with one ankle tucked awkwardly under the other knee. But there was nothing to identify the subject; only the name of the sculptor, Jeras Boehm, and the date, 1862.

I was examining the figure when M. Messinesi came out of his office to greet me.

'Ah,' he said, patting the statuette gently. 'Do you know who this is?'

I shook my head. M. Messinesi smiled.

'This,' he said, 'is your grandfather, Robert Ormond Maugham. We are very proud of him, and of his famous son, Somerset.'

It was a splendid find, because so far as I know there had never been even a photograph of my grandfather. After I left Paris, M. Messinesi had the terracotta photographed for me; and on my next visit to the Villa Mauresque I gave a copy to Willie. It was a touching moment. Willie held the photograph and peered at it closely.

'Der-do you know, in all these years since I was a boy in Paris,' he said, 'I have never remembered what my father looked like.'

'You cross your legs in exactly the same way as your father did,' I said.

'Now I come to think of it, so I do,' Willie replied with a smile.

*

The two and a half years between the deaths of my grandmother and my grandfather must have been very lonely for Willie – and for his father too. Willie recalled this period in *The Summing Up*.

After my mother's death, her maid became my nurse. I had till then had French nurses and I had been sent to a French school for children. My know-ledge of English must have been slight. I have been told that on one occasion, seeing a horse out of the window of a railway carriage, I cried: '*Regardez, Maman, voilà un 'orse*' . . . I had been taken away from the French school and went for my lessons every day to the apartment of the English clergyman at the Church attached to the Embassy. His method of teaching me English was to make me read aloud the police-court news in the *Standard*, and I can still remember the horror with which I read the ghastly details of a murder in the train between Paris and Calais. I must then have been about nine . . .

Despite the fact that there was little understanding between the nine-year-old boy and his sixty-year-old father, I think that at the time Willie must have been deeply shocked as he watched his father's health decline to the point of death. Tuberculosis had killed his mother. Cancer and grief were soon to kill his father.

I have heard that his illness made Robert Ormond Maugham rather irritable and that he had 'words' with his old friend and partner Albert Dixon, who managed the London side of their business. Dixon had refused to let him sign some document regarding the future of the Paris office, as he thought it detrimental to the financial interest of the four

Maugham sons. We know that the friendship between the Maugham and Dixon families survived this lapse, but the time came when my grandfather was so ill that he had to ask Albert Dixon to approach the Law Society to find a young solicitor with a sound knowledge of French to come and help him in Paris. The young man chosen was John Thomas Beadsworth Sewell, who entered into partnership with my grandfather in 1883 or early in 1884. And it was J. T. B. Sewell who carried on the business after my grandfather's death, until my uncle Charles joined him in 1889.

One of the documents which I obtained from Paris through the efforts of M. Messinesi was a copy of the *Dépôt de pièces, concernant la succession de Monsieur Robert Ormond Maugham*. It is a strange tangle of legal phrases – all in French but partly a translation from a will and a codicil which were made in English and which I suppose must have been lost. In the will – made exactly one month after his wife's death – my grandfather appointed two executors to administer his estate. These were his only surviving brother, the Reverend Henry Macdonald Maugham, Vicar of Whitstable, and another Englishman who was subsequently ousted by the codicil which nominated, in addition to the vicar, 'mon ami Albert Dixon' and 'l'Honorable Alan Herbert[22] ... mon ami très estimé'. Another part of the document concerns the instructions given by the executors to J. T. B. Sewell, empowering him to realise my grandfather's estate and to pay his debts. It must have been quite a shock to his four sons – though Willie was hardly old enough to understand – when the sale of all their father's possessions, all his stocks and shares, his books and furniture, and all the 'Tanagra statuettes, Rhodes ware and Turkish daggers in hilts of richly decorated silver' with which he had filled the apartment in the Avenue d'Antin, left them only with the sum of £4,690 18s. 6d. between the four of them.

The end of the story is told in a brief notice in *The Times* for January 26, 1884:

Our Paris correspondent telegraphs that Mr Maugham, solicitor to the British Embassy at Paris, and well known to English residents having legal business, died yesterday morning,[23] after long suffering, from cancer in the stomach. Mr Maugham had practised in Paris upwards of 30 years.

*

I think it must have been my grandfather's young partner, J. T. B.

Sewell, who arranged for Willie to make the lonely nine-hour journey to England, in the care of his French nurse. Willie loved the nurse. She had been his mother's personal maid for many years, and Willie must have felt some comfort in the belief that she would remain his companion in the strange life that awaited him in Whitstable, with the uncle and guardian he had never met.

That journey, in 1884 – all for the modest cost, second-class, of £1 8s. 6d. for adults and half-price for children like Willie – was one of the few incidents of childhood that Willie could recall eighty years later, as if it had happened yesterday. He clutched his nurse's hand tightly as the jetties and beaches of Calais disappeared in the distance, and he stood on the rails of the steamer as he saw, for the first time, the white cliffs of Dover. Like any child, he was excited by the prospect of a new country. And then, suddenly, it was all over. The ship berthed beside the quay, the English officials and stevedores came aboard, and Willie and his nurse stepped down the gangway – on to what was, for both of them, a foreign land. Willie was so confused that he quite forgot all the English words he had learned. All he could say, as he spotted the gang of porters and the waiting rank of horse-drawn hackney carriages, was *'Porteur! Cabriolet!'*

Part Two

WILLIE'S SCHOOLDAYS

WHEN Willie was ten years old, standing on the quay-side at Dover holding up his hand and crying, '*Porteur! Cabriolet!*', the most bitter period of his life began.

'I shall never forget the misery of those next few years,' he told me.

With his nurse he travelled to Whitstable and arrived at the vicarage, where they were greeted by his uncle, the Reverend Henry Macdonald Maugham, and his German-born wife. They were then in their middle fifties and childless. Henry Maugham, the vicar, was severe, pedantic, and bigoted; and, as I mentioned earlier, he was lazy and self-centred. He was also a great snob. His wife, Barbara Sophia von Scheidlin, was a pleasant ineffectual *Hausfrau* who was completely dominated by her husband; she was prim and respectable, kindly but straitlaced. Both of them appear with stark clarity as the Reverend William Carey and his wife Louise in Willie's autobiographical novel *Of Human Bondage*. The earlier chapters of the book are almost pure autobiography. Whitstable, where Willie spent so much of his painful adolescence, becomes Blackstable; Canterbury, where Willie went to the King's School, becomes Tercanbury; and – most important of all –Willie's stammer becomes Philip Carey's club foot, but otherwise the book gives an almost exact description of my uncle's childhood.

'I wrote *Of Human Bondage* to rid myself of an intolerable obsession,' Willie said. 'I wanted to lay all those ghosts, and I succeeded.'

But did he succeed? I don't think so. The days that followed his arrival at Dover were seared deep into his memory.

'As soon as we arrived that night at the vicarage,' Willie told me, some eighty years later, 'my uncle broke the news to me that my nurse was to be sent away because they couldn't afford to keep her on. After both my mother and my father had died my nurse was the only person in the world I loved. She was my one link with all the happiness and affection I'd known in the Avenue d'Antin. She was the only real friend I had. You see, my brothers were older than I was. But my nurse had been with me constantly since my mother died. She'd been my mother's maid, you know. And I think she was as fond of me as I was of her. She was my last link with my mother and all that she had meant to me. And they took her away from me that very night.'

Eighty years is a long time, but there were tears in my uncle's eyes as he spoke of it.

'*Of Human Bondage* is not an autobiography,' Willie wrote,[1] 'but an autobiographical novel; fact and fiction are inextricably mingled; the emotions are my own, but not all the incidents are related as they happened, and some of them are transferred to my hero not from my own life but from that of persons with whom I was intimate. The book did for me what I wanted, and when it was issued to the world . . . I found myself free from the pains and unhappy recollections that tormented me.'

This is what Willie tried to persuade himself to believe. Yet some thirty years after the book had been published Willie signed a contract to make a record of *Of Human Bondage*. He went to the studio in New York and began to read. He had not looked at the novel since he corrected the proofs in 1914 and, as he began to read out aloud the first few pages, bitter memories of his childhood in Whitstable came surging back, and he broke down and sobbed uncontrollably. He could not go on, and the contract had to be cancelled, for the unhappy recollections still had power to torment him. And in part, *Of Human Bondage* is so autobiographical that Willie might have been reading his own diary. Here, for instance, is the description of little Philip and his dying mother:

Her voice was so weak that it seemed to come already from a great distance. The child did not answer, but smiled comfortably. He was very happy in the large, warm bed, with those soft arms about him. He tried to make himself smaller still as he cuddled up against his mother, and he kissed her sleepily. In a moment he closed his eyes and was fast asleep.

And after his mother's death:

Philip opened a large cupboard filled with dresses and, stepping in, took as many of them as he could in his arms and buried his face in them. They smelt of the scent his mother used.

Nowhere else does Willie write so tenderly. Later in the book there comes the horribly vivid description of the bullying that Willie suffered when he was sent at the age of ten to the junior annexe of the King's School, at Canterbury.

Then one of them had the brilliant idea of imitating Philip's clumsy run. Other boys saw it and began to laugh; then they all copied the first; and they ran round Philip, limping grotesquely, screaming in their treble voices with shrill laughter. The game was forgotten in the entertainment of Philip's deformity.

The deformity was, of course, Willie's stammer. Even one of the masters – Mr Gordon in the novel – attacked him because of his infirmity:

'Don't mumble,' shouted the master.
Something seemed to stick in Philip's throat.
'Go on. Go on. Go on.'
Each time the words were screamed more loudly. The effect was to drive all he knew out of Philip's head and he looked at the printed page vacantly. Mr Gordon began to breathe heavily.
'If you don't know, why don't you say so? Do you know it or not? Did you hear all this construed last time or not? Why don't you speak? Speak, you blockhead, speak!'

But young Willie couldn't speak because of his stammer. And he prayed to God to remove his affliction – just as young Philip did in the novel. 'Oh, God, in Thy loving mercy and goodness,' Philip prayed, 'if it be Thy will, please make my foot all right . . . before I go back to school.' But in the novel Philip's prayer remained unanswered, and Willie stammered to the day he died.

*

A few years ago I dined one night alone with Willie at the Dorchester. He was ill and in pain, and his mind sometimes wandered. Suddenly he muttered: 'I shall never get over her death. I shall never get over it.' For an instant I supposed that he was referring to my much-beloved sister Kate who had died recently, but as he went on talking I realised from the context of his words that he was thinking of his mother, who had been dead for over eighty years.

His stammer and the death of his mother, whom he adored, were not the only afflictions that Willie had to bear when he was a boy. He had been brought up to believe that his family was rich. As we have seen, his father and mother had lived in fine style. But when Robert Ormond Maugham died it was discovered that his wealth existed only in his imagination. The sons were each left with barely one hundred and fifty pounds a year. Charles, the eldest son, eventually succeeded his father in the Paris firm, assisted at times by Harry; my father only managed to get to Cambridge because he won two scholarships; there was only just enough money to pay for Willie's education. The social position in which he now found himself was an added humiliation to Willie's life. In Paris every luxury had been available; in Whitstable his uncle and aunt scraped carefully and constantly to make ends meet: even their daily newspaper – *The Times* – was shared with two other houses close by. In Paris, famous and titled people had attended his mother's *salon*; in Whitstable, Willie was shamed by his uncle's deference to the landed gentry.

'My uncle toadied to the local squire,' Willie told me. 'And the man was just a vulgar lout. He'd *never* have been tolerated in my mother's drawing-room. My uncle was a cracking snob. I was never allowed even to speak to the local tradesmen.'

*

I believe that those early years in Whitstable moulded Willie's character. For instance, it was the humiliation of watching his uncle 'toadying' to the local squire that made Willie relish friendship with the great, the titled, and the affluent later in his life. Their friendship was a compensation for the years when he was poor and felt himself disdained. All his own success and all his own wealth were insufficient to heal the wounds he had suffered. To the very end of his days Willie delighted in telling stories about rich and powerful acquaintances and about celebrities or royalty as if living on the edge of their importance somehow produced a balm to soothe his still-aching pangs of inferiority. Thus, whenever I stayed at the Villa Mauresque, Willie would tell me stories of his wealthy friends on the Riviera. For example, he told me of a neighbour of his who heard that a woman recently widowed had acquired a villa on Cap Ferrat.

'My neighbour was informed that this woman was extremely rich,' Willie said, clasping and unclasping his hands as he sometimes did when telling a story. 'Extremely rich. But my neighbour was quite indignant.

"'Nonsense," he replied, "pure nonsense. I happen to know that she wasn't left more than thirty million."

'You see, though I'm a millionaire,' Willie explained to me, 'compared to some of my neighbours here on the Cap, I'm a *very poor* millionaire. One of my neighbours is so rich that he practically controls the whole French government,' Willie continued. 'I asked him once why he didn't go into politics.

"'Why should I?" my neighbour replied. "I tell the Ministers what to do as it is."'

Willie once complained that a female visitor to the Mauresque had failed to admire his pictures.

'Why should you care that she didn't admire them?' a friend asked.

'Because they cost a lot of money,' Willie replied.

On another occasion a young man was lunching at the Mauresque for the first time. Towards the end of the meal Willie suddenly turned to him.

'You may think you're eating ger-gruel,' Willie said. 'But it is in fact zabaglione – and very expensive to make.'

The poor young man was speechless.

*

The years at the vicarage in Whitstable may have made Willie a snob, but the most important influence on his life was his stammer. The impediment was an anguish to him – particularly when he was young. Willie told me a story that revealed this clearly.

'One day,' he said, 'I'd gone up to London for the day with my uncle, and late in the afternoon he decided that he would stay the night in town. But he wanted me to go back to Whitstable, so he sent me off to the station alone with the money for my ticket. But there was a long queue outside the third-class ticket office. So I took my place in the queue. But when it came to my turn to ask for my ticket to Whitstable I couldn't get the word out. I just stood there stammering. People behind me were getting impatient, but I still couldn't say "Whitstable". Suddenly two men stepped out of the queue and pushed me aside. "We can't wait all night for you," they said, "stop wasting our time." So I had to go to the back of the queue and start all over again. I'll never forget the humiliation of that moment – with everyone staring at me.'

Willie seldom spoke about his stammer, but what he felt about it is clearly shown in an essay on his old friend Arnold Bennett. Willie wrote in a preface for *The Old Wives' Tale:*

Everyone knows that Arnold was afflicted with a very bad stammer; it was painful to watch the struggle he had sometimes to get the words out. It was torture to him. Few realised the exhaustion it caused him to speak. What to most men was as easy as breathing, to him was a constant strain. It tore his nerves to pieces. Few knew the humiliation it exposed him to, the ridicule it excited in many, the impatience it aroused . . . the minor exasperation of thinking of a good, amusing, or apt remark and not venturing to say it in case the stammer ruined it. Few knew the distressing sense it gave rise to of a bar to complete contact with other men. It may be that except for the stammer which forced him to introspection, Arnold would never have become a writer.

As he grew older, Willie learned to use his stammer to give point to a particular word in a sentence, but when he was nervous or distraught his words came out painfully, slow and distorted, and evidently 'it was torture to him' also. For this reason when I have quoted his speech in this book I have only given a slight indication of his stammer when I felt it helped to reproduce the flavour of a particular comment.

It is probable that if Willie's childhood prayer had been answered and he had lost his stammer he would not have been an agnostic; it is almost certain that without an impediment in his speech Willie would not have been a writer; he would have been persuaded to become a lawyer – like his brothers. But Willie's stammer made him reserved; it forced him to remain an onlooker; it made him into the detached observer of life who became the first person singular of his writing. His stammer made his prose pithy, crisp, and succinct, and made the dialogue of his plays neatly turned and well balanced. Perhaps Willie's impediment made his fame. But if Willie's stammer was responsible for turning him into a superbly successful writer, the suffering and humiliation of his early years turned him into a strangely diffident character. Willie was emotionally crippled by his childhood. He was a classic example of what psychologists call 'the deprived child', and this was borne out by his constant and sometimes frantic search for happiness and reassurance throughout his life.

*

Willie *knew* that the early years had maimed him. He found it out when he came to write *Of Human Bondage*. But he was determined that if he must remain a cripple then at least he would be a strong cripple, and he had the most unusually firm willpower.

'I have a certain force of character which has enabled me to supplement my deficiencies,' Willie once said to me.

His force of character was strengthened by his discovery that every humiliation and defect that he suffered as a person could be turned into rich material for him as a writer. His power was further increased by his early decision that his craft was more important to him than his private life. Personal relationships were of less consequence to him than artistic achievement. In order to become a great writer Willie deliberately used his strength of character to train himself arduously and to discipline himself mercilessly. As a cloak to protect an abnormally sensitive and shy person from the frosts of an indifferent world, he adopted a pose of cynicism and worldliness. Gradually the pose became part of the man. But imprisoned behind the seemingly impassive, ruthless, world-famous, world-weary author was a lonely person who still craved for affection. Sometimes that person was released by the death of a friend or by a sentimental scene in a film, and Willie would cry bitterly. But the tears would soon be wiped away and the mask replaced.

'I shall never get over her death,' he said to me.

And he never did.

*

When Willie made his sad journey to England with his nurse, in 1884, Charles, the head of the family, had already gone up to Cambridge, but two of his brothers were still at Dover College. My father was then seventeen, and Harry was sixteen. All three of Willie's brothers seem at that period to have been hearty, normal and robust, and content with the guardianship of their father's old friend Albert Dixon. Before he went up to Caius College, Charles had been Head Prefect at Dover College and 'Victor Ludorum'; Harry had played for the rugger XV; my father became Head Prefect and editor of the school magazine, and he won his cap for rugger and cricket. The three older brothers were absorbed in their own careers and could spare no time for the sorrows of their very much younger brother, Willie. After all, he had been sent to a different school, and during the holidays a gap of six or seven years separated both my father and Harry at Dover College from their little brother at the vicarage in Whitstable.

I think it is significant that in Willie's autobiographical novel *Of Human Bondage*, Philip Carey – the hero – has no brothers or sisters. He is an only child and alone – because that is what Willie felt himself to be. He inhabited a very different world from his games-playing, tough elder brothers at Dover College.

*

My father seldom talked to me of his years at school, but he recalled them briefly in his autobiography *At the End of The Day*.[2] It is interesting to note that even my robust parent suffered from his French upbringing. He wrote:

My life at Dover was very unhappy for the first year or two, for I was a shy and doubtless unattractive boy with a slight French accent, and no knowledge of games. My brothers and I were at first called 'froggies' since we came from Paris and, I suspect, wore French clothes. Nor does a boy know of his own peculiarities of speech. It took me many years to acquire an English pronunciation of a good many words derived from the French; I still cannot without deliberation pronounce (or mispronounce) the words 'liqueur' or 'blouse' or 'landau' and other French words as an Englishman does. Schoolboys have a natural dislike for the unusual in other boys. It took us some time to live down these disastrous abnormalities. But fortunately we were strong, sturdy, and energetic and showed a remarkable aptitude both for work and games.

It was not only a gap of seven years in age that separated my father from Willie; it was the gulf that lay between their temperaments.

Dover College [my father wrote], was a very good school with about two hundred boys and a very fair set of masters. About a third of the boys were the sons of Army officers of no great means. None of the parents so far as I know were aristocratic or plutocratic, and we were not encouraged in any form of extravagance ... One advantage of our comparatively small numbers was that everyone had a chance to play games and that there were no loafers.

Willie did not enjoy my father's autobiography. 'When I was at school,' Willie said, 'I *was* a loafer. And I'm proud of it.'

My father was as great a success at Dover College as Willie was a failure at King's School, Canterbury. My father's book continues:

I slowly worked my way up to the top of the school, winning all the exhibitions and most of the prizes on my journey. Examinations had no terrors for me in those days . . . At the same time I became a very useful player at Rugby football, a good field, and a fair wicket-keeper . . . It was with many regrets that I left; for my later years there had been very successful and I had some close friends. Looking back I think I was a very easy boy to teach, and at that period of my life full of energy and high spirits.

*

In May 1963 I stopped at Dover College on my way to Canterbury. Derek Peel and I had driven across from Brighton through the hop-fields and orchards of Kent. The school lies on flat ground beneath Dover's imposing castle where I had once stood during the early days of the war, watching – as soldiers before me had watched for a thousand years – for invaders who might dare to cross the narrow channel from France. The school is built on the site of the former monastery of Dover Priory which was founded in the twelfth century. On that spring day in 1963 the grounds looked very lovely, with all the chestnuts in blossom and the sun shining on the old stone gatehouse, the guest house and the refectory, which had once been used by the monks. Now they are part of the school buildings. We called on the Bursar, Mr N. F. Burt, a straight-spined, soldierly figure who spoke proudly of all he showed us. I was quite surprised to learn that despite the venerable relics surrounding the broad lawns, the College did not come into existence until 1871, only six years before my two uncles, Charles and Harry, and my father were sent there. At first there were only fifteen boys, so the school must have grown with astonishing speed, for my father remembered about two hundred boys when he left in 1885. The school had to be evacuated in both World Wars, Mr Burt told us. The buildings were badly damaged by bombs during the last war and 'nearly ceased to exist', but now there are over three hundred pupils again and many of them, I was glad to see, came from countries in Asia.

Mr Burt led us into the little chapel – once the 'Guesten House' of the Priory – and then into the School House, the principal residence of boarders, which was built during my father's days there. I saw much that my father would have remembered – the high wooden partitions in the study rooms; the dining-hall, laid for tea, and stale with that smell which pervades all school dining-halls and which has the power to fill me with stark terror and gloom to this very day; and the narrow little bedrooms on the first floor. No doubt, at the end of the last century, the walls of these small cells were adorned with stern engravings of suitable heroes and heroines from the classics, but in 1963 I caught glimpses of the smoother profiles of wide-eyed pop-singers.

As we walked back to our car, boys were playing tennis on the broad green sward of the Close; their voices when they shouted out the score mingled with the plaintive cries of the seagulls swooping overhead, and from the flower-beds surrounding School House arose the scent of wallflowers which mixed with the smell of new-mown grass. I wondered how Willie would have fared at Dover College. I don't think he would have minded being called a 'froggie' as much as his brothers did. And certainly he wouldn't have felt that the place had 'the look of a prison' – as the King's School, Canterbury, did in young Philip's view. Willie might have become as happy at Dover College as my father had been – and as much of a success. And he might never have written a single book in his life.

*

From Dover we drove to Canterbury through one of the loveliest stretches of countryside I know, travelling along the road by which the faithful trudged to the shrine of St Thomas à Becket at Canterbury Cathedral. In the royal and ancient city we put up at Slatter's Hotel, and in the quiet of the early evening we wandered towards Christchurch Gate and entered the Precincts of the Cathedral, which contains the King's School. I thought of nine-year-old Philip – or ten-year-old Willie – 'sick with apprehension . . . pale and silent' staring up at 'the high brick wall in front of the school' which 'gave it the look of a prison'. I suppose that most small boys feel sick with fear on their first day at school; I shall never forget my misery and terror when the family car first took me to Eton. Yet the setting of cloistered tranquillity at Canterbury with the old stone of the Cathedral deceived one into forgetting that boys – and masters too – can be brutally unkind. This deception was encouraged by the first person we spoke to in the Precincts. He was a friendly scholar, about sixteen years old, and I had asked him the way to the headmaster's house where I was to lunch the next day. He was neatly dressed in the same school uniform that Willie must have worn when he was a senior boy – black coat, black striped trousers, starched wing collar, and black tie, and a straw boater worn at a jaunty angle. His manners were as immaculate as the crease in his trousers, and he gave up almost an hour of his leisure to show us round the Cathedral and the buildings of King's School – and appeared to enjoy it. We were surprised to see a huge placard outside the Deanery with the words written in bold Italic script against a blue background. The placard read: CHRISTIANS BAN NUCLEAR WEAPONS. It seemed an incongruous notice in such a place, but our friend informed us that it was the whim of the outspoken 'Red Dean', Dr Hewlett Johnson, who had just retired.

'But we get our own back on him,' the boy said. 'On *our* side of the quadrangle we put up a large dirty brown banner, with the words: CHRISTIANS BAN COMMUNISTS.'

The boy didn't know our names, so I thought it would be interesting to ask him about my uncle.

'Have you heard of Somerset Maugham?' I asked.

'Oh, yes,' he replied enthusiastically. 'He is one of our most famous old boys. I like his novels, especially *Of Human Bondage*. Isn't it strange that he's done so much for the school when he was so unhappy here?'

*

At half-past twelve the next day when I walked through Christchurch Gate on my way to lunch with the headmaster the Precincts were busy with tourists, and a group of young Flemish students were clustered round their guide, pressing in on him closely as if afraid he would escape their eager questions. I met the headmaster, the Reverend J. P. P. Newell, at the gate of his house on his return from Saturday morning school, and we went into his drawing-room where his wife gave us a glass of sherry. There was no 'massive, ugly furniture' as in the head-master's room in Philip's day. The room was pleasantly informal and so was the conversation.

'You know, some years ago your uncle was invited to lunch in hall with the boys,' the headmaster said with a smile as we sat down to an excellent meal. 'He'd come here for a Governors' meeting, and it was thought that he'd be amused to have a meal with the boys and eat the same food as they did. Afterwards your uncle happened to be telling a friend of mine about it and he said, "I was invited to lunch at King's School, and I must tell you . . .", and when your uncle paused my friend expected a nice compliment, but your uncle continued, "I must tell you it was one of the worst lunches I've ever eaten in my whole life.'"

Another of Mr Newell's stories about Willie also concerned lunch. Soon after he had succeeded Canon F. J. Shirley as headmaster in 1962, he received a message from Willie inviting him to lunch at a local hotel. They made small-talk throughout the meal, and the headmaster was beginning to wonder why he had been invited when Willie leaned forward.

'I've come down to ask you one single question,' Willie said. 'And it's this. Are you happy?'

'I'd always heard that your uncle was a rather cynical and some-times a rather hard man,' Mr Newell told me. 'So I was at once surprised and a little disconcerted by the question because it was obviously sincere. And I answered it to the best of my ability.'

Mrs Newell interrupted.

'Tell what Mr Maugham said when you invited him back to lunch here.'

The headmaster smiled across the table.

'When we came to say goodbye,' he told me, 'I said to your uncle, "Next time you come to Canterbury, I hope you'll lunch at our house because my wife's looking forward to meeting you." But your uncle shook his head. "I don't think you should invite me," he said, "because I'm sure I shall say all kinds of things that will shock her terribly."'

'They wouldn't, you know,' said Mrs Newell cheerfully.

*

Willie's odd question 'Are you happy?' was typical of his sense of the dramatic. Mr Newell was far too discreet to tell me Willie's motive for asking the question, but I found a possible clue from an acquaintance in the neighbourhood. The reason for Willie's question may well have been the lively influence of Dr Shirley, who had ruled King's School for twenty-seven years – since 1935 – and who was still living in the Precincts and continuing to cast his critical eye over all that his successor was doing. I am sure that Dr Shirley will forgive me – I hope with a

chuckle – if I credit him with effacing Willie's boyhood loathing of
the school and for transforming him into one of its most honoured,
and generous, benefactors. For it was Dr Shirley who saw to it that
various distinguished old boys, such as Field Marshal Lord Montgomery
and William Somerset Maugham, were co-opted as Governors; and in
return his long régime was identified by an astonishing revival in the
fortunes of the school, which now educates about 650 boys. And
despite Willie's published statement that he hoped to be cremated
with no funeral service, Willie certainly cherished a wish that the Dean
and Chapter of Canterbury would reward his generosity by burying
him within the Precincts.

*

My father, who enjoyed great prestige at Dover College, never even
presented his school with a silver-plated cup to perpetuate his memory.
Yet Willie, who was wretchedly miserable at the King's School,
Canterbury, gave quite a fortune. His first donation was in 1936 when
he paid to build hard tennis courts. Other gifts followed in the form of
books, furniture, and pictures. In 1953 he provided £3,000 to build a
boat-house for the boys.[3] A few years later he gave £10,000 which
was used to build some new science laboratories, and he came over
especially from France in June 1958 to perform the opening ceremony.
And in the autumn of 1961 he visited Canterbury yet again to open the
library building he had given to the School – the 'Maugham Library' –
which was to house his own private collection of books and the manuscripts of his first and his last novels, *Liza of Lambeth* and *Catalina*.

I was given the numbers of *The Cantuarian*, the School magazine, in
which these ceremonies are described. They are full of pictures of
Willie looking suitably academic, and they are laden with compli-
ments about his 'overwhelming generosity' and his 'extensive benefits
to the School'; but Willie's own words have been shorn of their
spontaneity by being paraphrased by some cautious editor who has
missed Willie's delightful remarks when he was interviewed on the
first occasion. However, Mr Richard Cordell quotes them in his book.[4]
Willie said: 'When I was young and travelled a good deal, I found that
the English were detested all over the world because they were so
class-conscious and sniffy. The public schools were, in my view,
largely responsible for creating this class-consciousness. So I suggested

to the headmaster that I should provide a certain sum to educate a working-class boy at King's School. But the scheme was a flop; for one thing, working-class parents didn't seem to want their sons contaminated. So after a number of years I said the money should be spent on something else. Hence the Science Building.' Willie then stated his own personal conviction that the public school system was bound to die out in a generation, and continued: 'I think grammar school competition is an excellent thing. I can't see why England needs public schools. They seem to get on all right without them in France and Italy and the United States.' As Mr Cordell points out, Willie's comments 'were hardly of a nature to endear the benefactor to either the staff or the boys of King's School'. But then at times Willie could be violently anti-establishment.

*

Why did Willie give so much money and devote so much attention to the school where he had been profoundly unhappy as a boy? Was it the vanity of an old man? Was it a desire to provide others with the pleasures he had been denied in his youth? Was it a way of avenging the misery of his boyhood? Or was it, perhaps Hugh Walpole?

Hugh Walpole had also been educated at the King's School, Canterbury; he had also been unhappy there – on occasions he had been forced by his jeering schoolmates to stand naked while they stuck pins into him. And he was also a popular novelist. By 1930 he was almost as well known as Willie, though he was ten years younger. But in some literary quarters Walpole's reputation stood even higher than Willie's. Important critics had begun to refer to Walpole as 'a great novelist', 'a genius', and 'the twentieth-century Dickens'. Late one evening in September 1930, Walpole came home from the theatre, went into his bedroom and, sitting on the edge of his bed, half-undressed, 'picked up idly Maugham's *Cakes and Ale*'.[5] It was an advance proof copy of Willie's new novel. Walpole read on 'with increasing horror', for the main character was an 'unmistakable portrait' of himself. Later he told Miss G. B. Stern that the first realisation that he had been reading without moving for over an hour came when he slid to the floor with cramp.

Willie had flung his darts with unerring accuracy. The character of Alroy Kear in the book is a novelist and a lecturer, a cautious careerist,

W. Somerset Maugham
as a schoolboy

W. Somerset Maugham at the
opening of The Maugham Library
at The King's School, Canterbury,
with Dr. F. J. Shirley, 1961

W. Somerset Maugham
aged about seventeen

W. Somerset Maugham
as a young man

and a literary and social snob who is 'determined at all costs to build himself up into a grand old man of letters'.

Willie, in the character of the first person singular, wrote of Alroy Kear[6]:

I had watched with admiration his rise in the world of letters. His career might have served as a model for any young man entering upon the pursuit of literature. I could think of no one among my contemporaries who had achieved so considerable a position on so little talent.

The dart must have struck home. Willie continued:

He was perfectly aware of it, and it must have seemed to him sometimes little short of a miracle that he had been able ... to compose already some thirty books. I cannot but think that he saw the white light of revelation when first he read that Thomas Carlyle ... had stated that genius was an infinite capacity for taking pains. He pondered the saying. If that was all, he must have told himself, he could be a genius like the rest ...

As Mr Myrick Land points out,[7] the figure of 'some thirty books' was 'dangerously close to Walpole's own thirty-one'. A few pages later, Willie's attack was aimed still closer to Walpole's heart:

Roy was very modest about his first novel. It was short, neatly written, and, as is everything he has produced since, in perfect taste. He sent it with a pleasant letter to all the leading writers of the day, and in this he told each one how greatly he admired his works, how much he had learned from his study of them, and how ardently he aspired to follow, albeit at a humble distance, the trail his correspondent had blazed. He laid his book at the feet of a great artist as a tribute of a young man entering upon the profession of letters to one whom he would always look up to as his master. Deprecatingly, fully conscious of his audacity in asking so busy a man to waste his time on a neophyte's puny effort, he begged for criticism and guidance. Few of the replies were perfunctory. The authors he wrote to, flattered by his praise answered at length ... Here, they felt, was someone worth taking a little trouble over.

By the time he reached this page the unfortunate Hugh Walpole must have known that for 'Alroy' the literary world would certainly substitute 'Hugh', for he had sent the manuscript of his first novel to Charles Marriott, Ethel Coburn Mayne, and E. M. Forster, and all three of them had answered at length; and other flattering letters, sometimes accompanied by manuscripts, had helped him win the friendship of useful celebrities such as Henry James, Thomas Hardy, Kipling, Arnold Bennett, Virginia Woolf, H. G. Wells – and W. Somerset Maugham.

The next jab followed swiftly:

... when someone has written a stinging criticism and Roy, especially since his reputation became so great, has had to put up with some virulent abuse, he does not, like most of us, shrug his shoulders ... he writes a long letter to his critic, telling him that he is very sorry he thought his book bad, but his review was so interesting in itself, and if he might venture to say so, showed so much critical sense and so much feeling for words, that he felt bound to write to him. No one is more anxious to improve himself than he, and he hopes he is still capable of learning. He does not want to be a bore, but if the critic has nothing to do on Wednesday or Friday will he come and lunch at the Savoy and tell him why exactly he thought his book so bad? No one can order a lunch better than Roy, and generally by the time the critic had eaten half a dozen oysters and a cut from a saddle of baby lamb, he had eaten his words too. It is only poetic justice that when Roy's next novel comes out the critic should see in the new work a very great advance.

Flattery and invitations to lunch were known to be part of Walpole's technique for dealing with hostile critics. No wonder the poor man slid to the floor with cramp. Walpole's wounds were slightly assuaged when he discovered that people in the literary world had fastened their attention as much on the second character in the book as on Alroy Kear, for the world-famous old writer with an Order of Merit was taken to be Thomas Hardy. But the pain remained.

A few days later Walpole wrote a letter of protest to my uncle; he received a bland reply.

I am really very unlucky [Willie wrote]. As you may have seen, I have been attacked in the papers because they think my old man is intended to be a portrait of Hardy. It is absurd. The only grounds are that both died old, received the O.M. and were married twice ... Now I have your letter. I cannot say I was surprised to receive it because I had heard from Charlie Evans[8] that Priestley and Clemence Dane had talked to him about it. He told them that it had never occurred to him that there was any resemblance between the Alroy Kear of my novel and you; and when he spoke to me about it I was able very honestly to assure him that nothing had been further from my thoughts than to describe you. I can only repeat this. I do not see any likeness. My man is an athlete and a sportsman, who tries to be as little like a man of letters as he can. Can you really recognise yourself in this? ... Nor is the appearance described anything like yours ... The only thing you can go on is the fact that you also are a lecturer. I admit that if I had thought twice of it I would have omitted this. But after all you are not the only English man of letters who lectures, but only the best known ... The loud laugh is nothing. All big men with the sort of heartiness I have described have a loud laugh ...

We now know that Willie wrote this letter with his tongue fixed deliberately in his cheek. He had used Hugh Walpole as his model for Alroy Kear and he was afraid of a libel action. The letter continues suavely:

I certainly never intended Alroy Kear to be a portrait of you. He is made up of a dozen people and the greater part of him is myself. There is more of me in him than of any writer I know ...

Walpole was mollified by the letter. 'Hugh wrote a short answer,' says Mr Hart-Davis, 'signed himself "Alroy Maugham Walpole" and commented: "That's that."' Nine years after Walpole's death, in a new introduction to the Modern Library edition of *Cakes and Ale*, published in New York in 1950, Willie confessed that Walpole had been in his mind when he described the character called Alroy Kear. He excused himself by stating his belief that 'no author can create a character out of nothing. He must have a model to give him a starting point; but then his imagination goes to work, he builds him up, adding a trait here, a trait there, which his model did not possess ... It is only thus that a novelist can give his characters the intensity, the reality which makes them not only plausible, but convincing.'

Various friends of Walpole's believe that *Cakes and Ale* spoiled the last eleven years of his life and marred his reputation. But as a writer, Willie was completely ruthless: he believed that Alroy Kear was an essential character in his novel, and the pain he caused Walpole was of less consequence in Willie's mind than the creation of a perfect novel. And if *Of Human Bondage* is Willie's most important novel, *Cakes and Ale* is certainly his most brilliant and the most perfect in shape and style. However, Willie's attack on Walpole did not go unavenged. In 1931 there appeared in America a novel called *Gin and Bitters*, written under the pseudonym 'A. Riposte'. It was a vicious and obvious attack on Willie, who appeared as Leverson Hurle, the successful novelist and traveller. Even the physical description of the character was evidently intended to be accurate: 'Leverson Hurle was a small dark man, proud of his smallness; rather sallow; showing, even then, yellow pouches under his dark eyes: eyes as sad and disillusioned as those of a sick monkey.'

Leverson Hurle is ambitious, he is 'old, bored and disgusted' with life, and he is a snob who speaks of 'people out of the top drawer'. He travels around the world accepting lavish hospitality and repaying it by putting into his books his hosts' 'most private affairs, their loves and hates and sorrows'. He also indulges in 'lambasting his fellow writers alive and dead . . . one living writer in particular'. At first it was thought that Hugh Walpole was the author, but it was soon discovered that the book had been written by Elinor Mordaunt, 'a facile and prolific writer of novels, of stories for women's magazines, and of travel books'.[9] And one of Willie's biographers, Karl G. Pfeiffer, suggests that the woman had 'followed in Maugham's footsteps in Tahiti and other South Sea islands, and collected everything unpleasant about him that she could'.[10] The novel is confused, repetitious and boring.

According to Karl Pfeiffer, when Willie read *Gin and Bitters* he professed surprise and lofty indifference. I'm sure he did. But Mr Pfeiffer continues: 'He was, in fact, far from indifferent. Gerald Haxton told me he somehow got hold of the page proof of the book, before it was published, and the two of them sat up all one night feverishly reading it.' But I think this is just another of Gerald's stories. Gerald Haxton, my uncle's secretary and companion in those days, may well have used the book's arrival as an excuse for a late night, but I doubt if Willie allowed it to disturb his sleep. He did, however, arrange for a copy of the book to be sent immediately to my father so as to get free legal advice. My father decided that it would be a mistake for Willie to sue for libel because the case would lend publicity to the book, but he advised Willie to instruct his solicitors 'to write round to the various publishers' to ensure that the book was not produced in England.

'I thought from the beginning that my publishers were making too much fuss about the book,' Willie said later to my father. 'I read it and it left me undisturbed. I can't help thinking that if my reputation can be damaged by such a dull work it can't be worth bothering about.'

Willie's publishers in England, Heinemann's, had sent Walpole a copy of *Gin and Bitters* and had asked him to try to persuade Willie to bring an injunction to prevent the book's publication in England.

'The irony of this situation was not lost on Hugh,' writes Mr Hart-Davis, 'and it is greatly to his credit that he made no capital out of it whatever.'

'The book is *foul* and you ought to stop it,' Walpole wrote to Willie. But though the book eventually appeared in England its sale was modest. In America it had sold three thousand copies.

*

Most of us tend to like those to whom we have done a good turn and to resent those whom we have harmed, so it is not surprising that Willie was irritated by Walpole's continued success and vexed when Walpole was given a Knighthood in 1937.

'I was offered a Knighthood long before *that*,' Willie once told me.

'Why didn't you accept it?' I asked.

'Ber-because I didn't want to look a fool,' Willie replied. 'I felt I'd look so silly if I went to a literary party and they announced "*Mr* Arnold Bennett, *Mr* H. G. Wells, *Mr* Bernard Shaw – and Sir-Sir Somerset Maugham."'

Meanwhile Walpole was growing 'more and more attached' to King's School, Canterbury, and 'when in 1935 the enterprising and energetic F. J. Shirley was appointed headmaster, opportunities arose for tangible benefactions. Hugh paid for the re-turfing of the Mint Yard, he presented valuable furniture to the school, his portrait by Augustus John, and finally his collection of manuscripts, which is housed in the gate-room of Prior Sellingegate over the Dark Entry. One of the boarding houses is now called Walpole House, there is a Walpole Society, and there are Walpole Prizes, to keep his memory green.'[11]

When the Junior School, to which Willie had been sent as a boy and which he had described in detail in *Of Human Bondage*, was renamed Walpole House I believe that my uncle was nettled, and I believe he saw the Walpole gifts as a challenge. Let Hugh Walpole re-turf Mint Yard, *Willie* would provide hard tennis courts. Let Hugh give furniture, *he* would give furniture and pictures *and* a boat-house. Let Hugh present his collection of manuscripts. *Willie* would donate a whole library. Poor Walpole! Even in his gifts to his old school he was outbid by Willie. It seems unfair – particularly since from most accounts Walpole was a pleasant, charming character. I met him once. He and

H. G. Wells were dining with my sister Kate Mary Bruce in Cadogan Square, and I was invited in after dinner. I brought a girl I had been dining with. It was 1937, and we were both young. We were introduced to the celebrities and sat down together on a sofa in the corner of the room. For some reason the sight of the two of us sitting close together immediately inspired Walpole to a panegyric on romantic love. I can't remember the exact words he used but I recollect that the moon shimmered quite a bit on the still waters of woodland lakes, Daphnis and Chloe flitted around, and so – come to that – did Romeo and Juliet, the sun rose – and set – in an extraordinary assortment of colours, and we both squirmed with embarrassment until H. G. Wells interrupted him.

'Nonsense, Hugh,' Wells said. 'There's no such thing as romantic love. Every normally constituted young man wants to pop into bed with every normally constituted young woman. And vice versa. And that's all there is to it.'

Death never softened Willie's opinion of a man. 'Walpole's reputation was never very great,' he wrote in 1961. 'Hugh was a ridiculous creature.'

*

My next appointment at the King's School was with the librarian, Mr H. M. P. Davies, so I set off through the Precincts towards Mint Yard – since 1559 the centre of the school's life,[12] where money was coined in the seventh century and turf laid down by Hugh Walpole in the twentieth. Few of the buildings here are of any great age, but they blend pleasantly with the mellow stone of the Cathedral and seem to breathe the feeling of peace that the first scholars must have enjoyed long ago. Mr Davies, an energetic, studious-looking young master, met me near what is known as the 'Dark Entry' and took me to the School Library – a classroom in Willie's day – built on the site of what was once a dormitory for 'poor pilgrims'. Then he led me briskly through the Memorial Court and up a flight of steps into the smaller but brand new 'Maugham Library', which even before Willie's death was half-filled with the books he had given to the school. It gave me an odd feeling to run my hands over the spines of some of the exquisitely bound books, for I had seen many of them before in the drawing-room of the Villa Mauresque. I was shown a fine set of twelve volumes of

The Lives of the Saints by S. Baring Gould. In each volume was carefully written 'W. Somerset Maugham. Sep. 98'. But I doubt if even the most benign of Willie's biographers will claim that the whole bunch of saintly volumes considerably influenced my uncle's behaviour. I spotted a presentation copy of Hugh Walpole's *Extracts from a Diary*, specially bound in vellum, signed and numbered but not – I observed without surprise – read by Willie, for it was still in mint condition. There were my father's three books, *The Case of Jean Calas*, *The Tichborne Case* and his autobiography *At the End of the Day*, and one by Henry Neville Maugham – my uncle Harry – *The Husband of Poverty. A drama of the life of St Francis of Assisi*, published in 1896. There were even two of my own books, *Journey to Siwa* and *The Servant*.

Each book – and there were 1,391 volumes in the inventory – bore a plate with the words 'The King's School, Canterbury, Maugham Library. Presented by W. Somerset Maugham, O.K.S.' (There was an ironic touch about 'O.K.S.', for in 1901, when a list of Old King's School Boys was compiled, Willie did not even bother to pay the subscription of five shillings to have his name included.) Some of the books contained lively and affectionate inscriptions. Dame Edith Sitwell had written a *double* inscription in *The Song of the Cold*: 'For W. Somerset Maugham with homage from Edith Sitwell' and 'For Willie with love from Edith'. And H. G. Wells, in the first of a beautiful twenty-eight-volume set of his Complete Works, which he gave to my uncle for Christmas in 1934, had written 'To Willie, God bless him, H.G.' and drawn a comic sketch of himself in the nude with all his 'works' churning round in his stomach like a machine.

In his speech at the opening of the library in 1961 Willie said: 'The books I am giving you are the working materials of the author I have been. It may surprise you to find books not only in English, but in French, German, Spanish and Italian ... I like to think that no school the size of King's will have such a substantial library as I am providing you with ... When I look back on my long life, I realise reading has been one of the most enduring pleasures life has offered me. I hope that you may have that pleasure too.' The breadth of his reading as revealed in the 'working materials' is quite remarkable – scientific treatises, poetry, philosophy, *belles-lettres*, biography, novels in half a dozen languages, religious tracts, and anthropological works of all kinds. (The splendidly enlightened attitude of the school authorities is shown by the fact that they allow books such as Malinowski's *The Sexual Life of Savages* and René Guyon's *The Ethics of Sexual Acts* to stand on the shelves; they would have been in the *arcana* section at my school.) And from their condition it was obvious that almost all the books had been often read: many of them were annotated by Willie, and various passages had been marked for future reference. Glancing through the copy of Bertrand Russell's *An Outline of Philosophy* I was amused to see that Willie had underlined the sentence, 'Good is, to my mind, mainly a social concept.'

'It's a fine field of research for anyone who wants to write a thesis on my uncle,' I said to Mr Davies, the librarian.

'Yes,' he replied. 'Scholars come to the Walpole Collection from all over the world to see the books and I expect they will come here too. One has already come from France to study the two manuscripts. Would you care to see the manuscripts of *Liza of Lambeth* and *Catalina*?'

'Very much,' I said.

He darted away and reappeared with the manuscripts of Willie's first novel and last novel in his hand. I sat down at the large green leather-topped table at the end of the library, and turned over the pages of *Catalina* – 381 pages of neat writing, all beautifully bound in pale blue leather, the calligraphy exquisitely level, the few corrections wonderfully clear, and the whole a model of what a good manuscript should be – but I felt not a twinge of emotion, for I find the book one of the dreariest that Willie ever produced. When he begins a novel with a sentence such as, 'It was a great day for the city of Castel Rodriguez',[13] or 'Biagio Buonaccorsi had had a busy day',[14] my heart sinks, for I know that I'm in for one of his historical pieces, and historical novels were never his strong point. In my copy of *The Making of a Saint*,[15] Willie has written with characteristic brevity, 'A very poor novel by W. Somerset Maugham'. If only this awareness that his second book was a disaster had made Willie realise that his talents were ill-suited for historical romances, he would never have attempted to write *Then and Now*, a drab reconstruction of Machiavelli's play *La Mandragola*, and he would not have laid himself open to Edmund Wilson's scathing and unbalanced attack.[16]

Edmund Wilson uses *Then and Now* as a spring-board to launch his onslaught.

It has happened to me from time to time to run into some person of taste who tells me that I ought to take Somerset Maugham seriously [he begins], yet I have never been able to convince myself that he was anything but second-rate ... His new novel, THEN AND NOW – which I had sworn to explore to the end, if only in order to be able to say that I had read a book of Maugham's through – opposed to my progress, through all the first half, such thickets of unreadableness, that there were moments when I thought I should never succeed ... The language is such a tissue of clichés that one's wonder is finally aroused at the writer's ability to assemble so many and at his unfailing inability to put anything in an individual way ...

Mr Wilson then demolishes the novel without much difficulty, but he is not prepared to rest there. His offensive now becomes deployed on a wider front. He criticises Willie for managing 'to sound invidious when he is speaking of his top-drawer contemporaries', and claims that Willie 'does not know what he is talking about' when he writes of Proust. Mr Wilson concludes with a frontal attack:

Admirers of Somerset Maugham have protested that this article[17] was unfair to him and have begged me to read his short stories. I have therefore procured EAST IS WEST, the collected volume of these, and made shift to dine on a dozen. They *are* readable – quite entertaining. The style is much tighter and neater than it is in THEN AND NOW – Mr Maugham writes best when his language is plainest. But [... by the time one had read through this vitriolic review one knows that a 'but' is coming ...] these stories are magazine commodities ... on about the same level as Sherlock Holmes; but Sherlock Holmes has more literary dignity, precisely because it is less pretentious. Mr Maugham makes play with more serious themes, but his work is full of bogus motivations that are needed to turn the monthly trick. He is for our day, I suppose, what Bulwer Lytton was for Dickens's: a half-trashy novelist, who writes badly, but is patronised by half-serious readers, who do not care much about writing.

I have never ceased to be astonished by the *intensity* of the disapproval Willie's work has excited in various intellectuals.[18] Is it because subconsciously they resent his world-wide success? Or is it because they are annoyed that by living to the age of ninety Willie 'got away with it' and became the grand old man of English letters? Calmer critics than Mr Wilson have been perplexed by the problem. Reviewing *The Razor's Edge*, Mr Cyril Connolly wrote: 'It has puzzled me, considering the sheer delight that I and all my friends have received from this novel, that it has been so uncharitably reviewed. Are

we becoming incapable of recognising excellence when we see it?'
And his answer is clear: 'I think prejudice is to blame – prejudice
against any book which so perfectly recaptures the graces that have
vanished, and against any writer who is so obviously not content with
the banal routine of self-esteem and habit, graced by occasional orgies
of nationalisation and herd celebrations, with which most of us...
fidget away our one-and-only lives.'[19]

Mr Connolly called Willie 'the greatest living short-story writer'.
Critics such as Sir Desmond MacCarthy, Mr Frank Swinnerton, and
Sir Harold Nicolson believed he was an important, underrated literary
figure. None of these four critics could ever be considered as 'half-
serious readers, who do not care much about writing'. Willie's style
may sometimes be uneven and jerky and his historical novels may be
dull, but he was nonetheless a fine artist, who, with his detachment and
his suffering, and his unique slant on life, had – like every true artist in
his time – seen life whole and seen it crooked; for crooked it must have
been, since he had seen it through the distortion of his own eyes. This is
how Theodore Dreiser ended his review of *Of Human Bondage*:

Vicariously, it seems to me, he has suffered for the joy of the many who
are to read after him. By no willing of his own he has been compelled to take
life by the hand and go down where there has been little save sorrow and
degradation ... The cup of gall and wormwood has obviously been lifted
to his lips and to the last drop he has been compelled to drink it. Because of
this we are enabled to see the rug, woven of the tortures and delights of a life:
we may actually walk and talk with one whose hands and feet have been
pierced with nails.

In most of the studies of the modern novel that appeared during his
lifetime Willie was either treated with condescension or ignored. He
is not even mentioned in *The Novel and the Modern World* by David
Daiches, in *Twilight on Parnassus* by G. A. Ellis, or in *Modern English
Fiction* by Gerald Bullett. But, as Richard Cordell says in the last
paragraph of his book published while my uncle was still alive,

Although denied the supreme accolade bestowed by the New Criticism on
Joyce, Proust, Faulkner, Kafka, Camus, and James, Somerset Maugham can
be proud of his admirers: W. H. Auden, Frank Swinnerton, Theodore
Dreiser, Max Beerbohm, Christopher Isherwood, Desmond MacCarthy,
St John Ervine, Carl and Mark Van Doren, Richard Aldington, Mary

Colum, Cyril Connolly, Harold Nicolson, Glenway Wescott, V. S. Pritchett, William Rose Benét, S. R. Behrman, and many other fellow writers. Perhaps he is equally proud of the fact that his books have afforded pleasure to hundreds of thousands of intelligent readers who know or care little about literary criticism.

*

I was not excited by the immaculate manuscript of *Catalina*. But I was fascinated to see *Liza of Lambeth* – Willie's first novel, begun when he was twenty-one, only four years after he had left the King's School. The novel is written in three cloth-and-cardboard exercise-books which still have the stationer's label inside – 'Papeterie F. Brocchi, 30 Faubourg Saint-Honoré, Paris'. The handwriting is jerky and uncertain, there are frequent corrections, and the manuscript throughout is untidy and at times almost illegible. Moreover, there are two surprises. On the opening page the title is written as *A Lambeth Idyll*, and the author is stated to be 'William Somerset'. Perhaps young Willie had realised that his novel might cause a stir and his first nervous thought had been to conceal his identity. The third slim volume of the manuscript ends on page 212, but six pages have been added in Willie's handwriting some thirty-five years later with the explanation: 'The last four pages of this MS written on loose sheets have vanished in the course of years, so to complete it I have rewritten them. 15 July 1931.' And below this he has added: 'P.S. This novel, my first, was written in 1895 at 11 Vincent Square, Westminster. W. Somerset Maugham.'

In 1895 Willie was in his fourth year at St Thomas's Hospital and was working as an obstetric clerk in the Lambeth slums. At the age of seventeen he had persuaded his uncle, the vicar of Whitstable, to let him go to Heidelberg for a year. On his return to the vicarage, Willie had refused to consider the Church as a career, and for two months he had been articled to a chartered accountant; but as he loathed the work he suggested that he should study medicine, and his uncle and aunt had agreed. So he was now a medical student living in his digs in Westminster. His term of duty as an obstetric clerk lasted three weeks and he attended sixty-three confinements.

You had to be on hand day and night [Willie wrote some thirty years later].[20] You took a lodging immediately opposite the hospital to which the porter had a key, and if you were wanted in the night he came across the street and woke you. You dressed and went to the hospital where you found waiting for you the husband or perhaps the small son of the patient, with the card which the woman in labour had earlier obtained from the hospital . . . The messenger led you through the dark and silent streets of Lambeth, up stinking alleys and into sinister courts where the police hesitated to penetrate, but where your black bag protected you from harm. You were taken to grim houses, on each floor of which a couple of families lived, and shown into a stuffy room, ill-lit with a paraffin lamp, in which two or three women, the midwife, the mother, the 'lady as lives on the floor below', were standing round the bed on which the patient lay . . . This was the material I used for this book. I exercised little invention. I put down what I had seen and heard as plainly as possible.

Willie was twenty-three and in his final year at medical school when *Liza of Lambeth* was published – only a few weeks before he qualified as a doctor, with the initials M.R.C.S. and L.R.C.P. after his name. The novel created a sensation and appalled the conventional society of his day.

'I think it not unfair to describe Mr W. S. Maughan's* story as dirty,' wrote the reviewer for *Vanity Fair* on September 16, 1897. 'It is many a long day since I got up from reading a book with a feeling of absolute disgust; yet with such did "Liza of Lambeth" inspire me. Mr Maughan has been nosing in the gutters, and has brought the result of his investigations to light; a rank result – unpleasant, unhealthy. . . . M. Zola has written dirtily, but he is always more or less artistic – Mr Maughan never . . . Mr Maughan should drop this kind of work; or else, if he will continue it, it should be labelled orange-red.'

The review was signed FAITHFUL.

I am delighted by the line 'M. Zola has written dirtily, but he is always more or less artistic – Mr Maughan never.'

My uncle's novel was generally considered to be in bad taste and shocking. Even my mother who was devoted to him wrote in her diary, 'Willie's book came out, *Liza of Lambeth*, a most unpleasant story.' But it was the first English novel of any consequence to treat the slums realistically and objectively, and it attracted considerable attention. Some of the reviews praised its literary merit, and Willie was very proud when his beloved landlady, Mrs Foresman, heard Bishop Wilberforce[21] make it the subject of a sermon one Sunday

* Misspelt 'Maughan'.

evening in Westminster Abbey. The book was the turning-point in Willie's life. When his publisher, Fisher Unwin, told him that a second edition was to be produced at once, Willie determined to abandon his career as a doctor. So he never practised. But he once told me that he regretted he had not spent three or four years in medicine after he qualified. He felt it would have given him splendid material. But the death of his uncle had removed the last barrier to his independence, and he decided to become a writer. First he went to Spain, then to Italy, and later he settled in Paris where he shared a studio with Gerald Kelly. The first World War only partly interrupted his triumphant success as a novelist and playwright, for after he had been recalled from France, where he was serving with a Red Cross ambulance unit, he was given a job in British intelligence. His profession as a writer was a useful cover – first in Switzerland, where he wrote his famous *Ashenden* stories; then in the Pacific, where he wrote *Rain*; and finally in Russia, where he was sent on a secret mission to try to stop the Revolution and to keep the Russians in the war on the Allied side.

Liza of Lambeth decided the shape of the rest of his life.

*

At the King's School in Canterbury I had seen and heard so much of my uncle's beneficent old age that it was quite a relief to be shown two souvenirs of his boyhood. The first was an old number of *The Cantuarian* for August 1888, which showed that W. S. Maugham, then aged fourteen, had won three 'minor prizes' – for Divinity, History, and French. The second relic was a photograph of about the same date – perhaps a little earlier – in which Willie looked very small and insignificant and rather attractive in a group of about a hundred and thirty boys flanked by a number of sour-faced, bearded, unsmiling masters. In *The Summing Up* Willie said that the masters of the lower forms were 'frightening bullies', and I must say in that photograph they look it.

*

There remained the one building that I most wished to see within the Precincts of the King's School – the Junior School, now known as Walpole House, the school to which Willie's uncle, the Reverend Henry Macdonald Maugham, had brought him on the train from Whitstable 'one Thursday afternoon towards the end of September', in 1884. But the place was not at all as I had imagined it. The 'high brick wall' was still there, and a very small boy might well think that it was high enough to give the school 'the look of a prison'. But there was nothing grim about the atmosphere of the place. As we approached the house, boys were sprawling on soft rugs stretched across the lawn; others in open-necked white shirts and grey flannels were perched on the window-sills. And from one room – perhaps the very room in which Mr Watson, the huge red-bearded headmaster, had changed his mind about caning Philip Carey, because, as he put it, he couldn't 'hit a cripple' – there came the strident gay sound of 'pop' music.

Schools have changed since Willie was a boy.

WILLIE AT THE VICARAGE

BEFORE we left Canterbury on Sunday morning, Derek Peel and I wandered down to the King's School and took one last look at the 'high brick wall' that had made young Willie think of a prison. Then we drove six miles to Whitstable, the little seaside town which has been famous for its oysters, we read, 'from time immemorial'. Most of Whitstable – which Willie called Blackstable in *Of Human Bondage* and *Cakes and Ale* – has greatly changed in the past eighty years, but the High Street is still much as he described it as 'a long winding street that led to the sea, with little two-storey houses, many of them residential with a good many shops'; and the 'congeries of narrow winding alleys' still exist around the harbour. The Canterbury road drops down quite sharply as you approach the town, and the house now known as the Old Vicarage, where Willie had lived with his guardian the Reverend Henry Macdonald Maugham, lies at the bottom of the hill on the right-hand side of the road. We had been invited to lunch by the present owners, Dr and Mrs Nesfield.

As soon as we drew near the house we noticed the big five-barred gate – once red, now white – on which Willie had been forbidden to swing, and we had a glimpse through the trees of the 'fairly large house of yellow brick, with a red roof, built . . . in an ecclesiastical style'. We opened the gate, resisted the temptation to swing on it, and walked up the short gravel drive. The description in *Of Human Bondage* was completely accurate. 'The front door was like a church porch, and the drawing-room windows were Gothic.' I have never walked straight into a novel before, and it was an odd sensation.

Our welcome from Dr and Mrs Nesfield was as warm and friendly as we had expected from their letters. They took it for granted that we should pry into every corner and cupboard of the house as others had frequently tried to do during the seventeen years they had lived in the place, and they paid us the compliment of giving us not only a delicious lunch but devoting to us a large part of their one day of leisure in the week. Far from resenting our intrusion it was obvious that they took real pleasure in Willie's associations with their house. His novels came very much to life in their conversation, and they were anxious to show us everything that would help in our quest. The doctor, a big, handsome man in his early fifties with a look of Robert Louis Stevenson about him, took us first into the drawing-room – the room, I recalled, that was 'used only by Mr Carey on Sunday afternoons for his nap'; Mrs Nesfield introduced us to her mother and daughter, and gave us a glass of sherry and led us through the french windows into the garden – a pleasant expanse of green lawn, with tall trees and tidy flower-beds contrasting with a wild shrubbery in which they had installed an ornate gipsy caravan. The doctor showed me the foundation stone, set low down in the wall of the house, with the inscription, 'This stone was laid by the Right Rev. Edward Parry, D.D. Bishop Suffragan of Dover, June 27, 1871'.

'That was the year when Vicar Maugham came to Whitstable,' the doctor said. 'The house was really built for him.'

'What happened to the previous vicarage?' I asked.

'That fell down,' said Mrs Nesfield. 'It started to rock one night and completely collapsed only ten minutes after the previous vicar and his family were safely out.'

I remembered that Willie's uncle had enjoyed the privilege of twenty acres of glebe land attached to the vicarage, but Dr Nesfield told me that it had all been built over.

'We've only got one and a half acres,' he said. 'In Vicar Maugham's day there was nothing but open country between this house and All Saints Church which is almost a mile away. In fact, Vicar Maugham used to drive to church in his carriage along a track through the fields. He used a brougham in winter and a trap in summer. The stable's now our garage, but the horse's manger is still there. Before all those houses were built on the glebe land, you could see the clock on the church tower from this lawn.'

We lunched in the old dining-room which is still used throughout the year as the main living-room of the house, as it was in my uncle's childhood. ('In the winter Mr and Mrs Carey lived in the dining-room so that one fire should do, and in the summer they could not get out of the habit . . .') It is still a 'large and well proportioned' room with 'windows on two sides of it'.

W. Somerset Maugham
the author of *Liza of
Lambeth*, an 'unpleasant,
unhealthy' novel (*Vanity
Fair*)

First page of the MS of
W. Somerset Maugham's
first novel, *Liza of Lambeth*

W. Somerset Maugham

'It's the one room in the house we can keep really warm,' said Mrs Nesfield. 'And have you noticed the ceiling? It's made from the same wood as the pews in the church which were put in during Vicar Maugham's day. There's more of it in the kitchen and the study.'

One wall of the room was lined with books – including several of Willie's.

'Has my uncle ever been back to Whitstable?' I asked.

'Twice since we've been here,' said Mrs Nesfield. 'The first time was soon after the war, in November 1948 – the day before he gave those two manuscripts to the King's School. It must have been about ten o'clock in the morning when I noticed two men poking around in the garden. I couldn't imagine what they were doing. Then I recognised him from photos I'd seen. I think his secretary, Mr Alan Searle, was with him. Your uncle couldn't have been sweeter. I showed him all over the house – the little bedroom he had as a boy, the study – he asked if the fire still smoked – and I showed him the pond in the garden which no longer holds water, I'm afraid.'

Mrs Nesfield got up from the table and took down a book from one of the shelves. I saw that it was a copy of Willie's *A Writer's Notebook*.

'When your uncle came here again three years later, he inscribed this book for us,' she said.

I opened the book and read, 'I write this in the dining-room of the Old Vicarage at Whitstable where I spent all my holidays when I was at school. In this room I had my first lessons at Whist. W.S.M. November 11, 1951.'

'What sort of reception did my uncle have in Whitstable when he came back?' I asked.

Dr. Nesfield smiled.

'Well, you know, his novel *Cakes and Ale* annoyed a lot of local people, and they've never quite forgotten it or forgiven him. When he arrived in 1951, he put up for two nights at the Bear and Key. Usually the arrival of the most minor film star causes a commotion in Whitstable and gets a full page in the local press. But your uncle's visit was dismissed in one small paragraph.'

*

At the time I visited Whitstable, there were at least two people of my uncle's generation still living who had a clear recollection of Willie as a

boy and who remembered old Vicar Maugham. One of them was
Mr James Robert Smith, then aged eighty-seven. And, after lunch, we
met him. We had moved to the back of the house outside the former
laundry which Dr Nesfield's daughter uses as a studio – the old copper
is still there in the corner – and we were drinking our coffee in the sunshine when Miss Nesfield appeared with a splendid old gentleman on
her arm. Mr Smith was only two years younger than Willie. Born of
poor parents he had started life as a paper-boy in Whitstable. He used
to deliver the newspaper each day to the Old Vicarage – it was *The
Times* which Vicar Maugham shared for reasons of economy with two
of his neighbours: Tom Gann in the white house opposite, which was
called 'The Limes', and a retired pork-butcher named Robinson who
lived at the 'Manor House'. Seventy years later Mr James Robert
Smith was believed to be one of the most prosperous citizens of
Whitstable. He was short, lean, and dapper with a long narrow face
and a wonderful moustache waxed into points at the end. He wore a
neat well-cut dark suit of serge. He looked very trim and spruce. His
smile was gentle and his soft voice still held the trace of a Kentish burr.
He began by telling us that he had left Whitstable back in the 1890s at
the age of eighteen – with not even a shilling in his pocket – to seek his
fortune. He found work in a bicycle shop in London and eventually
invented a particular part of a bicycle's wheel – some bearing – which
he patented and which made him rich. Fifty years later when he
retired he decided to return to Whitstable in the rôle of the local boy
who had made good. He treasured the hope of being able to 'cut a dash'
with the people who had known him when his family were on poor
relief. But when he got back to his home town he discovered that there
was no one left who remembered him in those humiliating days, so
the whole point of his return was lost. But Mr Smith had enough sense
of humour to tell the story against himself; indeed, he still seemed to
derive a lot of fun from life, and he enlivened all he said with a chuckle.
To help prompt his memory, he had brought a bundle of photographs
of Whitstable as it was in his boyhood, and we looked in turn at faded
sepia prints of the old colliers in the harbour, the oyster porters and their
carts on the beach, and the station with its rank of horse-drawn cabs.
   'Of course, it's all different nowadays,' Mr Smith said. 'But when I
was a boy, people practically used to starve down here. Some families
had only two shillings a week and a couple of loaves apiece if they were

on parish relief. The clerk used to come out from Canterbury and pay
the poor people from the front room of a cottage. If the weather was
bad, people just had to wait in the rain . . . But we were very proud.
We didn't like strangers from places like Chatham and London coming
to use our beach. "Foreigners" we called them. In Whitstable a
foreigner is anyone not born in Whitstable. Very genteel we were, and
we didn't like foreigners. So nobody would dare to put a "Bed-and-
Breakfast" advertisement in the window of their lodging house. If you
wanted to take in a foreigner as a lodger, you had to do it furtively.
Of course it's all different now.'

I steered the conversation round to my uncle Willie.

'His description of Whitstable in *Cakes and Ale* is very good,' said
Mr Smith. 'Of course he upset a good lot of people, didn't he?' He
paused and chuckled to himself. 'Especially the Gann family,' he added.
'He took the sacred name of Gann in vain.'

He did indeed. Rosie, the heroine – and easily the most attractive
female character that Willie ever created – was 'Rosie Gann before she
married . . . Gann was one of the commonest names at Blackstable.
The churchyard was thick with their graves.'[1] The name of Gann may
be common in Whitstable but it is unusual in the rest of England, and
when *Cakes and Ale* appeared Whitstable in general and the highly-
respectable Ganns in particular were enraged. In the novel, before she
marries Edward Driffield, the distinguished novelist, Rosie 'carries on
with' a coal merchant called George Kemp who is generally known as
Lord George 'owing to his grand manner'. In real life Rosie Gann was
alive when *Cakes and Ale* was published, and she taught in a Sunday
school. Lord George was a well-known character in Whitstable. I wonder if Willie's publishers ever guessed how close they were to a libel action. The Kemps in Whitstable were as highly respected as the Ganns.

'Do you remember my great-uncle, the vicar?' I asked Mr Smith.

'Well, in all the four years that I delivered *The Times* to his vicarage,
he never spoke to me once,' Mr Smith replied. '"Old Maugham" we
called him – like you'd talk about the Pope. He didn't have much to do
with ordinary working people. Very remote, he was. He kept two
maids, I remember, and gave them twelve pounds a year on top of
their uniform and keep.'

'What did he look like?' I asked.

Mr Smith thought for a minute. 'Not like *anybody* in particular,' he said at length. 'A bit like George Reeves the baker, but then *he* didn't look like anybody in particular either. Quite undistinguished. The sort of man you'd meet in a crowd and not notice.'

Dr Nesfield asked Mr Smith if he had ever heard my great-uncle preach.

'Oh, no,' Mr Smith answered. 'We didn't go to his church, because my parents were Baptists, and Old Maugham didn't talk to chapel folk. But I did attend the church school. Most boys paid in a penny or tuppence or threepence a week, but those of us who were on poor relief didn't have to pay anything at all, and we had to sit on a separate side of the schoolroom. Old Maugham only came once – in 1887. He seemed a bit peeved at how little the boys knew about religion, so he offered a book as a prize for scripture. We only had five books at home, and one of them was the Bible, so I knew it pretty well. And I won the prize. I have the book still. *The Fortunes of Hassan*² it was called. But it wasn't a very popular win, my parents being Baptists.'

Mr Smith laughed and gave the waxed ends of his moustache a quick twirl.

'Of course I couldn't stay long at school as I had to get work and earn some money,' he continued. 'First, I tried to get a job as a lather-boy in the barber's shop down in the harbour. The long-shoremen used to come in on a Saturday night for a shave at a penny a time, and the lather-boy had to go round with the pot and the brush and lather all their beards ready for the barber. Well, in those days I had curls right down to my shoulders. All done up in paper at night by my mother they were. But they said I'd have to have all my curls cut off if I was going in for the job. So I went to the barber and said, "You must cut off my hair." But he refused. He said it was too beautiful. When I got home that night I told my elder brother, and right away he took up a pair of shears and cut the lot off. That caused a blazing row in the family that lasted for years. But I still didn't get the job of lather-boy, so I had to deliver papers instead.'

Time was getting late, but there was one more question I was determined to ask him.

'Did you ever meet Willie Somerset Maugham when you were both young boys?' I asked.

Mr Smith shook his head. 'No,' he replied. 'I never actually met him – not to talk to, that is. But I used to see him sometimes when he was home on holiday from school. I don't think he liked school much, and *he* probably wanted to be free and living at home the same as I was. Of course all I wanted was to be in *his* shoes. I remember one occasion when I saw him. In fact I shall never forget it. He must have been nearly fifteen then. He was standing outside the gate at the end of this drive. He had on his school uniform and a straw hat. His box was beside him and a pile of books. It must have been the end of the holidays and he was just off back to school. And he looked very sad. We didn't say anything. We just took a long stare at each other, as boys do. But I'll never forget how sad he looked. And I remember I thought at the time, "If only I could change places with you."'

*

The second person alive in Whitstable who remembered Willie as a boy was Miss Charlotte Etheridge. Her father had been one of the two doctors in the town. He was succeeded in the practice by one of her brothers whom Willie rather unkindly described in *Cakes and Ale* as being 'shabbily dressed and unkempt' when he met him one day in the High Street on his return to Whitstable as a grown man. When Dr Etheridge read the book he said that he remembered the actual meeting with Willie in the High Street perfectly well, and he had noticed that Willie's coat was very dusty.

'And since Maugham has made so much money from his books, I should have supposed that he could afford to have his coat properly brushed,' the doctor said tartly.

Miss Etheridge had evidently forgiven Willie for his description of her brother, because she told Mrs Nesfield that she would be 'delighted' to tell me what she could remember about him. I did not meet Miss Etheridge in Whitstable but she wrote a long letter. Her family, she said, were 'the most constant visitors at the Old Vicarage' and young Willie was given lessons at her parents' home, Ivy House, during the year before he attended King's School. She remembered 'his very bad stammer and how they laughed at him', and she had 'a vivid picture of him standing on the verandah, clad in a velvet knickerbocker suit with a white lace collar'. The other children called him 'Little Lord Fauntleroy'. (This may have accounted for odd complexes in my uncle's character.) Miss Etheridge also remembered Vicar Maugham and his curate, Mr Ellman, whom they used to call 'The Devil' – partly because of a pun on his name. Willie described him in *Cakes and Ale* as 'a tall, thin, ungainly man with untidy hair and a small, sallow dark face'. It is interesting that in this later novel the character of his uncle, the vicar, is less harsh than in *Of Human Bondage*, for Willie had now mellowed with success and could afford to look back more leniently on the narrow-minded but virtuous parson.

Miss Etheridge, however, did not like the vicar, 'on account of his long beard and because he used to try to kiss the children'. The children used to hide from him, 'but he liked to show them his goldfish', and she felt that he was 'fond of children but unable to understand them'.

'Once during the annual carnival,' she said, 'the vicar's effigy was carried through the streets in a cart – with the people laughing at it.' She added that he 'was not, it seemed, much liked or respected'.

The old vicar must have looked rather odd. He suffered from bad teeth, and whenever a toothache came on he used to drive out in his carriage with his face completely swathed in a black veil.

*

Before starting on my journey to Whitstable I had tried to discover a few facts about Willie's uncle, the Reverend Henry Macdonald Maugham. But apart from Willie's various descriptions of him, surprisingly little seemed to be known about him. We did not even know the exact date of his death – until, thumbing through old copies of *The Church Times*, we came on a short entry under 'Clerical Obituaries' in the issue of September 24, 1897. It read, simply: 'MAUGHAM. On the 18th inst., the Rev. Henry Macdonald Maugham, 27 years Vicar of Whitstable.'

The next step was to find an account of his funeral, but the files of the local journal, the *Whitstable Times*, had been destroyed in a bombing raid during the war, and it seemed unlikely that any Canterbury paper would have made much of the death of an ordinary country priest when there were so many fine prelates and deans and canons on their very doorstep. However, we were lucky: while I was lunching with the headmaster of the King's School, Derek Peel buried himself in the basement of the Beaney Institute, the public library and museum in Canterbury's High Street. There, among the dusty old piles of *The Kentish Gazette and Canterbury Press* in the issue for Saturday, September 25, 1897, was the notice, 'DEATH OF THE VICAR OF WHITSTABLE.'

The news that spread through our town on Saturday evening last that the Rev. H. M. Maugham had passed away at about six o'clock, came to most of the inhabitants as a shock, for although it was generally known that he had been in failing health for some time past, and that for the last three weeks he had been confined to bed, the serious nature of his illness was not realised by the majority of the parishioners.[3]

Mr Maugham entered his 70th year while on his sick-bed. He came to Whitstable in the year 1871 . . . He was twice married, his first wife being a lady of German birth, who died and was buried at Ems, where she was staying with her husband for the benefit of her health. About two years ago Mr Maugham married Miss Matthews, daughter of the late General Matthews, of Bath, who survives him. He leaves no children.

The funeral took place on Tuesday last, and was an impressive ceremony. Most of the places of business in the town were closed from 1 to 3 o'clock. The procession left the Vicarage at half-past one. The chief mourners were Mr Henry Maugham and Mr William S. Maugham, nephews, who were accompanied by Mr J. W. Hayward. The trustees of the local charities . . . followed, as did also a number of Freemasons, wearing white gloves, and each carrying a sprig of acacia, which they dropped into the grave at the conclusion of the burial, Mr Maugham having been for many years a member of the local Lodge, of which he was a Past Master, holding also the rank of Past Provincial Grand Chaplain. Many other inhabitants formed part of the long procession.

Arrived at the Churchyard, the coffin was received by the Clergy. . . . The whole of the Choir were present vested in surplice and cassock, and the *cortège* moved to the west door of the Church while the accustomed sentences were intoned. The coffin, which was covered with beautiful wreaths and crosses, was deposited in the Chancel, and the 90th Psalm was sung to *Felton's* mournful chant. The Lesson was read by the Rev. E. Ellman, and then, preceded by the Choir and Clergy singing the hymn 'O Paradise!' the coffin was borne to the grave . . . the anthem 'I heard a voice from Heaven' being beautifully sung by the choir, who also, at the close of the service, sang with great feeling the hymn 'Now the labourer's task is o'er' . . .

In addition to those who followed from the Vicarage a large number of persons were present in the church and the churchyard. Mr O. Holden attended the funeral of the Vicar as the representative of his uncle, Mr George Holden, of Belmont, who was unavoidably absent.

*

I had never realised that Willie was present at his uncle's funeral. I

wonder what his feelings were on that day. Of course, he was grown
up by then; he was twenty-three years old and in his final year at the
medical school. He had already received the first six advance copies
of his first novel *Liza of Lambeth* which was published the following
month. He had cut himself free from the Vicarage. Yet for all his
independence I doubt if Willie had lost what Mr Cordell describes as
the 'cold-blooded yearning for his uncle's death' which he had made
Philip Carey feel so deeply.[4] Willie's emotions must have been mixed
as he heard the choir singing 'O Paradise!'. On September 2, 1897,
only sixteen days before the Vicar died, Willie had sent him an advance
copy of *Liza of Lambeth*. Did Willie wonder sardonically whether the
shock of reading this 'dirty, unpleasant, unhealthy work' had hastened
his uncle's death? And what could Willie's thoughts have been during
the anthem when the choir 'heard a voice from Heaven'? Willie had
never heard a voice from heaven in his life and never intended to. He
must have felt relieved when the choir began to sing 'Now the
labourer's task is o'er' and it was evident that the service would soon be
finished.

The funeral, however, must have been quite an impressive ceremony – with almost all the local bigwigs present. Mr Hayward, who
accompanied my uncles Willie and Harry to the funeral, was one of the
two doctors in Whitstable and a former churchwarden. 'People called
him "Mr" out of courtesy,' Dr Nesfield told us, 'because as well as
being a doctor he was also a surgeon and used to take out tonsils on his
kitchen table.' And there was an amusingly snobbish note at the end of
the newspaper account concerning the representative of 'Mr George
Holden, of Belmont, who was unavoidably absent'. When I asked old
Mr Smith about George Holden he chuckled. 'That was "Gentleman
Holden,"' he said. 'You might say he was one of the industrial aristo-
crats of the town. He was related to the Gann family – needless to say.
A big shipowner, he was, with luggers carrying hay and wheat to
Tower Bridge, and schooners that took Kentish coal to Bermuda.
Everyone called him "Gentleman Holden" because of his fine clothes.'

But the line in the newspaper cutting that caused me most surprise
was that the Vicar had married for a second time – 'Miss Matthews,
daughter of the late General Matthews, of Bath,' who survived him.
Willie had never even mentioned her existence. We knew about the
first Mrs Maugham. Willie had written about her twice. The second

description, in *Cakes and Ale*, being the most charitable. 'She was a simple old lady, of a meek and Christian disposition, but she had not, though married for more than thirty years to a modest parson with very little beyond his stipend, forgotten that she was *hochwohlgeboren*.' What could the second Mrs Maugham have been like? Miss Etheridge helped to answer the question for us. The first Mrs Maugham, she wrote, was 'a very quiet, gentle lady', who had given her an embroidered text of *Home Sweet Home*.[5] The second Mrs Maugham was 'an entirely different lady, very jocular and merry', and she and the Vicar 'seemed happy together'.

*

Our last appointment in Whitstable was with the present vicar, Canon C. E. Waynforth, at the new Vicarage, close to the Church of All Saints. We drove slowly along the narrow main street, past the Railway Arms where Rosie Gann served as a barmaid and met the notorious Lord George Kemp in *Cakes and Ale*, past the imposing Congregational Chapel and the 'dingy yellow brick' two-storey house with a bow window – now a 'Gents' Outfitters' – where Rosie lived with her husband, the celebrated novelist Edward Driffield, down to 'the little space' between the Bear and Key and the Duke of Cumberland – which Willie calls the Duke of Kent. Then along to the pretty beach by the Royal Native Oyster Stores, which are now, unhappily, put to little use, for the oyster industry in Whitstable no longer flourishes as it did when Willie's uncle could buy the succulent 'natives' for a shilling a dozen. Away to the left was the famous Neptune Inn. Young Willie used to swim from the broad beach in front of it. But gone are the swing boats, the bathing machines and the booths where he used to enjoy a shrimp tea for sixpence. Gone, too, are most of the oyster dredgers and dirty old colliers, and in their place are the signs of a new prosperity brought in by the 'foreign' holiday-makers – gleaming yachts and catamarans, and luxurious cabin-cruisers moored in the outer harbour alongside the timber freighters that ply twice a week between Whitstable and Esbjerg in Denmark.

The new Vicarage is a well-proportioned house set far back from the road with a pleasant border of flowers running between a fine spread of lawn. And within we discovered at a glance there was none of the usual Church of England gloom. Great bowls of flowers were

reflected by gleaming floors and shining furniture, and Mrs Waynforth had prepared a tea of such splendour that I wished I had not
lunched so fully. The third guest was a tall African priest, handsome and
firmly-built, with an enchanting smile that would, I felt sure, win
converts in towns or jungles alike.

Presently Canon Waynforth led us through his garden into the
churchyard. I already knew a little about All Saints from a booklet
I had read about the church.[6] It was written not only with a sense of
history but a sense of humour. I was pleased by the account of the
'swearers and cursors' and 'common ale haunters' who were reported
by the Vicar to his superiors during the sixteenth and seventeenth
centuries.

1599. We present John Wilkins for going about the street in woman's
apparel, being the parish clerk at the time.

1611. John Wighton, for extraordinary swearing and blaspheming, for
ribaldry in undoing his hose, being very unseemly in the ale house.

1614. That Thomas Fox the elder, upon the Twenty-seventh day of the
month of June last past, being in a drunk distemper did in the Church of
Whitstable . . . in the service time interrupt the preacher by rude repetition
after him, and by his most profane swearing of most horrible and fearful
oaths, to the great profanation of God's holy name and evil example and
offence to others.

There has been a church on the site of All Saints for more than eight
hundred years, but the records only go back to the thirteenth century
when a new church was built in about 1220 and a splendid square tower
was erected beside it to serve both as a landmark for sailors and as a
watch-tower against invaders. (Even during the last World War the
old tower was manned by spotters who kept watch for enemy aircraft
coming up the Thames Estuary to bomb London.) The thirteenth
century was a time of power and prosperity in the history of the church.
But by the end of the eighteenth century All Saints was so financially
encumbered that it could no longer afford to care for the actual structure of the church. When Willie's uncle became Vicar in 1871, 'he was
faced with the problem of a decaying fabric which could no longer be
made serviceable with minor repairs. A complete rebuilding was the
only possible solution.'

It seems that the Reverend Henry Macdonald Maugham, for all his
evident lack of talent both as parish priest and guardian of children,

deserves at least some praise for devotion to his church. Within five years of his arrival as the forty-fifth incumbent of an office that had once been held by priests with such names as Walter de Albiniaco, Robert de Kemesinge, Henry Bokelonde, and William Orgodeby, the old tower had been restored and most of the rest of the church rebuilt. Vicar Maugham's great day came on May 31, 1876, when the church was reopened by no less a prelate than the Archbishop of Canterbury.[7] In 1888, and four years after young Willie Maugham had come to live with his uncle, the Rural Dean made an official inspection and recorded 'I visited the Church of Whitstable, and was met by the Vicar. I found everything connected with the church, both inside and outside, in excellent order.'

The Rural Dean would have been no less delighted with the condition of the church in 1963, for it was as bright and immaculate as the Vicarage. A few bell-ringers were preparing to call the people to Evensong as we walked through the West door into the empty church, past the octagonal font which belongs to the same period as the tower and is surrounded by coats of arms all brightly painted – as they were in the thirteenth century. On the south side of the nave we saw the pulpit which Willie's uncle had given to the church four months after his first wife died[8] – an ornate circular stone-and-marble edifice designed in the most florid Victorian-Gothic style. I stooped down to read the inscription on the brass plate near its base.

To the Glory of God and in loving memory of
Barbara Sophie Maugham
this Pulpit is dedicated by her Husband
the Rev. H. Macdonald Maugham, M.A., Vicar.
20th Dec. 1892.

'And is there a memorial to Vicar Maugham himself?' I asked Canon Waynforth.

'Only his tombstone,' he replied. 'Shall we go and look at it? It's out in the churchyard.'

About thirty yards from the south-west corner of the church, I saw the low coffin-shaped stone slab, its apex fashioned as a cross, that covered the tomb into which sixty-six years before the Freemasons had cast the sprigs from an acacia, their sacred tree. On one side of the slab I read the words, 'Jesus said I am the resurrection and the life,' and on the other side, 'In loving Memory of the Rev. Henry Macdonald Maugham, for 27 years Vicar of Whitstable, died Sept. 18th, 1897.'

But the world only remembers the Vicar because of a few chapters in *Of Human Bondage* and *Cakes and Ale*.

*

In *Of Human Bondage*, truth, fact, and fiction were so inextricably mingled that Willie himself became confused. Thus at the beginning of the book Philip's father is called Henry Carey, but by the end of the book he has become Stephen.[9]

The description of the Vicar's death – the 'horribly frightening' loud rattle while the bluebottle buzzed noisily against the window-pane may not be accurate, and we know that the settling of the Vicar's modest estate is inaccurate. In the novel, the Reverend William Carey left everything to his nephew Philip. This was most likely wishful thinking on Willie's part, for in real life the Reverend Henry Macdonald Maugham left his nephew nothing. Willie received not a penny. The whole estate, valued at £1,677, went to the Vicar's widow, the second Mrs Maugham, who has no counterpart in the novel.

But we know that the incident of finding the letter from his beloved mother while going through his uncle's papers is factual, for Willie refers to it again in *The Summing Up*.[10] Fifteen years had passed since her death, and finding the letter among 'the Vicar's dreary correspondence' after his death must have given Willie a sudden stab of pain. Willie's mother had written to her brother-in-law, the Vicar, asking him to be godfather to her latest-born son, William Somerset, and we have only to replace the fictional names in *Of Human Bondage* with the real names to read the letter exactly as Willie's mother wrote it.

My dear Henry,

Robert wrote to you to thank you for your congratulations on the birth of our son and your kind wishes to myself. Thank God we are both well and I am deeply thankful for the great mercy which has been shown me. Now that I can hold a pen I want to tell you and dear Sophie myself how truly grateful I am to you both for all your kindness to me now and always since my marriage. I am going to ask you to do me a great favour. Both Robert and I wish you to be the boy's godfather, and we hope that you will consent. I know I am not asking a small thing, for I am sure you will take the responsibilities of the position very seriously, but I am especially anxious that you should undertake this office because you are a clergyman as well as the boy's uncle. I am very anxious for the boy's welfare and I pray God night and day that he may grow into a good, honest, and Christian man. With you to guide him I hope that he will become a soldier in Christ's Faith and be all the days of his life God-fearing, humble and pious.

Your affectionate sister,
Edith.

*

In the novel Philip pushes the letter away, leans forward, and rests his face on his hands.

He knew nothing of his mother, dead now for nearly twenty years, but that she was beautiful and it was strange to learn that she was simple and pious. He had never thought of that side of her. He read again what she said about him, what she expected and thought about him; he had turned out very differently; he looked at himself for a moment; perhaps it was better that she was dead. Then a sudden impulse caused him to tear up the letter; its tenderness and simplicity made it seem peculiarly private; he had a queer feeling that there was something indecent in his reading what exposed his mother's gentle soul.

But in real life Willie kept the letter, he never became a soldier in Christ's Faith, and he never got over his mother's death.

FAMILY TIES

WHEN I stayed with my uncle Willie in the South of France in the autumn of 1963, I tried to prod his memory in the hope that he could recall any stories about his uncle, the Vicar of Whitstable, and his uncle's two wives. But Willie could only remember what he had written in his novels, and he had no recollection whatsoever of the second Mrs Maugham, 'daughter of the late General Matthews of Bath', for the simple reason that he had never written about her. So that all I could do was to go back to the old books of reference and work forwards. First I obtained the marriage certificate from Somerset House, which showed that on June 6, 1894, Henry Macdonald Maugham, widower, of Whitstable Vicarage, was married in Bath to Ellen Mary Matthews, spinster, daughter of General Henry William Matthews. The wedding was at the parish church of St Mary, Bathwick. Then I found that Mrs Maugham returned to Bath after the Vicar's death, and that she died there, at 41 Bathwick Street, on October 2, 1928, at the age of eighty-four. And finally I got a copy of her will, which showed that she did not forget her nephew Willie – even though he seemed to have forgotten her – for she left him two hundred and fifty pounds. The other principal bequests were to her sister, Mrs Alice Harriet Smith, and her friend Theophilus Kellaway Northover, whom she appointed sole executor and trustee and residuary legatee.

All rather dull facts on the surface, but they led to another trail that proved quite fruitful. Also, they prompted my own memory, for as a boy I had lived with my parents and my three sisters in the country quite near Bath, and I vaguely remembered being taken to one of those elegant Georgian houses in the city to have tea with two old ladies. I was about seven or eight years old at the time, and the two old ladies must have been my great-aunt Ellen Mary Maugham and her sister. But who was the gentleman with the rather Trollopian name of Theophilus Kellaway Northover? Were there any Northovers still living in Bath? I searched the local telephone directory and came on

Dr P. T. Northover, who turned out to be the son of Theophilus. I wrote to him, and his answer was surprising. Not only did he remember the two old ladies, but he possessed several mementoes of General Matthews and his daughters, also letters written by both my father and my uncle Willie, and, more important still, some first editions that Willie had inscribed to his 'Aunt Ellen'.

So in November 1963, with an invitation to lunch with Dr and Mrs Northover, Derek Peel and I set off on yet another journey. We stayed the week-end in the enchanting village of Castle Combe; and on Sunday morning we motored twelve miles into Bath. On the way I caught a glimpse of Hamswell House where my parents had lived soon after the first World War.

We drove down into the city and then, within sight of the Abbey, we crossed the Avon river by Pulteney Bridge, to see the places associated with Vicar Maugham's second wife, before and after her brief marriage – first, to 8 Sydney Place, the elegant house crowned with a pediment, where old General Matthews, late of the Bengal Infantry, had died in 1884; next, the pleasant cul-de-sac named Darlington Place, where Ellen Mary Matthews was living when she was betrothed to the Reverend Henry Macdonald Maugham; then, the church of St Mary, built in the style known as 'Somerset Gothic' and smelling discreetly of incense to please its Anglo-Catholic congregation, where Ellen and Henry were married in 1894; and, finally, the severely plain exterior of the house in Bathwick Street, to which Mrs Maugham retired in 1897 and where she lived with her sister. This was the house to which my parents had taken me to tea almost forty years ago. Then we drove back across the Avon, up the hill by way of the ring of Georgian mansions known as The Circle, and thence to Dr Northover's house, high above the city. It was a strange coincidence that, like Dr Nesfield at the Old Vicarage in Whitstable, another doctor of medicine, in Bath, at the other side of England, should have so many souvenirs of the Maughams. Dr Northover, an earnest, friendly man, had a big box of papers and other treasures ready to show me – the campaign medals of General Matthews, several certificates of births, marriages and deaths (the old general had had three wives), and one which showed that Ellen Mary Matthews had been born on February 11, 1845, at Fatehgarh in India. He showed us relics of my own family – the Masonic certificates of the Reverend Henry Macdonald Maugham, and several letters from both my father and Willie. But these, unfortunately were dull – mainly concerned with an annuity of ten pounds which Willie had to pay to his Aunt Ellen under the conditions imposed by another aunt, Julia Maugham, in her will[1] made in 1910. By then, of course, Willie had become a successful playwright with plenty of money, but I fear that Aunt Ellen never got more than her annual ten pounds out of him.

'In fact,' said Dr Northover, 'she was really quite poor.'

'But how did your family come into the story?' I asked.

'My parents were great friends with Mrs Maugham and her sister,' he replied. 'My mother played bridge with them every Thursday, and your aunt, towards the end of her life, gave my father power of attorney, since she was very bad at managing her own affairs.'

I told the doctor that Aunt Ellen was remembered in Whitstable as being 'very jocular and merry'.

'Of course, she was quite elderly when I knew her,' Dr Northover said. 'She was a small, rather subdued old lady, overshadowed by the stronger character of her sister. Yet she had a bit of talent as a painter.'

The doctor showed me the only painting that seems to have survived among Aunt Ellen's possessions – a surprisingly strong and very competent portrait of an old peasant, perhaps painted on her honeymoon with Vicar Maugham in 1894. I remembered Miss Etheridge's remark that 'they seemed happy together'. So perhaps, for all the vicar's apparent coldness – which may have been due to thirty-five years of boredom with his first wife, Barbara Sophia – his second marriage really was a happy one.

Over coffee and liqueurs Dr Northover showed me more treasures – a pile of 'period' photographs, each mounted on a stiff board. There was old General Matthews, bewhiskered and bemedalled, in various military poses, and several of his daughters, Ellen and Alice, in stiff Victorian dresses. And then – and I had hardly dared hope to make such a find – a rather sinister portrait of a clergyman with drooping moustaches and rimless spectacles, taken by a photographer in South Kensington with the gentle name of Mendelssohn. It could be none other than Willie's uncle, the Reverend Henry Macdonald Maugham.[2] And there was yet another surprise. Dr Northover went over to the bookshelf and produced mint-condition copies of the first three novels that Willie ever wrote. They were *Liza of Lambeth*, *The Making of a*

Frederic Herbert Maugham as a small boy

Frederic Herbert Maugham at Cambridge, 1889. From a cartoon in *The Granta*, 1 March 1889

REGISTRATION DISTRICT	LAMBETH							

1904. DEATH in the Sub-district of Lambeth Church Ft. in the County of London

Columns:— (1)	(2)	(3)	(4)	(5)	(6)	(7)	(8)	(9)
No.	When and where died	Name and surname	Sex	Age	Occupation	Cause of death	Signature, description, and residence of informant	When registered	Signature of registrar
481	Twentyseventh July 1904 St.Thomas's Hospital Albert Embankment Lambeth	Henry Neville ~~Maugham~~ Maugham	Male	26 years	of no Occupation of 9 Cadogan Street Chelsea	Collapse following Poisoning by Nitric Acid Suicide while of unsound mind P.M.	Certificate received from J.Troutbeck Coroner for South Western London Inquest held 29th July 1904	Thirtieth July 1904	P.W. Ayers Registrar

Above: Harry Maugham's Death Certificate

Harry Maugham

Bernard Partridge's drawing in *Punch*
comparing W. Somerset Maugham to
Shakespeare, 1908

Saint, and *Orientations* – all published by Fisher Unwin at the end of the last century and all bound in dark green cloth. In the last two, the inscriptions were simply, 'Aunt Ellen – with the Author's love'. But in *Liza of Lambeth,* the first of all Willie's many novels, was the dedication, 'To the Vicar & Aunt Ellen with the Author's love. Sep. 2nd 1897'.

Here, then, was the only copy of the only book that Willie ever gave to the uncle he despised so much. It is interesting to note that he inscribed it not to 'Uncle Henry', but merely to 'The Vicar'. And the date is of especial significance, for it was an advance copy given to his uncle while he lay on his sick-bed. Sixteen days later, 'The Vicar' was dead.

*

Ellen Mary Maugham was the last of her generation of my family. She died on October 2, 1928. By then, of course, the next generation – Willie and his brothers – were middle-aged, almost elderly; all except Harry, who had killed himself by taking nitric acid, in 1904, at the age of thirty-six.

Mr Richard Cordell in his biography of Willie wrote that Harry was 'said to have been a prodigious bore'.[3] But my aunt Beldy – Mabel, the wife of Charles Ormond Maugham – had a very different opinion of him.

'If Charlie was the saint of the family,' Beldy said, 'Harry was the sweetest of the four brothers. He had great charm and he was very sensitive, and he showed very little of himself to the world. He needed a lot of understanding, and very few people could understand him.'

If Harry and Willie had been closer in age they might have had much to share. Their natures were strangely similar, and they were both attracted to the Bohemian life – quite unlike my father who – as Beldy stated scornfully – preferred to mix with 'clean, decent legal people in a decent society', as my mother described the circle in which they lived. Yet the gap of almost six years between Harry and Willie seemed to widen as they grew older, and Harry became envious of his younger brother's success in writing novels which he considered trivial and second-rate; while Harry's own works – mostly highbrow plays patiently written in blank verse – attracted little attention. I remember hearing a story of the party Willie gave to celebrate the first production of one of his own plays on a London stage – *A Man of Honour,* which opened at the Imperial Theatre, Westminster, on February 23, 1903. Harry arrived late for the party, in a very shabby blue suit, when everyone else was in full evening dress.

'I'm glad to hear that my little brother has had some success at last,' he said in a nervously loud voice.

Among the many family photographs that I found with my father's papers there were several of Harry. He was plump and he had a big moustache. But behind the conventional whiskers by which so many Edwardian males asserted their manhood I suspect there lurked a sad, rather timid soul who yearned for affection and was afraid of marriage. Beldy was the only woman mentioned in Harry's will. All the others in the will (excluding Charles and my father who were appointed executors) were young men with whom Harry had probably shared his Bohemian adventures in Paris when his day's work in the office was over. For Harry, like his eldest brother Charles, had also become a solicitor and had earned his living in the family firm at 54 Faubourg St. Honoré. This was the address he gave when he made his will early in 1895, but at that time he was living in Italy. Charles had realised how miserable Harry was working as a solicitor and had let him leave the firm. He roamed around for a while and eventually settled in Assisi where he wrote a play about St Francis. It is rather pathetic that in his will he ordered his executors to set aside a sum 'of not less than £120' to publish such of his works 'as a respectable London publisher thinks fit'. Actually Harry had the pleasure of seeing *The Husband of Poverty. A drama of the life of St Francis of Assisi* published during his lifetime, in 1896. He spent a year or more in Assisi, and it was there, according to Beldy, that his 'nervous trouble' began.

'When Harry came back to France he was odd in various ways,' Beldy said. 'For instance, he'd never take a train and he'd never go on a funicular. He had a kind of *vertigo*. If he came to stay with us in the country, he would always arrive on a bicycle.'

Later, Harry came to London. So far as I know he did no work, and he lived alone in rooms at 9 Cadogan Street in Chelsea. He saw little of the family. Charles and Beldy were mostly in Paris; my mother and father who had married in 1896 were too busy making their own lives in the society of other 'clean, decent legal people' to bother about him; and whatever sympathy Willie might have felt for him was not exactly encouraged by Harry's prim remark after reading the manuscript of *Liza of Lambeth* that his young brother should 'give up once and for all any ideas of authorship'.[4]

I think that Willie's increasing success as a novelist was partly responsible for Harry's increasing failure as a human being. He must have sunk into the depths of frustration and bitterness to have killed himself in such a dramatic and painful fashion. Swallowing a corrosive acid is not the easiest way out of this world. It is ironical that it should have been Willie's fate to find his brother Harry in a state of collapse, lingering half-way between life and death, when he called on him in Cadogan Street that fine summer's day of July 27, 1904. But for all Willie's knowledge as a doctor he was too late to save his brother. He rushed him off in a cab through the busy streets of Westminster, past the Houses of Parliament and over the bridge to St Thomas's, the hospital at which Willie had studied a few years before. But nothing could be done, and later that day Harry died. At an inquest two days later, following a post-mortem which revealed the nitric acid, the coroner for South-West London gave his short verdict, 'Suicide while of unsound mind'.

It was only after Harry's death that Willie realised how fond of him he had been.

'Harry was charming, and he was gifted,' Willie told me. 'You can find some of his verse in the anthologies of his day. Unfortunately, he wrote all his plays in blank verse at a time when theatre managers were getting sick to death of plays in blank verse. So it wasn't very surprising that they weren't produced. But I'm afraid Harry cared desperately . . . And he made an awful botch of his suicide, you know. He was in anguish for three days before we found him . . . I'm sure it wasn't only failure that made him kill himself. It was the life he led.'

*

My aunt Beldy told me that if she and Charles Ormond Maugham 'had not been abroad at the time, Harry would never have killed himself'. I think she loved Harry almost as much as her own husband; but Beldy and Charles lived in Paris so there was little they could do for him after Harry returned to England. And, like any other young married couple, they were preoccupied in making their own lives.

Beldy and Charles had married in London – at St Stephen's Church in Paddington, on June 21, 1894 – but they had met in Paris. After leaving Caius College, Cambridge (where he took his Law Tripos and gained his degree as Bachelor of Laws in 1886), Charles became a solicitor in 1889 and went immediately to join J. T. B. Sewell in the office in Paris. As he was the junior partner, the firm was known as 'Sewell and Maugham'. In the same year, Beldy, then aged fourteen, persuaded her parents – her father was Heywood Hardy the artist – to let her attend the Paris Conservatoire. Five years later she and Charles were married. They must have been happy together. Charles was, by all accounts, 'a saint' as well as a considerable scholar; Beldy had inherited her father's talent as an artist, and she made beautiful pictures out of coloured stuffs, many of which have been shown in public exhibitions. They seem to have got quite a lot of fun out of life. One of their first possessions was a Gardner-Serpollet steam car. In those days cars of any sort were rare on the roads and sometimes in towns had to be preceded by a man bearing a red flag. Léon Serpollet was a client of Charles, for cars were always getting into trouble with the law and he needed a good solicitor. Later, when people became less frightened of such monsters, Charles and Beldy used to race their 'steamer' between Paris and Marseilles – until one year when the races were stopped after fourteen people had been killed.

'Tell me about Uncle Charles's steam car,' I once said to Aunt Beldy.

'It wasn't *his* steam car,' she replied indignantly. 'It was *our* steam car. *I* used to drive it too. I wore a tricorne hat with gold braid on it. But I had to stop one day when a man came up and spat in my face and said that women shouldn't be allowed to drive steam cars. People were very prejudiced then. I even remember when some of them threw stones in Bordeaux at my daughter Clarisse, because she had cut her hair short!'

'What about Charles's grandmother, Mrs Snell?' I asked.

'I don't remember Mrs Snell at all,' Beldy answered. 'But I do remember that we drove down to Le Mans after her death and that we found her cat all alone in the house. I also remember that the cat was called Tom. He looked very lonely so we took him back with us to Paris.'

Charles and Beldy had four children – three daughters and one son, Ormond[5]. The only real sadness in their marriage came when Ormond, aged twelve, fell and was seriously injured while climbing a tree at school. He was paralysed for the rest of his life and he died on January 11, 1935, at the age of twenty-five. His family were then living

in a flat in London at 23 Cadogan Gardens, and it was there that
Charles also died six months later, on July 25, 1935. Later Beldy and
her three daughters moved to a mews flat in Kensington. When I last
saw Beldy, in 1963, she had been seriously ill, but at the age of almost
ninety she was up and dressed and extremely active, and she took an
obvious pleasure in showing me the latest of the beautiful pictures she
had made out of materials. But she regarded the purpose of my visit
with deep suspicion.

'I don't know why you want to write about the Maugham family,'
she said. 'With all the fuss in the papers and the way Willie has been
behaving lately, the less said about the Maughams the better.'

'What was your first impression of Willie?' I asked.

'I quite liked him in *those days*,' Beldy replied. 'I remember when
Clarisse was a child and we went out on a picnic and he took her on his
knee and peeled shrimps for her.'

'Did Willie take any interest in Ormond?' I asked.

'He used to call sometimes,' Beldy answered. 'But when I suggested
that his daughter Liza, whom Ormond had known when she was a
child, should come to see him, Willie said, "I don't think that would
be at all suitable."

'And then later,' Beldy continued, 'Willie took against me. I don't
know why. The last time I saw him was more than twenty years ago,
at the beginning of the last war, when he'd escaped from France on that
cargo boat. I went to see him at the Dorchester Hotel, and I told him
how upset I was about the fall of France. Suddenly he got very cross
with me and lost his temper completely, so I had to leave and I never
saw him again. He never really cared for any of us.'

But Willie had indeed been moved by the sight of young crippled
Ormond and he had been touched by Beldy's devotion to him. And,
using their misfortune as he used every scrap of experience that came
his way, he converted the situation into the plot of his famous play
The Sacred Flame.

THE LORD CHANCELLOR

WHEN I told Willie that I was thinking of writing a book about the family he looked at me for a while in silence before he spoke.

'You'll have your time cut out when it comes to writing about your father,' he said.

I had thought that my father's death might have softened Willie's aversion to him, but evidently I was mistaken, for Willie continued, 'He was an odious man. I have met many detestable men in my life, but your father was easily the mer-most detestable.'

The fact is that the two brothers grew to dislike each other intensely. Why did they?

First, one must remember that the Maughams had the intense respectability of the upper middle class. ('Who was that lady, Mama?' my father once enquired after a beautiful and well-dressed woman had passed by them at Deauville escorted by four gentlemen in top-hats. 'Nobody,' replied his mother. 'A Mrs Langtry.') When he decided to become a writer Willie determined to break free from the bonds of the class into which he had been born. As we have seen, his very first novel shocked the conventional society of his day, and even my mother found it 'a most unpleasant story', but she was fond of Willie as a person. My father, however, disapproved of his conduct in almost every way. He believed that his younger brother had made what he called 'an egregious error' in abandoning his safe career as a doctor to become a writer and he dreaded the moment when he would be called on for a loan. He was shocked by the books that Willie produced and dismayed by his apparent disregard for money. And when at last Willie began to make a success, my father disliked his way of life and his friends in general – and his young American secretary, Gerald Haxton, in particular. Nor did my father approve of Willie's marriage in 1916 to a *divorcée* named Syrie Wellcome. The scandal that arose when Syrie divorced Willie in 1927 did nothing to change his mind. My father by now resented Willie's attitude towards women generally.

In *Cakes and Ale*, which was Willie's favourite of all his novels, my uncle had written: 'We know of course that women are habitually constipated, but to represent them in fiction as being altogether devoid of a back passage seems to me an excess of chivalry.' My father considered this in extremely bad taste – and so, I suppose, it is.

On his side, Willie had reasons to dislike my father – and one of them was envy. When shy little Willie was sent at the age of ten to live with his uncle at Whitstable, my father was the head prefect of Dover College and a member of the rugger fifteen and cricket eleven. While Willie was being bullied at the King's School in Canterbury because he was bad at games, my father was rowing for Cambridge. While Willie was being cruelly mocked because of his stammer, my father's talent for debate helped him to become President of the Union. When Willie was only making a hundred pounds a year as a writer, my father was earning a thousand pounds a year at the Bar. The year after Willie was divorced by Syrie and decided to leave England, my father became a High Court Judge. The year that Willie was humiliated by the scandal caused by Gerald Haxton's wildly drunken behaviour on board his yacht, the *Sara*, in the South of France, my father was appointed Lord Chancellor of England. Willie certainly had reasons for envy.

*

'Various barristers I've met have informed me that your father was the most brilliant lawyer of our time,'[1] Willie said to me when I stayed at the Villa Mauresque for the week-end of his ninetieth birthday. 'Unfortunately, when he became Lord Chancellor he treated the Peers in the House of Lords as if they were hostile witnesses.'

I supposed that Willie was referring to my father's handling of the Coal Bill in May, 1938.[2] In his chapters about my father Mr Heuston refers to it thus: 'Maugham adopted a somewhat hectoring tone which the Peers resented. In particular they objected to being given what one of them described as a lecture on the importance of not voting according to private pecuniary interests.'[3] My father, however, believed that he had made some good friends in course of the debates, including a number who were opposed to the Bill.[4] He was blissfully unconscious of the feelings he had aroused, but his brother wasn't. Willie believed that my father had adopted much the same supercilious attitude to his fellow Peers as he had meted out to Willie all his life.

'So far as I am concerned,' Willie continued, 'ever since I can remember, during all the years of my life until I was eighty, your father was beastly to me. He never had a good word to say to me. In 1908 I had four plays running at the same time.* I was quite a success. But if we met, your father wouldn't even mention one of them. If it hadn't been for your mother I would never even have been asked to the house. Your mother used to say to him, "Isn't it time we asked Willie to lunch?". Sometimes I'd go and have tea with her when your father was working and we'd have a lovely talk together. But as soon as *he* came in it all changed. It wasn't until I was eighty that he ever said anything pleasant to me. When I reached eighty he did deign to say that some book I'd written recently had something to commend it.'

Willie unclasped his hands and stretched out his fingers.

'I wonder if he was so sour because of your grandfather,' he continued. 'You see, we were orphaned. And your grandfather had lived very extravagantly with carriages and servants, entertaining lavishly. But as you know, when he died we were left with only a hundred and fifty pounds a year ... Anyhow, your father was never kind to me. But your mother was. I shall never forget her kindness.'

*

Willie was very fond of my mother. All the first editions of his books that he sent to the family as they appeared are inscribed to my mother – not to my father. And I believe that he understood her better than my father did. My mother was a Romer, and whereas the Maughams tend to be inhibited, reserved, introspective, and melancholy, the Romers tend to be extroverts, and – to use the words of my eldest sister, Kate[5] – 'friendly, affectionate, rumbustious, boisterous, demonstrative'. Here is my father's account of his first meeting with the Romer family[6]:

It was at my very first lecture at Trinity Hall that I sat beside my life-long friend, Mark Romer ... He asked me up to his rooms and from that day onwards we were constant companions during our time at Cambridge; for we sat in Hall together at meals, we rowed to a considerable extent in the

* See *Punch* cartoon, dated June 24, 1908, reproduced opposite p. 163.

same boats, we attended the same mathematical lectures, we went in for the same Tripos, and we had the same amusements. Nor was that all. He introduced me to his family in the Christmas vacation of 1885, and that event had a great and happy effect on my subsequent life. His father and mother were the kindest people whom I have ever met, and among the cleverest and most amusing. Robert Romer was Senior Wrangler in 1863, the first member of Trinity Hall to attain that distinction. His subsequent career is interesting. Having no private means except the fellowship which he was awarded, he applied for and obtained the post of Private Secretary in Paris to Baron Lionel de Rothschild; and on the strength of this position he married (in 1864) his first cousin, Betty Lemon, the daughter of Mark Lemon the part founder and first editor of *Punch*, and took her to Paris. No doubt the wise and prudent shook their heads over this 'improvident marriage'; but she was as intelligent as she was charming and there never was a greater success. He then went to Queen's College, Cork, as mathematical professor while he was eating his dinners at Lincoln's Inn. He was called to the Bar in 1867, and got together a practice in a very short space of time. When I first met him in London he was an eminent Chancery Q.C. attached to the Court of Mr Justice Chitty, and universally known as 'Bob' Romer. He became a Judge of the High Court in 1890 and a Lord Justice in 1899 . . . He had by this time five sons, of whom Mark was the second, and two daughters, of whom the eldest was then a young girl. She became my wife and after a very happy life she left me desolate in 1950. I spent many happy days with them as a guest both in London and at their grouse-moor in Ayrshire, where I learnt how to shoot. There will be more to be said of the family later; but I should like to state here that, being a shy and lonely lad without parents, the unstinted affection and friendship of Robert and Betty Romer were of extraordinary value to me in my early days, and to this good fortune I owe to a great extent my future success.

My mother used to tell me that she believed that my father had been fonder of her parents than of herself, and certainly the brief mentions of his wife in my father's long autobiography would appear to support that belief. But their marriage could never have been completely happy because of the sharp difference in their temperaments. My father was quiet, dignified, reserved, and solemn; my mother was irrepressibly cheerful and high-spirited. To use Cyril Asquith's words,[7]

she had the secret of disengaging the kernel of fun or absurdity which often lurks within the most unpromising material and bringing it to the surface, a process warming to the cockles alike of the heart and of the mind. It was this, along with her unforced, unposed approach to people and things which made her one of the happiest human beings, and a potent and pervasive cause of happiness in others. In her presence shyness was disarmed, diffidence melted, spirits rose, dullness began to emit sparks, or to think it was doing so, while the most exacting were held, charmed and exhilarated.

But my father was not exhilarated. What A. A. Milne described as my mother's 'ever-youthful spirits and sense of fun' were apt to irritate him; and while my mother 'bubbled over . . . with an absurd travesty of everything which had been happening to her; illness, war troubles, domestic difficulties . . . an irresistible saga of nonsense',[8] my father would sit tense and pale and silent at the other end of the table. On one occasion when he was Lord Chancellor I remember a large lunch party at which he had not said a word. But when his guests were drinking their second cup of coffee he suddenly leaned forward towards my mother. So impressive was his movement that people stopped in mid-sentence to hear what they expected to be an important political or legal pronouncement.

'Will you kindly pass me the sugar, Nellie?' said my father and relapsed into silence.

My mother's sense of humour was seldom shared by my father. My mother, for instance, in her simple Edwardian way, was always highly amused if anyone tripped over something and fell flat on his face. My father could see only the foolishness or the sadness of such an occurrence. On one occasion my father had asked for a stepladder to be carried up from the basement of the house in Cadogan Square to the drawing-room because he wished to hang a picture he had just bought at Sotheby's. Half an hour later he appeared in my mother's sitting-room, limping badly and pallid.

'It will amuse you, Nellie, to hear that I have fallen off the step-ladder,' my father said in a hollow mournful voice. 'It will further amuse you to learn that I have hurt myself considerably.'

*

My father was fifty years old when I was born, and the half century that separated us was certainly one of the factors that made our relationship difficult. But he never managed to establish any warm communication with my three sisters when they were young.

When I first became aware of my father [Kate, my eldest sister, wrote], he was pale and grave and silent, always bent over a brief. I suppose he was then thirty-four or five, a hard-working, painstaking barrister. At the time of his marriage with my mother, he was making about £300 a year. He had no money beside what he earned at the Bar; my mother had an allowance from her father of £100 a year. They started their married life in a small house in the Boltons. My mother told me that when I was on the way she fed on rice pudding for two reasons: firstly because it was the cheapest and most filling thing to eat, secondly because she liked it. In those days everyone in the upper middle classes had a servant. Impecunious though they were, my parents had two – a cook and house-parlour-maid. And when I appeared I had a Nanny. I see now that my father must have been anxious and preoccupied about money. He worked late every night, even at the week-end, and we children were taught that he must not be disturbed.

I expect I was a sore trial to this struggling young barrister. I was a bois- terous child, greedy, merry, highly-strung . . . I was grown-up, married with three children of my own, before I discovered that he was human. In our early days we never saw him; he left the house after breakfast and came home just before dinner; after dinner he worked. He was congenitally unsuited to go down on all fours and play bears with us in the nursery, or to sit on our beds and hear us lisp our childish prayers. My mother kept us away from him as much as possible, for our games and our chatter disturbed him as he sat poring over his briefs. Small wonder that we grew up thinking him a bogey- man.

But when we were young we were largely compensated for our father's remoteness by our mother's affection, and all four of us chil- dren adored her. The deep and happy relationship we enjoyed was inevitably bound to make my father feel cut off and hurt and jealous. Though his wife's high spirits and robust humour frequently annoyed him, he was, in his own reticent way, intensely devoted to her, and he remained so all his life. When he saw his wife's emotions almost en- tirely absorbed by her children, he was intensely resentful, and as we grew older and unconsciously made it clear that we were not only united in love for our mother but devoted to one another, his jealousy increased. These emotions, combined with his bitter struggle to succeed as a lawyer and the long hours of work 'late every night', were proba- bly responsible for making him turn back into himself and revert to the 'shy and lonely' person he said that he had been before he found friends and affection during his days at Cambridge.

My father's three years 'among the Colleges and in the streets and on the river of beautiful Cambridge' were certainly the happiest he was ever to know. 'There was more real liberty than I have ever found elsewhere in the conditions of my life,' he wrote in his autobiography. He was popular and successful and without any disturbing responsibility, and he looked back on that period with undying affection. 'The railway station can only be described as dingy and sordid; but never have I emerged from it on a visit to Cambridge without a thrill. Old as I am, it is with a beating heart that I walk along a street with buildings of a lovely grey tint and I do not enter or pass the entrance gates of Colleges without emotion ... Trinity Hall was my only home.'

My father loved Cambridge, and he was loved by Cambridge in return. 'Mr Frederick Herbert Maugham,' said *The Granta* on March 1st, 1889,[9] mis-spelling his Christian name, 'is one of the best specimens of the all-round man that Cambridge can show at the present time ... His good sense is as strong as his manners are gentle, and his friendship as valuable as his presence in a crew. He is a universal favourite, in spite of his universal success.' The lonely shy boy came out of his shell and was basking in praise and triumph. No wonder even the memory of his rooms in College was precious to him.

The rooms were just under the tiles and were very cold in winter and sometimes unbearably hot in summer, but for me it was Heaven and for three years they were my home. My parents being dead, and there being no relatives who could take me in, I had in truth no other home,[10] and I think that Cambridge from that circumstance meant more to me than it did to anyone else of my acquaintance. All my clothes, my knick-knacks, all my books, in a word, all my scanty belongings were in those two small rooms.

Within six years his whole life had changed. Gone were the days when he 'followed the herd, and had a most enjoyable time'. In 1895 he was sitting day after day in a set of chambers on the ground floor of 3 New Square, Lincoln's Inn, waiting desperately for a brief.

When I was sitting at work in my room I could, of course, hear the door to the chambers being opened and some person entering the clerk's room, usually a client. Was it by a remote chance a set of papers coming for me? I could not help but hear the conversation with at times a disturbed heart. The necessity of getting briefs, especially if one has a wife and children to support, is of a very poignant kind ... A day, sometimes a whole week, would go by without any of these glorious sheets of paper tied up with red tape arriving with my name on the back. The waiting for work is a terrible drawback to a young barrister's life and tends to sour his whole existence. I shall never forget those unhappy days.[11]

It was the tragedy of my father's life that a seemingly ill-suited marriage, almost constant worries about money, and a neurotically violent jealousy allied to an intensely personal ambition did in the end 'sour his whole existence'. He withdrew into his cloak of loneliness and seldom, if ever, emerged again.

*

My first memory of my father is of a white-faced stranger coming into the nursery on the top floor of 3 Rutland Gate where my parents lived before they moved to Cadogan Square. I gazed up at him in alarm.

'Say "Good-evening, Daddy",' my Nanny prompted in a whisper.

'Good-evening, Daddy,' I mumbled.

'Good-evening, Robin,' he said in a sad, hollow voice.

For a few disquieting moments there was silence.

'What did you do this afternoon?' he asked in a stern and, it seemed to me, accusing voice.

What had I done? What misdeed had I committed within the last four hours that he had uncovered?

'We went for a walk in the Park, didn't we?' Nanny prompted in the spuriously cheerful voice that she always adopted when grown-ups were present.

'Yes, we went for a walk,' I muttered.

During the silence that followed my father searched in his pockets and produced a tuppenny bar of milk chocolate. He then examined it carefully, and for a while I thought that he was going to eat it, but with a quivering hand he held it out to me.

'Here is a present for you, Robin,' he said.

I stared up at him in surprise. Evidently no misdeed had been discovered.

'Now what do we say when we're given a present?' Nanny asked, smiling archly. 'We say "thank-you", don't we? Don't we now?'

'Thank you, Daddy.'

My father looked gloomily around the room. I suppose he was trying to think of something to say.

'May I eat it?' I asked.

My father looked startled. He glanced at Nanny, who beamed confirmation.

'Now?' I asked, unwrapping the silver paper that enveloped the bar. I had just eaten a large meal. Nanny sent out another beam of approval.

'If you want to,' said my father.

'But not all of it at once,' Nanny added warningly.

Her command came too late. I had wolfed down the lot.

'What do you intend to do tomorrow?' my father asked accusingly.

I was silent. The last thing I intended to do was to reveal my plans to this frightening person.

'After our lessons in the morning we're going to see the ducks on the Round Pond, aren't we?' Nanny said merrily. 'Aren't we?'

'Yes,' I said.

'How are the lessons going?'

Again I was silent, for so far as I was concerned the lessons were a disaster. There had been tears that very morning; and the strain of the man's fearful inquisition, combined with the unexpectedly large piece of chocolate I had devoured, were beginning to make me feel rather sick.

'They're going very well,' Nanny said swiftly. 'We can do our multiplication table right up to ten.'

'What are five times seven?'

'Thirty-two,' I said after a pause.

'Now that's not right, is it?' Nanny laughed brightly. 'We know better than that, don't we? We know what five times seven make, sure enough! Five times seven make . . .'

But she never completed her sentence, for at that moment I was sick on the floor.

*

My father never came up to the nursery again, but once or twice a week I was taken to his dark study to say good-night to him as he sat in his deep mahogany-and-wickerwork armchair going through a brief, and I can remember being fascinated by the strokes he made with a flat pencil that projected from a flat silver case, marking the side of the stiff white pages and underlining various passages of typescript. But though I was urged to call him 'Daddy' he remained a stranger to me. I knew the old gardener down at Hamswell, our country house near Bath, and King, the chauffeur, a hundred times better.

*

I suppose I must have been about seven when my mother first took me to the Law Courts in London to hear my father plead.

'One day when you're grown up, you'll be a lawyer – like your father,' she said. 'And you'll never forget the day when as a child you first saw him in court.'

I will certainly never forget the day nor what occurred. We walked along dank gloomy corridors that smelled faintly of cabbage soup and stopped in front of some tall doors panelled with frosted glass. A policeman nodded his head when my mother gave her name, and we were ushered into a large courtroom and placed on a shiny wooden bench behind the witnesses. My father looked more of a stranger than ever in his grey wig, and his voice sounded alarmingly hollow as he cross-examined a witness. He never raised his voice, but I could hear every word he said though I could not understand what it was all about. His questions were put calmly and evenly, one after the other, and I could see that they were making the unhappy-looking red-faced man in the witness-box very angry.

'Why is Daddy making that poor man so cross?' I asked my mother.
'Quiet, darling.'

The questions continued smoothly in my father's cold, dispassionate voice, and the red-faced man began to tremble and shake with rage.

'I think the poor man's going to be sick.'
'Hush.'
'But look! He's taking out his hanky.'
'You must keep quiet,' my mother whispered.

As she spoke, my father asked yet another question in his indifferent yet glacial voice, and the effect on the red-faced man was disastrous. His eyes bulged, his arms jerked about in the air like a clockwork toy, and froth covered his mouth; and at the height of his fit I burst into loud tears and was led by my mother, sobbing from the court.

*

I know so well the kind of son that my father would like to have had. 'One of the best specimens of the all-round man,' he would have been a magnificent games-player and a brilliant scholar. But I was neither. Though I fenced for my school, I was never much good at games, and I was more interested in learning the piano and editing a school magazine than in trying for a scholarship to Cambridge. By the time I reached Trinity Hall I had at least had the sense to realise that I was unlikely to be any good as a pianist, and my parents sternly told me that I must prepare to become a lawyer, for the Maughams had been lawyers for three generations and so had my mother's family, the Romers.[12] However, I was allowed to read English Literature for the first two years, provided I promised to take the Law Tripos Part II immediately afterwards and then to study in London for the Bar Exams, and this, as a dutiful son, I did, albeit unwillingly. However, when I began to write short stories for *The Granta* in my second year I kept the fact secret from my father. One afternoon he arrived unexpectedly to visit me with my mother, and as we wandered round the town I saw to my horror that the placards were emblazoned with my name in vast letters, 'New Story by R. Maugham', the posters proclaimed. So each time we approached a poster my mother, who knew the terrible truth, would engage him in fervent conversation while I moved hastily between his line of view and the blatant poster.

My father was still further disappointed in me when it dawned on him that I was a socialist. I took my duties to the cause most seriously. In order to learn about the iniquities of capitalism I worked in my spare time in the Cambridge juvenile employment office; I visited the East End of London to learn about housing conditions; and I was so keen a proselytiser that one day I tried to convert a hairdresser to socialism during the course of a haircut and shampoo. I loathed all forms of class-barriers, and I still do. The Tories in those days represented to my mind the devil undisguised, and Neville Chamberlain was Lucifer incarnate. When Lucifer came to lunch with my family at 73 Cadogan Square shortly after my father had taken his seat in the House of Lords, I glowered in resentful silence over the Dover sole and lamb cutlets, and bided my time. My opportunity came over the *crème brulée*. Poor Mr Chamberlain, noticing my concentrated silence, put some polite and trivial question to me about students and politics. I looked my father, the newly-made Peer of the Realm, straight in the face.

'Speaking as a member of the middle-class,' I began with slow deliberation. But before I got any further, my father had popped his monocle into his eye.

'Speak for yourself,' he said firmly.

*

W. Somerset Maugham and Frederic Herbert Maugham in Bad
Gastein, 1936

The first Viscount Maugham in his robes as Lord Chancellor, a portrait by Sir Gerald Kelly

Lady Maugham, the author's mother

My father was passionately loyal to Mr Chamberlain, and on December 14, 1938, after he had been Lord Chancellor for nine months, he combined a vehement defence of Chamberlain's policy at Munich with a violent attack on the activities of Mr Winston Churchill in a speech at the Constitutional Club. Politicians such as Churchill, who advocated war against another country without considering the probable results, said my father, 'ought to be impeached'. Politicians should consider the facts he had stated about the might of the German airforce before deciding what to do next. 'The men who did not ought to be either shot or hanged.'

It was unfortunate for me that my father made this speech three days before I was due to drive over to Chartwell for tea to meet Mr Churchill for the first time. At the time of the Munich crisis I had enrolled as a trooper in the Inns of Court Regiment, for as soon as Mr Chamberlain had returned to Downing Street and said, 'Peace for our time', and my father had echoed the words in agreement, I realised that inasmuch as my father had been wrong in all his prognostications, war was now inevitable. While waiting for war to break out I had become private secretary to Sir Herbert Morgan, who was the director of the National Service Campaign. And it was to seek Mr Churchill's support over various problems about National Service that it had been suggested I should visit him informally. As I drove down to the country house near Hartfield that my father had bought after he had decided that Hamswell was too far from London, I stopped to buy an evening paper and was dismayed to read the headline 'Churchill's Attack on Cabinet Ministers'. I read further. 'Mr Winston Churchill today issued a statement criticising a speech by the Lord Chancellor, Lord Maugham. The statement is as follows:

The Lord Chancellor, speaking last night at the Constitutional Club, is reported to have stated: 'The Germans had it in their power to let loose 3,000 tons of bombs in a single day', and further, 'that in the first week or two of war the Germans might do an amount of damage in London and other great cities which would amount in money to £500,000,000'.

No statement of this kind about the power of the German air force has ever been made upon official authority before.

But it must be remembered that the Lord Chancellor has access to the secret information at the disposal of the Government.

If his facts are true, how can they be reconciled with Mr Chamberlain's statement only the day before to the Foreign Press Association, namely, 'Nor can we forget that we have obligations not only to our own people at home, but to those for whom we are responsible in the British Empire and to the allies who are bound to us by treaty. Those obligations we must be ready to fulfil, and our preparations have now proceeded far enough for us to say with confidence that we are in a position to do so.'

This contradiction in statements about our defences, made on successive days, by the two highest Ministers of the Crown, glares out upon us. Which are we to believe?

The Lord Chancellor further asked whether we should not consider the facts he had stated before deciding what to do and he added judicially, 'The men who do not ought to be either shot or hanged.'

It may be doubted whether the highest legal luminary in the land, the head of our whole system of judicature, is well advised to use language which savours of lynch law and mob law abhorrent equally to the British character and Constitution.

But if persons are to be held worthy of being 'shot or hanged' for not giving due consideration to the evil conditions which exist, what penalty would the Lord Chancellor suggest should be reserved for Ministers of the Crown who, during many years of plenary power, have allowed such conditions to grow up, while constantly assuring the country that all is well?

*

I realised that my father was not going to be at all pleased if he learned that on Sunday I was going to have tea with his adversary who said that his language savoured of 'lynch law and mob law', so I decided to say nothing about it.

'I intend to play golf this afternoon,' my father said to me at lunch on Sunday. 'Are you coming?'

I dreaded games of golf with my father—and so probably did he. I became so nervous when he tried to teach me how to swing my club that at each hole I would slice the ball into dense gorse and lose it, and this annoyed my father – for 'no income could stand it'.

'I'm afraid I can't play golf this afternoon,' I said.

'And why not?'

'I'm going out for tea.'

'Are you?' said my mother in surprise. 'You never told me.'

'No, I didn't,' I mumbled.

'And may we ask with whom you're going out to tea?' my father enquired.

'I don't see why not,' I muttered stupidly.

'What was that? I fear I didn't quite catch what you said.'

'Yes, you may enquire,' I repeated, rigid with embarrassment.

'Then with whom are you having tea?' my father demanded.

'With Mr Winston Churchill,' I said.

Slowly my father fumbled for his monocle and put it up to his eye. He gazed at me sadly.

'Well,' he said, after a long pause. 'There is no accounting for tastes.' The monocle fell from his eye and he relapsed into silence.

*

The sequel occurred just over four years later. By then I had been wounded in the head in the Western Desert and down-graded medically, and I had joined the Middle East Intelligence Centre. While in Syria I had worked out a plan for small units of Arabs, led by British officers, to stay behind in hiding should the Germans invade North Arabia in strength – which was generally expected at that moment.* I argued that if this German invasion did not take place, the plan could easily be converted to peacetime use. (And indeed out of my plan grew the Middle East Centre of Arab Studies.) At that time I had obtained the support of General Glubb and General Spears, and of Sir Kinahan Cornwallis. General Wilson and Arab experts such as the late Colonel Altounyan favoured the plan, and I now only needed political blessing from on high. But when I reached Cairo the shrapnel in my head gave trouble again and I was sent to the 15th General Hospital.

Visitors were not allowed until afternoon, so that when one morning my friend John Adam Watson, the Second Secretary at the Embassy, stole like a fugitive into my room in the officers' ward I knew this meant some development in my plan, which he had helped me to draft.

'Churchill is back from the Adana Conference,' he said. 'He wants to see you at four o'clock this afternoon.'

'Go on,' I said. 'I suppose Hitler wants to see me afterwards.'

'It's true. Do you think you'll be allowed out?'

'I'll get out somehow.'

But Dr Michael Kremer, who was looking after me, was away for the day, so my only hope was to approach the stern-faced Sister in charge of the ward.

* See *Nomad*, by Robin Maugham (Chapman & Hall, 1947).

'Can I possibly go out for an hour this afternoon?'

'Certainly not.'

'It's awfully important.'

'I'm sorry, Captain Maugham. But that's quite impossible.'

I glanced at her heavily-creased face and at the rows of medals on her breast. She was obviously reliable.

'At the moment it's top security, but if I tell you why, do you promise to keep it to yourself? It's important.'

'Yes.'

'Churchill is at the Embassy. I've got an appointment with him at four o'clock.'

She looked at me for a moment. Then she said, 'All right. So long as you're only out an hour.'

I felt sick and feeble as I got out of my taxi and walked into the Embassy. The ante-room was so full of generals that I recoiled and would have tried to escape if I had not been rescued and led into another office where the Prime Minister's staff sat about in attitudes of exhaustion.

The double doors at the end of the room swung open and disclosed Churchill in a boiler suit. He was radiant with vitality.

'Whiskies and sodas for all,' he said, and disappeared within.

Suffragis sprang up from nowhere with drinks, and I was offered one which I accepted, feeling that at least it could not make me feel any iller. It did not: it went to my head so that I felt almost capable of conversation with Churchill. The doors swung open again, and I was brought up to him.

'How are you? Come into the next room.'

He beckoned me into a large armchair and offered me a drink and a cigar.

'Well,' he said, 'this is a far cry from Chartwell.' Then he leaned back and looked at me with a smile. 'And how is your father?' he chuckled. 'Does he still love the Germans?'

An hour later, as I walked happily back along the corridor which led to my room in the hospital I met the bemedalled Sister.

'Well, at least you kept your word,' she said.

'Of course I did.'

'But next time you want to spend an afternoon with your girl-friend,' she said, 'just tell me outright, and don't tell fibs to make an excuse. Do you understand?'

'Yes, Sister,' I said.

*

In defence of my father I must state that though he had been a passionate supporter of the Munich Pact, he had never loved the Germans, and during the war he was most active in helping in their defeat. He spoke constantly in the House of Lords, he wrote vigorous war pamphlets – including the famous *Lies as Allies* – and when he learnt from secret reports from me that the tanks in which we were fighting in the Western Desert were defective, he devoted his few spare hours to visiting the factories that were making the tanks in England and to long conferences with the experts who were responsible for their design. On one occasion he even drove a tank round the test area of the factory – to the general alarm of all about him.[13]

*

For many years after I had returned from my travels in the Middle East I lived on the top floor of my father's house in Cadogan Square. The rooms had formerly been used by servants. But the two old maids who now looked after my parents could not climb so many stairs and I was allowed to use the rooms as a flat. One evening I had dined happily at the Travellers' Club with my friend and mentor Harold Nicolson, who had become a kind of godfather to me in my struggles to become a writer, and we had returned to my flat for a night-cap. My father and mother were already asleep, so we had crept gingerly up the steep winding stairs that led past their room. At about midnight Harold announced that he must go home. At the top of the staircase he turned.

'Don't bother to see me down,' he said. 'By now I know the way blindfold.'

Unfortunately on the cue word 'blindfold' he somehow caught his foot in the carpet and fell headlong down the stairs, landing up finally with a crash against the door that led into my father's bedroom. Such was the force of the impact that the woodwork splintered, but the door remained closed. I rushed down the stairs, picked up my distinguished guest and found that he was not seriously injured, so I was able to help him down the stairs and find him a taxi.

When I came down rather late to breakfast the next morning *The*

Times was trembling violently in my father's hands – a sure omen of trouble.

'Good morning,' I said brightly.

My mother nodded her head in my father's direction and gave me a warning wink. After I had helped myself to bacon and eggs from the hot-plate and had taken my place at the table, my father lowered the paper.

'Now, Robin,' my father began in a mournful tone of voice, 'your mother and I have been having a long talk about you, and we have decided that it is high time you changed your present mode of life – and your present friends. And even before my discussion with your mother I have been giving the matter some considerable thought. Now I personally would like to see you consort with people *older* than yourself instead of young flibbertigibbets. I would like to see you make friends with some important politician or someone who has won renown in the world of letters rather than with common riff-raff. *Who*, for example, was the drunken young hooligan who crashed against my bedroom door last night?'

'Harold Nicolson,' I replied truthfully.

*

Success over the years mellowed both my father and Willie sufficiently for the two brothers to meet on odd occasions with interest and a certain admiration for their mutual longevity, combined with a solicitude for their health.

'We must face it,' Willie said to his brother–when my father was ninety and Willie was eighty-three–'we must face it that both of us were endowed with very frail constitutions.'

But though they sometimes met quite affably, my father's disapproval of Willie persisted, and my uncle's resentment of my father's attitude grew to a violent dislike. Unfortunately neither brother was capable of appreciating the full extent of the other's success – and for this reason: my father was convinced that if he had stooped so low as to adopt the career of a professional writer he would have written far nobler and more eloquent works than Willie; whereas Willie was calmly certain that if he had decided to adopt a political career he would have done better than end up as Lord Chancellor for a year or two.

These convictions did nothing to improve the relations between the two old and distinguished brothers.

Whereas Willie was interested by my father's legal works he disliked his pamphlet in defence of the Munich agreement[14] and he told me that he found the short stories that my father published under the pseudonym of Ormond Greville 'both inept and inane'. But Willie, as has been seen, was biased. For a completely detached view of my father's career I prefer to quote from Mr R. F. V. Heuston's *Lives of the Lord Chancellors: 1885–1940*:

Maugham's literary interests also found an outcome in three successful volumes. One dealt with the judicial error in the case of Jean Calas of France in 1761. Maugham followed Voltaire in holding that Calas was quite innocent and the victim of religious intolerance. The work is a clear and valuable account which was written mainly in the intervals of Maugham's heavy work as a Chancery silk. After he became a judge his interest in the conflict of human testimony was awakened by the Tichborne case, and in 1936 he published what is still the best short account of that extraordinary affair. Maugham's skill in the elucidation of complicated facts and his ability to analyse with clarity a complicated chain of evidence is here shown at its very best. In addition there are some interesting remarks not merely about the conduct of the various judges and Counsel engaged in the trial (Maugham had a poor opinion of Coleridge as a cross-examiner), but also on the reasons why the public at large should have believed for so long in the incredible case put forward by the claimant. Maugham said:

'It is doubted whether the hypnotic effect of repeated statements however ill-founded has ever been sufficiently appreciated in this country. Suggestion of a falsehood acts like cumulative poison dropped into the ears of the victims, until at length reception of the unwelcome truth becomes for some people almost impossible . . . In view of documentary evidence which could not be disputed, and of the claimant's own mistakes and foolishness, it is really impossible to explain these long-drawn-out trials except on the hypothesis that at least half the world was so hypnotised before the civil case began into a belief in the genuineness of this impostor that no one could be certain that a unanimous verdict would be obtained from either of the juries.'

Maugham also contributed an interesting chapter to a work edited by Sir George Clark entitled *The Campden Wonder*. In 1661 three persons were tried and executed for the murder of the steward of Lady Campden at Chipping Campden in Gloucestershire. The three persons concerned were a fellow-servant of the steward together with his mother and brother, and the conviction was obtained mainly on the confession of the fellow-servant. Two years later the murdered man returned to Chipping Campden with an extra-ordinary story of having been kidnapped and sold into slavery. The problem of the proof of murder in the absence of a corpse is one well known to criminal lawyers, but Maugham was also fascinated by the conflict of human testimony involved, as he had been earlier by a similar conflict in the Tichborne case. He was also of the opinion that in 1661 there was no settled rule against the reception of hearsay evidence.

Maugham also wrote, but did not publish, a number of miscellaneous works. His papers contain a sketch for a play, and a short essay of interest to Dickensians entitled *Was Edwin Drood Murdered?* He also wrote, and occasionally published in *Blackwood's Magazine*, short stories under the pen name Ormond Greville. Their plot is a trifle slow-moving and elaborate for modern tastes but the interest is maintained throughout, and on the whole they are not unworthy to be compared with the more famous productions of his brother, Somerset Maugham. Maugham's relations with his brother were distant. When the present author wrote to Mr Somerset Maugham in 1959 to ask if he had any reminiscences of his brother, he received the following reply:

7th September, 1959.

'I am very much afraid that I cannot be of any help to you. My brother was a very strange, reticent and difficult man. I saw him very seldom, and if it hadn't been for my sister-in-law, his wife, I should not have seen him from year's end to year's end.

I don't suppose you have ever read a novel of mine called *The Painted Veil*. I used my brother as my model for the doctor in that story.

My nephew Robin can tell you much more about his father than I can, and on the whole what he tells you can be relied on. You probably know that he was very unpopular in the House of Lords, because, as one member told me, he treated the Peers as hostile witnesses.'

*

On my way back from North Africa in 1949 Willie invited me to stay at the Villa Mauresque. I had been away from England for a year.

'It may have escaped your notice,' Willie remarked, 'but during your absence abroad your sainted father deigned to spend a fortnight as a guest in this house.'

'Did he?' I exclaimed in surprise.

'Indeed he did,' Willie said. 'And he managed to spend fourteen days beneath this roof without passing one single civil remark.'

The visit, I discovered, had been a failure from the very beginning. In those days Willie knew three princesses in Monte Carlo, and when he wanted to impress a guest, Jean his chauffeur was sent off to collect them for lunch. They were fetched for my father's benefit, and Annette, who had the reputation of being the finest cook on the Riviera, was given special instructions for the lunch party.

'Tell me, Lord Maugham,' said the youngest princess, aged seventy, towards the end of a luxurious meal, 'tell me, how do you find the Riviera suits you?'

My father took out his monocle, raised it with a trembling hand to his right eye, looked at the princess for an instant without speaking, and then let the monocle drop from his eye. The dignity with which this ploy was accomplished was such that it reduced the whole table to silence – which was precisely its purpose.

'Does the Riviera suit you?' the princess quavered.

'Yes,' replied my father. 'I find this plain cooking agrees with me.'

The remark did not endear him to his host. Then, while Willie was still silent, the eldest princess addressed my father.

'Your nose is exactly like your brother's,' she remarked.

My father looked at her reproachfully.

'You mean my brother's nose resembles mine,' he corrected.

After lunch Willie had news that an Empire table he had recently bought in Paris for a high price was being delivered during the afternoon, and he determined to invite a few friends up to the villa for a drink to celebrate its arrival. By now he realised that my father's presence would dampen the party, so he suggested to his brother that he should rest in his room until it was time to dress for dinner.

'You're looking very pale and tired,' Willie said firmly. 'And a long rest would do you good.'

My father departed rather sadly to his room, and Willie's friends were invited. But in the evening, as they stood admiring the new piece of furniture, suddenly the door into the long living-room was flung open and there stood my father looking quite stricken. Willie did not know that for the last twenty years of his life my father could look like King Lear on the blasted heath at the drop of a hat. Willie moved forward nervously and introduced my father to his friends. My father did not speak.

'I asked a few people in to celebrate the arrival of this new piece,'

Willie said, pointing to the intricately-carved gilded table in its place of honour at the far end of the room.

Slowly my father raised his monocle up to his eye. Then he spoke.

'Rather florid, isn't it?' he remarked.

*

My father's visit to the Riviera in 1949 still rankled with Willie in November 1963, when I stayed with him at the Villa Mauresque two months before his ninetieth birthday.

'Did I ever tell you the story about your father and the glass of port?' Willie asked me.

'No,' I replied.

'Well, Alan and I had been invited to Portugal,' Willie said, 'and we'd been invited to the vintage on the Douro and they'd given us six bottles of port. So next time your father came to dine I opened a bottle. As you know, your sainted father always thought he knew best about everything. And after he'd tasted the port he looked up at me and he said:

'"It's quite nice wine. But it isn't port."

'I was furious with him,' Willie said with a dry chuckle. 'But what could I do? I tried to protest.

'"But I brought the bottle back myself from Portugal," I said, "and I know it's port."

'You would have thought that would have persuaded your father. But no. Nothing would ever persuade him that he was mistaken in any opinion.

'"I've been buying port now for Lincoln's Inn for over forty years," your father replied. "So I do know port. And I can tell you this with complete authority. *This isn't port.*"

'I was enraged,' Willie said, laughing at the recollection. 'But I had to give up trying to convince him.'

Willie glanced down at his glass of brandy.

'You know, he was a perfectly odious man,' Willie said. 'Nothing was ever right for him. On one occasion when he was staying here he looked round at all the shelves of books running up all the walls as they did at the time in this room, and he turned to Alan and said: "And *where* is my brother's library?"'

Willie dropped his cigarette into an ash-tray.

'But he was a brilliant lawyer,' he continued. 'The trouble with him was that he didn't like the human race. And he'd got no patience with fools. And as we know, most human beings *are* fools. And there's nothing we can do about it.'

*

To the end of his life my father resolutely ignored my uncle's increasing fame, although at various times such as Willie's eightieth birthday it became quite difficult to do so. One day my father received a letter addressed to Viscount Somerset Maugham. He opened the letter and found that it was intended for Willie, so he sent it to the Villa Mauresque with a tart covering note.

'I was greatly disturbed by the letter you sent on to me,' Willie replied by the next post. 'I know exactly what it is going to be. Shakespeare and Bacon all over again. Posterity will say that as an eminent lawyer and Lord Chancellor it was impossible for you to acknowledge that you had written plays and novels under your own name, so they were produced and published under the insignificant name of your younger brother.'

I was in my father's sitting-room when this letter arrived.

'I detect a distinctly unpleasant flavour about Willie's remarks,' my father commented. 'I think I shall feel myself obliged to make some suitable reply.'

And indeed he did reply – in words to this effect:

Dear Willie,

You may well be right in thinking that you write like Shakespeare. Certainly I have noticed during these last few months an adulation of your name in the more vulgar portions of the popular press. But one word of brotherly advice. *Do not attempt the sonnets.*

*

It is sad that the last book my father wrote was by far the most unsatisfactory. On the jacket of the book is written: *At the End of the Day: an autobiography*, but unfortunately the autobiographical passages occupy less than a seventh of a very long book. During his last years my father became obsessed with the campaigns that had been waged in the two World Wars he had lived through. Why he became so absorbed in grand strategy I shall never know. He had no first-hand knowledge of military problems; he had never fought in a battle; and, so far as I am aware, he never heard a shot fired in anger in his life. But he became determined to give his balanced judgment on complicated plans and manipulations of forces that have baffled most historians. The result was unhappy, for while he devoted only twenty pages to a description of his early days, thirty pages to Cambridge, and thirty-seven to the Bar, his account of the beginning of the first World War, the Dardanelles Campaign, the Battles of 1915, Jutland, Verdun, and of the Somme runs to nearly a hundred pages. As Mr Heuston says, 'The account is, as with everything Maugham wrote, clearly written and trenchantly argued. It is certainly a remarkable performance for a man aged 88 years, but the verdict must be that it is not a permanent contribution to military history.'

One morning, when my father had been at work for three years on his voluminous memoirs, he summoned me to his sitting-room in Cadogan Square.

'I have a question to put to you,' he said. 'It is this. Do you think people would consider it odd if in the autobiography I am now engaged in writing I made no mention of my immediate family?'

For once my father had asked me a question to which I could give a short and simple answer.

'Yes,' I replied.

My father gazed at me mournfully with his large brown eyes.

'I was afraid you would say that,' he said. 'But I have already written nearly a quarter of a million words, and so I'm afraid I can't spare the family very much space. I must therefore ask you to write out for me a brief description of your three sisters and of yourself and of my brother Willie – *in that order*.'

'How brief?' I asked.

'Four lines,' my father replied. 'I can't spare more than four lines in all. And you will kindly bring me those four lines before lunch.'

My father turned his attention back to revising his intricate description of the Battle of the Somme which had been troubling him for some months. The interview was at an end. I went upstairs to my little flat and began my task. The time was half-past twelve.

'My daughter Kate Mary Bruce is a novelist and playwright,' I wrote. And that took one line. 'My daughter Honor Earl is a well-known portrait painter.' That was another line. 'My daughter Diana

Marr-Johnson is a novelist, playwright, and short-story writer.' And there went the third line, leaving only one line for Willie and me to share. And my orders were to put my name next. 'My son Robin writes novels, plays, and stories.' And that was all of half a line gone. How in heaven's name could I describe Willie in six words? I was still trying to solve the ghastly problem when the gong rang for lunch. 'My son Robin writes novels, plays, and stories . . .' I repeated frantically to myself.

'And so does my brother Willie,' I scrawled in despair and went downstairs to hand over my homework.

'That will do very nicely,' my father said after he had read the four lines through.

And thus, in the main, it appears in the book – except that my father changed 'And so does my brother Willie' to the colder-sounding 'I need not describe the works of my brother William Somerset Maugham'. Willie gets only three brief mentions by name in all the five hundred and eighty-seven pages of the book.

*

Kate, the eldest of his four children, did eventually establish a close friendship with my father.

One day, [Kate writes in her unpublished book] it fell to my lot, being the only serious golfer in the family, to accompany my father on a golfing expedition. The filial ice was broken by a niblick so to speak. We made a habit of it. Venturing next into the world of culture, he took me to Denmark, Sweden, Italy, Paris. I found out that he was human; he, I hope, found out that I wasn't entirely half-witted. There is a shaming story about my sisters and me when we were very young: in an unusually expansive mood, our father asked us what we thought was the oldest thing in the house. With one accord we answered, 'You, Daddy.' I had developed since then, however, a thirst for knowledge. I never met a man so generally well informed as he, nor such an indefatigable sightseer. He walked me off my feet in most of the capitals of Europe. Faint and foot-sore, I used to point wistfully to the patient, straw-hatted horses drawn up beside the curb, flies buzzing about their twitching ears, a dusty open carriage behind them, an ancient driver hunched on the box. 'We could always take a clip-clop,' I would point out. But my father was made of sterner stuff. We walked on . . .

*

When Kate at the age of twenty-two sent Willie her first novel,[15] he

wrote to say that he found 'the humour delightful and the whole story
... carried through with vivacity, high spirits and verve'. The words
might well be used to describe Kate's character. He concluded, 'You
have a natural humour which is very valuable and a power of sincere
observation which is admirable ... but do not think success can be
achieved without hard work. It is because they will not work that
women on the whole write less well than men. It is for you to decide
whether you think it worth while to take an infinite amount of pains.
Personally I think it is.'

But Kate, bless her heart, didn't. To Kate, with her vitality and her
wonderful capacity for friendship and sympathy, the business of living
to the full each day was an excitement more rewarding than the labour
of constructing a book. A date for lunch was worth more than a chapter; a friend's troubles poured out into the telephone took precedence
over an afternoon's work. Although these distractions did not affect
her short poems, some of her novels suffered in consequence, but Kate
enjoyed herself when she could, and gave happiness to her family and
to all her friends until the day she died.

*

I would like, at this stage, to write of my sisters Honor and Diana,
but I am stupidly inhibited by affection from doing so. When I was
young I took the warm relationship that existed between us for
granted, but I have since learned that the close understanding the three
of us enjoy today is unusual. Perhaps, as I have mentioned before, it
came as a compensation for the awkwardness we felt in our father's
presence. Certainly it has made up for the sense of deficiency and guilt
that I so often experienced when I was alone with my father. A similar
inhibition prevents me from writing about Kate's son, David Bruce,
who is only a few years younger than I am and who has been more
like a brother than a nephew.

I like to believe that my father forgave me my shortcomings before
his death, for when he was dying he sent for me. I walked through the
dimly-lit gloomy hall of his house in Cadogan Square and entered his
bedroom on the ground floor which looked out on to a narrow lawn,
sparsely covered with grass like a threadbare carpet. My father was
lying in a small bed propped up by pillows, but did not appear to
recognise me. I sat down in the chair beside the bed. After a while I

thought he had gone to sleep, but presently he stirred and turned towards me. He looked up at me with watery eyes.

'Hullo, my boy,' he said. And slowly he stretched out an arm and took my hand. I stayed with him until he went to sleep again. Soon afterwards he died.

WILLIE'S LAST YEARS

THERE were obvious reasons for William Somerset Maugham's un-happiness in his youth. The poor little stammering orphan led a lonely existence in his uncle's bleak vicarage in Whitstable. But when Willie became rich and successful – during the middle period of his life when his plays were being performed throughout Europe and America, when his novels and stories were being published all over the world, when he became one of the best-known writers alive – why did he still seem so discontented? Why did every chance of permanent happiness elude him?

I found out some of the answers to these questions during the frequent visits I made to the Villa Mauresque in the last years of his life.

*

One spring morning my uncle Willie's temper had been uncertain from the moment he awoke. When I went into his bedroom I found him sitting up in bed with a pillar-box red shawl round his shoulders. He was reading the Bible. The photograph of his mother stood, as it always did, on the table beside his bed.

'Good morning, Willie,' I said.

He glared at me with his small, yellowish eyes.

'*What* was that?' he demanded, trembling in a sudden rage. '*What* did you say?'

'I said "good morning",' I shouted.

This seemed to appease him. His hands stopped shaking and he looked up at me more calmly.

'Well, at least your remark is to the point,' he said. 'It is both apt and truthful – for it *is* a good morning. And I have been amusing myself by reading in the Book of Samuel about Saul and David and Jonathan. *That* was a queer ménage if ever there was one. I can't imagine what the parsons do when they have to preach about it. What *can* they make of it? They must realise that all three of those men were in love with

W. Somerset Maugham (*right*), with his daughter Liza and his brother
Frederic, at an exhibition of his manuscripts and first editions, 26 January,
1954

W. Somerset Maugham and Alan Searle

each other. It's a quite fascinating story. Think what a play it would make! By the way, we're lunching in Nice today with some old friends of mine. We shall leave here at half past twelve. So don't be late.'

'I won't,' I promised.

As I left the room he gave me a benign smile. His good humour had returned.

But when at half past twelve he came down the marble steps of the Villa Mauresque leaning on the arm of Alan Searle, his friend, companion, and secretary, his bad temper had returned. His mouth was pursed, and he looked cross and sulky, like a small boy who has been dragged out of bed and dressed in his best clothes by his nanny to be presented to the grown-ups in the drawing-room. And he sat in grim silence while the old Rolls, driven by Jean his faithful chauffeur, clattered and bumped its way along the Corniche in the brilliant sunshine. As we drove past the old port in Nice, Alan turned to Willie.

'What time would you like the car to come to take you back?' Alan asked.

'As soon as we arrive,' Willie snapped.

Alan gave me a worried look. Willie at ninety was unpredictable. Anything could happen from one moment to the next. And it was Alan – untiring, loyal, patient Alan – who had to cope. I honestly believe that had it not been for Alan's unceasing care and devotion during the last years of Willie's life my uncle would have gone mad or killed himself.

'Millicent is an old friend of yours,' Alan said. 'And she's giving a little lunch-party in your honour. She'll be very disappointed if you don't come.'

'Then she'll have to be disappointed, won't she?' Willie replied.

But when the car drew up outside the block of flats behind the Promenade des Anglais we managed to persuade Willie to get out of the car and we escorted him to the lift. Our hostess was waiting on the landing outside her flat to greet us as we stepped out of the lift door.

'Willie!' she cried. 'Welcome, darling!'

And she gave him a smacking kiss on both cheeks. For a moment Willie did not move. He stared at her in silent distaste. Then he spoke.

'There's only one excuse for plump women like you,' he said. 'And that is that they should have no clothes on.'

'Oh, you're so witty, Willie!' Millicent tittered a trifle nervously.

'No, I'm not,' Willie replied. 'I'm perfectly serious. Take off all your clothes. I want to see what you've got.'

Millicent gave a strained laugh and turned to us.

'Isn't he witty!' she exclaimed once again.

'If you don't take your clothes off, I shan't come to lunch,' Willie said firmly.

Millicent's smile froze and she fixed her faded eyes on Alan in appeal for help. As usual Alan saved the situation, and a few moments later, while we were being introduced to Millicent's guests, Willie was his usual courteous self. And the lunch party was a success.

But when he got back to the Villa Mauresque Willie looked exhausted. Alan went to answer the telephone. Suddenly Willie buried his head in his hands.

'I've been a failure,' he stammered. 'The whole way through my life I've made mistake after mistake. I've had a wretched life. And I've made a hash of everything.'

It was no good my trying to remind him of his achievements as a playwright and a novelist and as the greatest short-story writer of the century. He was plunged in self-pity.

Why was William Somerset Maugham so convinced he was a failure? Why was he so miserable?

The first reason, I believe, is that his character was permanently warped by the bitter years he spent in his uncle's vicarage and by the lean period that followed his decision to give up being a doctor in order to become an author. My uncle Willie never forgot his experience of what he called the 'grinding agony of poverty which befalls persons who have to live among those richer than themselves'.

'I hated poverty,' he said. 'I hated having to scrape and save so as to make both ends meet.'

He never forgot his disappointment that the success of his first novel *Liza of Lambeth* brought him only £20 in royalties, due to an astute contract drawn up by his publisher Fisher Unwin. For a while he was tormented by the prospect of being forced to give up his career as a writer, to admit defeat and to make use of his medical knowledge by taking a job as ship's doctor. The humiliations that Willie suffered during those early years throbbed bitterly to the end of his life.

*

No wonder my uncle was so desperately nervous at the first nights of his early plays. Each one was a threat of defeat.

'Went to the first night of Willie's play *A Man of Honour*,' says an entry in my mother's diary for February 1903. 'Very enthusiastic audience, and it was quite well acted. Willie was pale with terror!'

But the Stage Society gave only two performances of *A Man of Honour*, and theatre managers continued to reject Willie's plays for the next four years. Then at last his luck changed. Otto Stuart, the manager of the Court Theatre, needed a play to fill in six odd weeks while he was casting another production, and he took a gamble on *Lady Frederick*.

'To dine at the Berkeley and then on to Willie's play *Lady Frederick*,' my mother wrote on October 26, 1907. 'Willie was very pale and silent. He sat at the back of the box. The play was an enormous success. It is very witty and interesting. I believe it will prove a success with the public. Willie gave a supper-party for 22 of us at the Bath Club, all the cast.'

My mother was right about the play's success. It was a smash hit. Within a year three more plays of Willie's were produced, and at last the money began to pour in. It has flowed in copiously ever since. The sad thing is that it did not bring him happiness.

'Money,' he said once, 'is a sixth sense without which you can't make the most of the other five.'

Even after the triumph of his talent had made him a millionaire, my uncle's attitude towards money was tinged by the memories of his penury. And he was appalled by the extravagance of the younger members of his family and particularly my own.

In 1945 I was staying with Willie at the Ritz-Carlton in New York, and both of us were being treated by the same doctor. One day Willie discovered that his appointment with Dr Max Wolf was at five in the afternoon and mine was at five-thirty.

'I'll wait on there for you,' Willie said. 'And we can go back to-gether.'

'Fine,' I said.

When Dr Wolf had finished examining my head injury I collected Willie from the waiting-room and we left the building together. It was a bitterly cold night, and snow was lying thickly on the sidewalk. I was just about to hail a taxi when Willie spoke.

'Which bus stop do you find the closer?' he asked. 'The one on Fifth Avenue or the one on Park.'

'I find them much the same,' I replied quite truthfully, for I had always taken a taxi back from Dr Wolf's consulting room.

'I believe the one in Fifth Avenue's the best,' Willie said, and began to trudge slowly through the snow towards it. I followed, feeling rather guilty. If Dr Wolf had seen my uncle's green, frozen face as we waited for that bus I think he would have been most annoyed. After all, Willie had recently made half a million dollars out of *The Razor's Edge*, so for the sake of his health you might have thought that he could afford a taxi. But no. There we stood at the bus stop shivering in an icy wind.

But worse was to come. When at last we clambered stiffly into the bus, Willie fumbled in his pockets and then turned to me.

'I've got no small change on me,' he stammered. 'So you'll have to pay for us both.'

At that moment an enormous bus conductor bore down on me with a huge slot-machine slung round his neck. I had never been on a bus in New York before, but I didn't dare tell Willie, and it was obvious that the conductor expected me to put a coin in his slot. But what coin? I panicked. I felt wildly in my pocket and produced a quarter. Frantically I tried to push the coin into one of the slots but it wouldn't fit.

'Guess it's your first time on a bus,' the conductor said, breezily.

'Yes,' I hissed.

And Willie didn't help. He just looked at me very mournfully and said nothing. But he had a lot to say about it later.

*

Willie delighted in the fortune he had amassed and he frequently contemplated and drew attention to the plight of authors who had failed on the road to success or fallen by the wayside. This concern with their misfortune led to his generous gifts and bequests to such societies as might benefit struggling writers; it also occasionally led to his convincing himself that some famous author was 'poverty-stricken' when in fact he was flourishing.

Every evening after dinner at the Villa Mauresque, in the days before the war, Annette, his famous cook, would come in with the menu book and stand behind his chair, and Willie would put on his spectacles to order the meals for the following day. This would be the moment when all of us staying at the villa would know who was coming to lunch the next day. If a successful author was coming – let us call him Vivian Parry – Willie would take this opportunity to begin his ploy of making us believe that the man was penniless.

I took notes each time that this happened, so I am able to reproduce a specific occasion in 1938.

As Annette stood behind his chair Willie removed his spectacles and looked up at us mournfully.

'Vivian is coming to lunch tomorrow,' he announced.

We all murmured approval. We all knew Vivian Parry, and we all liked him.

'Poor Vivian,' Willie said sadly, 'I suppose you know that he's right down on his uppers?'

'Down on his uppers!' someone exclaimed in astonishment. 'I thought he was rolling in money.'

'He *was*,' Willie said, 'but it's all gone. Every penny of it. His novels don't sell as well as they used to. His last two plays were a flop. His backers lost their shirts. And I'm told that all poor Vivian's investments have gone down the drain. He hasn't got a cent left.'

We were all left speechless by this information.

'He won't have had a square meal for weeks,' Willie continued. 'So we'd better give him something substantial.'

Willie turned to Annette.

'*Alors pour commencer on prendrait une soupe à l'oignon,*' he said. '*Et ensuite un steak-et-kidney pudding. Et pour terminer un soufflé au chocolat.*'

'*Bien, monsieur,*' said Annette. '*Bonsoir, monsieur.*'

'*Bonsoir, Annette,*' said Willie, and turned once again to us.

'You know, when people are down on their luck they're apt to get rather touchy,' he said. 'So I must ask you to be here waiting for him at a quarter to one tomorrow when Vivian arrives. I don't want him to feel ser-slighted.'

By this time Willie had managed to convince even the most doubtful of us that Vivian wasn't quite as successful as we had supposed. So punctually at a quarter to one on that hot summer day we were assembled waiting to greet the famous (but apparently now down-at-heel) writer. And punctually Vivian Parry arrived. He looked very well-fed and extremely affluent, and indeed we were subsequently to discover that he was both.

'Willie!' he cried. '*Cher maître!*' And he embraced him warmly. Willie gently detached himself.

'I'm sure you need a cocktail,' Willie said with a meaning look towards us.

'I'd love one,' Vivian said, sprightly as ever.

Vivian was given his cocktail first, and by the time the shaker had been handed round the room, Vivian, who was rather disconcerted by our surreptitious glances towards his shoes, had finished his glass.

'Vivian would like *another* cocktail,' Willie said.

And Vivian's glass was refilled.

'*Monsieur est servi,*' the butler announced.

And in we went to lunch – with Vivian still sparkling gaily but perhaps slightly nervously.

By the time he had finished the steaming bowl of onion soup, beads of sweat stood out on Vivian's forehead and the bright torrent of his conversation had been reduced to a trickle. When the steak-and-kidney pudding was brought in, he raised his eyes in silent anguish to the ceiling.

'*Servez bien Monsieur Parry,*' said Willie. '*Il a l'air d'avoir faim.* He looks quite famished.'

Vivian stared down in dismay at the vast helping on his plate. But Vivian was always polite and splendidly gallant, and he finished every bit of it. Then, round came the chocolate soufflé sizzling in the torrid Riviera heat, and Vivian's eyes once again rolled plaintively to the ceiling. But once more he got through it manfully, though his shirt was now drenched with sweat.

After coffee and liqueurs I escorted Vivian to his car. He was exhausted by sheer weight of food. It was with an effort that he spoke at all.

'Wonderful old boy!' Vivian said. 'But a trifle over-hospitable, don't you think?'

'I suppose you noticed how quickly he drank his first two cocktails.' Willie was saying when I came back into the house. 'He obviously needed a decent drink. And did you see how he wolfed down the steak-and-kidney pudding? *And* the chocolate soufflé? He probably hadn't had a ser-square meal for weeks.'

*

I discovered a second reason for Willie's unhappiness a few days later during my stay on that occasion at the Villa Mauresque.

We had dined alone together, and Marius the butler had come into the drawing-room to clear away our coffee cups and to say goodnight. Willie had been silent for a while. I looked up and saw tears flowing down his wrinkled, sallow cheeks.

'I've been such a fool,' he cried. 'And the awful thing is that if I had my life all over again I'd probably make exactly the same mistakes.'

'What mistakes?' I asked.

'Mer-my greatest one was this,' he stammered, 'I tried to persuade myself that I was three-quarters normal and that only a quarter of me was queer – whereas really it was the other way round.'

It was in 1913, when my uncle Willie was thirty-nine years old, that he met the woman he later married. Syrie was the daughter of the well-known philanthropist, Dr Thomas Barnardo, and still married to Henry (later Sir Henry) Wellcome, of the firm of Burroughs, Wellcome, the chemists. She was small and smart and pretty. She had radiant brown eyes and a beautiful skin; she had high spirits and was endowed with a brilliant vivacity that lasted until the day she died. Willie was flattered when she made it clear that she was attracted to him. He very much wanted to lead a normal sex-life, and it is interesting that in his autobiography, written when he was well over eighty years old, he was proud to be able to write, 'In the circles in which we moved it was an understood thing that I was Syrie's lover.'

He married Syrie in 1916. But quite apart from the obvious incompatibility of temperaments, the marriage was bound to have failed – because even before he married Syrie, Willie had met the young American named Gerald Haxton.

'There's no point in trying to change your essential nature,' Willie had said after he had told me of his meeting in the Ritz-Carlton with his American cousin. 'One hasn't a hope.'

But Willie still tried to change. He was socially ambitious and he kept up his heterosexual pretence in public to the end of his life. This was displayed in its most unpleasant form in the sections of his autobiography which were published in the *Sunday Express* in England and in *Show* magazine in America. In it Willie dismisses Gerald with the words, 'I had found him a very useful companion,' and he puts all the blame for the failure of his marriage on to Syrie.

The truth is that with a few exceptions Willie did not like the opposite sex. The only really pleasant heroine in any of his books is Rosie in
Cakes and Ale, and he cannot resist bringing her back at the end as a
stout, over-made-up, seventy-year-old matron with a double chin and
rubber corsets. Women irritated him – particularly those who seemed
pleased with themselves – as the following story shows.

I had lunched with him and we were waiting for his car outside the
Dorchester. There were half-a-dozen Rolls Royces but not one of
them belonged to Willie. It was a cold windy day and after we had
waited for ten minutes Willie looked quite green. I suggested taking
a taxi.

'No,' Willie said. 'The car's bound to turn up any moment now.'
At that instant a large, sleek Rolls drew up in front of us.

'This one's mine,' Willie said, and moved quickly towards it.

But the Rolls didn't belong to Willie; it belonged to a stout mink-
clad lady of about sixty with dyed hair and heavy make-up. The porter
opened the car door for her and she got out followed by a handsome,
flashily-dressed young man who was obviously a gigolo. Suddenly she
recognised Willie who was looking very crossly at the Rolls that didn't
belong to him.

'Willie!' she cried and teetered over to him and kissed him on both
cheeks.

Willie did not move. He stared at her calmly without a flicker of
recognition.

'You remember me,' the woman said, beginning to lose her nerve.
'I'm Mabel Swope.'

My uncle gazed at her with silent loathing.

'You stayed with us in our penthouse in Johannesburg,' the woman
continued. 'Surely you remember. It's not all *that* long ago.'

At last Willie spoke.

'I remember,' he said. 'But I was sorry to hear that you'd lost all your
money.'

The woman swung round as if she had been stung.

'What's that?' she cried.

'That's what I was told,' Willie said. 'Every cent of it.'

The woman forced herself to smile at him brightly.

'I'm afraid there's some mistake,' she said. 'I haven't lost any money.'
Her smile by now was stretched tight.

'Every penny per-piece,' Willie said firmly.

'I can assure you that your informant must have been mistaken,' the woman said, fingering a thick diamond bracelet. 'Completely and utterly mistaken.'

And she swept off into the Dorchester followed by a crestfallen gigolo. I turned to Willie.

'Who in heaven's name was that?' I asked.

'I haven't the fer-foggiest idea,' Willie answered placidly.

'Then *why* did you tell the poor woman that you'd heard she'd lost all her money?' I asked.

'Because she looked so pleased with herself,' Willie replied, moving towards his car that had appeared at last.

*

I stayed with Willie frequently during the last years of his life, and I can see him with odd clarity as I now write these words.

His face was very lined and the colour of parchment. His fading eyes looked out on the world without any illusion and without much interest, for he had seen it all so many times before. His hands and feet were small, and he was short in height, but he moved with dignity and his gestures were full of authority. In the evening when he had changed into a double-breasted quilted smoking-jacket and black trousers, and put on his black velvet shoes with his monogram stitched on the toes in gold braid, he looked like a Chinese mandarin – ancient, fragile, wise, and benign, and almost wholly detached from the trivial problems of the world.

At ninety Willie led a quiet but comfortable life at the Villa Mauresque. He had six servants and four gardeners. He was looked after by Alan Searle, who had been with him constantly since the end of the war. If ever the over-used words 'loyalty and devotion' meant anything, Alan Searle exemplified them. The villa ran smoothly.

But Willie had retired from work. He no longer climbed the narrow stairs each morning that led up to his writing-room built on the roof of the house. He now stayed either in the patio or in the drawing-room, reading books – mainly detective stories. Time seemed to hang on his hands. In the Villa Mauresque one could hear the clocks ticking.

His mind often rambled, but he still enjoyed displaying his skill as a *raconteur*. Certainly I have never known anyone tell a story so well as

Willie. Even as a child I can remember listening with fascination to the stories he would relate when he came to lunch with my father and mother. Somehow he seemed to be able to use the stammer that occasionally checked him as a lever to lend balance to his sentence or to give dramatic effect. From time to time Willie would tell a story as well as ever – the tale which was still in his mind but which he no longer had any inclination to write.

We were talking about Fiji which I had recently visited.

'I was in Fiji,' Willie said, 'but it was during the first World War so I expect it's all changed since then. But I remember I got a very unusual story when I was there. It's always stuck in my mind, but I never wrote it.

'There were two Englishmen who lived out in Fiji together. I can't remember what their jobs were. I think they may have been Government officials. Anyhow, they shared a house on the outskirts of Suva, and they were close friends. They'd lived together perfectly happily for over ten years.

'Now both of them were fond of dogs, but strangely enough they hadn't had a dog since they'd been out there together.

'One evening at the Club an old friend of theirs asked them if they'd like a spaniel. He was going back to England and he didn't want to take the dog with him, and he wanted to find a good home for it.

'And since they'd always wanted to have a dog they said they'd take the spaniel.

'So they put the spaniel in the back of their car that very night and drove home to the *bure*, their shack by the Pacific. And the dog was a great success. Both of them became devoted to it. Each of them did his best to make the dog happy and to make it forget the loss of its previous owner.

'But gradually as the weeks passed by, the two friends began to get desperately jealous of each other.

'Each of them wanted the dog to like him best. Each of them wanted the dog to come up to him and make a fuss of him. And as the days wore by, their jealousy of each other became intense, and their fiercely possessive obsession over the dog began to poison their relationship. They began to quarrel almost incessantly. They began to hate each other.'

Willie paused in telling me the story – as he always did to obtain dramatic effect.

'At last one of them could bear the strain no longer. And he realised there was only one solution. He took out the dog they both loved so much,' Willie said, clasping and unclasping his hands as the story's dramatic value gripped him. 'He had taken the revolver that he kept locked up in his desk. He led the spaniel away from the shack, and he shot the dog stone dead.'

Willie took a sip of the pink champagne that Marius had poured into his glass.

'You must admit that it's an unusual story,' he said. 'And you know, I'm sure it's a true story. It's got the ring of truth about it. I live alone with Alan, and we have a dachshund as you know. And I notice I am quite upset if the dog makes more fuss of Alan than of me.'

*

'But I think that was almost the only story that I got in Fiji,' Willie continued. 'As you know, you don't just get a story. You have to wait for it to come to you. I've never written a story in my life. The story has come to me *and demanded to be written.*'

Willie sighed.

'You know, when I look back on all the stories I've had published,' he said, 'I simply don't know how they ever came to be written.'

Willie was silent as Marius handed round some roast partridge and hot slaw.

'But I suppose I *must* have written the stories, because I'm famous now,' he said. 'And now I'm famous, people invite me to meals and to parties just so that they can show me off.

'In Singapore we were invited out to dinner, and when we arrived we discovered it was a great party. All the ladies were in long dresses with their jewels on. All the men were in black ties. And we stood about drinking, and I was introduced to one person after another. At about eleven, Alan went to our host and asked when we were going to have dinner. And our host said, "Oh, about midnight I expect". So Alan said I was very old and must eat at once. But they wouldn't do anything about it. So we left them and went back to our hotel and dined there.'

Willie lit a cigarette and watched the smoke he exhaled rising into the air.

'People simply want to show me off,' he repeated. 'Now I'm famous everybody wants to meet me. People I haven't seen for thirty years write me letters saying, "Darling Willie, we must meet." Each one of them thinks they're the only pebble on the beach. And it isn't really me they want to meet at all. They don't care a rap about me.'

At that moment he looked very old and tired.

'Sometimes I wish I'd never written a single story,' Willie muttered.

'But all the same,' I said to cheer him up, 'it must be satisfactory to have done something better than anyone else.'

Willie smiled.

'I must confess that I'd never seen it in that light before,' he said. 'Though now you mention it I have to admit that I do see your point,' he added with a chuckle. 'But it doesn't give me pride, and it doesn't give me pleasure. And being so famous has a lot of disadvantages.'

Over coffee we talked about a mutual friend who lived in Bangkok.

'You know, in Siam they're sensible,' Willie said suddenly. 'They don't regard homosexuality as anything abnormal. They accept it as something perfectly natural. . . . And I believe that one day people will realise that there are people who are *born* homosexual. And there's nothing whatsoever that they can do about it . . . Did I tell you the astonishing story I was told when I was in Japan?'

'No,' I said.

'Well, there was a European banker who had a young Japanese friend, a boy of about eighteen. The boy was devoted to him, and they lived together. But their relationship became so notorious about town that the banker's employers came to him and told him that the scandal was such that he must break with the boy for good and all, or be sacked . . .

'So the banker broke the news to his friend and invited him out for a farewell dinner. And after dinner they went back to his apartment. And the boy asked him, "Are you certain that we've got to part?" And he said "Yes." And the boy asked, "For good?" And the man said, "I'm afraid so." And the boy took out a knife and plunged it into his stomach and disembowelled himself . . . You know, that was really true love, wasn't it?'

Marius handed round an ice-cream made from the avocado pears that Willie grew in his garden. Willie continued reminiscently.

'It must have been in 1916 that I was out in Fiji. It was the year before I was sent to Russia. You know, in 1917 I was sent to Russia on a secret mission. I'd been in the secret service for some time. That's why I'd been sent out to the Pacific. But Sir William Wiseman, the head of British Intelligence in America, recalled me to Washington. And I was given a vast sum of money by the American and the British Governments. And I was sent to Petrograd. You see, they sent me out there because they thought that I could stop the Bolshevik Revolution.'

Willie clasped and unclasped his hands again.

'With the money they'd given me – half of it was provided by America and half by England – I was supposed to help the Mensheviks buy arms and finance newspapers so as to keep Russia in the war and to prevent the Bolsheviks from seizing power. I told them I was the wrong man for the job, but they wouldn't believe me. They thought that my being a writer was a good cover for my activities. You see, on the surface of it I was visiting Russia to write articles on conditions there for the *Daily Telegraph*.'

For a while Willie was silent. Into his eyes had crept a look of intense sadness.

'I feel a deep sense of failure,' he said, 'complete and utter failure.'

'Why?' I asked.

'As I've told you, my job was to stop the Revolution. It was a huge responsibility. I can't imagine why they ever chose me. If they'd known me better they'd never have picked me, I'm sure of that. I'd no experience of that kind of thing at all. I didn't know where to begin. I was the wrong man for the job. And then they asked me to go down into Roumania, and I might have had some hope there. But I didn't go. And I should have.'

Alan leant across the dinner table and spoke slowly and clearly.

'You didn't go because if you *had* gone you'd have died of tuberculosis,' Alan said.

'I daresay,' Willie replied, 'but if I'd been more competent and if I'd been less sick, perhaps I could have gone, and perhaps I'd have been able to stop the Revolution as it then happened.'

Willie took a cigarette from the little silver box beside him and lit it.

'But apart from anything else, you can have no idea what a disadvantage my stammer was to me when I was a secret agent. One morning in the autumn Kerensky sent for me and gave me a message for Lloyd George. It was so secret that he wouldn't put it in writing. But when I got back to London I wrote the message down because I knew that when I came to tell it to the Prime Minister I'd begin to stammer. Lloyd George was in a hurry when I met him, so I just handed him what I'd written out. And he only glanced at the note. If I'd read the memo out to him it might have made all the difference. And perhaps the world today might be a very different place. But I made a hash of the whole business. And that's why I consider myself a failure.'

*

It is difficult to write objectively about a close relation one has known intimately, but I have tried to be as kind as I can about my uncle Willie. However, kindness and truth do not always coincide. So far, I have tried to explain that my uncle was unhappy in his youth because he was shy and lonely, and unhappy in his middle age because of the unresolved social conflicts in his life. I would like to be able to say that in old age – all struggles past, all conflicts resolved – he lived from seventy into his nineties in placid contentment. But I cannot. During the last years of Willie's life, certainly a benign acceptance of the defects of human nature calmed the surface of his character, but beneath this benevolence there smouldered fires of hatred that occasionally erupted. And he neither forgot nor forgave. For instance, he never forgave his former wife Syrie for the harm he imagined she had caused him. During the second World War he happened to meet her at a party and she came up to greet him.

'I am crossing the Atlantic and I am terrified of torpedoes,' she said. 'And I can't swim, so what should I do if the boat were to sink, and there was I floundering in the water?'

'Ser-swallow,' Willie stammered. 'Just ser-swallow.'

Syrie died in July 1955. Willie heard the news of her death when he was sitting playing patience at a card-table at the Villa Mauresque: immediately he put down the pack and began to drum with his fingers on the table in a triumphant tattoo.

'Tra-la-la-la,' he sang. 'No more alimony. Tra-la, tra-la.'

But though Willie did not mourn her death, Syrie had a host of admirers who did. For many years she was a professional interior decorator, and her flair was responsible in the 1920s – both in England and in America – for the vogue of the off-white drawing-room. Like most of us she could be bitter about her enemies, but she was devotedly loyal to her friends, who displayed their affection by subscribing for a memorial to her – a magnificent marble bust of Catherine the Great by Fedot Shubin – which was presented in October 1964 to the Victoria and Albert Museum. *How appropriate!*

*

Towards the end of his life, Willie's eyesight was so impaired that he could seldom read; he was very deaf; and his mind appeared to be tormented by remorse.

'I've been a horrible and evil man,' he said to me. 'Every single one of the few people who have ever got to know me well has ended up by hating me.'

Restless and distraught he would wander past the marble-and-gilt furniture in the high-ceilinged rooms and drift like a shaking ghost through the whitewashed patios. In the long drawing-room his magnificent collection of Impressionists had gone – the money from its sale at Sotheby's had given rise to an unfortunate law-suit which continued to distress him even after it had been settled. His Zoffanys and other theatrical paintings had been put back on the off-white walls. He had made them over to the National Theatre at his death, and he had made over his villa to his daughter Liza, who is now Lady Glendevon.

Sometimes his mind was pathetically confused. 'You know, all of this only belongs to me during my life-time,' he said to me mournfully, as we walked along a green glade between the eucalyptus and pine trees in his garden. 'When I die, they'll take it all away from me – every tree, the whole house, and every stick of furniture. I shan't even be able to take a single table with me.'

For a while he was silent as we walked through a grove of orange trees.

'Jesus Christ could cope with all the miseries I have had to contend with in life,' Willie said. Then he stopped walking and peered gloomily across the tops of the trees towards the blue sea beyond. 'But then Jesus Christ had advantages I don't possess,' he added.

On the way out to the terrace after lunch that day, he leaned his head against the wall at the top of the steps and burst into tears.

'I'm so miserable,' he said. 'Why can't they let me die?'

His grief was heart-rending, yet later that afternoon he was making plans to visit the famous clinic in Switzerland that gave him life-preserving injections. Though some part of his nature clung to life almost to the end, he tried to make himself believe that he was not afraid of death itself.

'There are moments when I have so palpitating an eagerness for death that I could fly to it as to the arms of a lover . . .' he wrote in *The Summing Up*.[1] 'I am drunk with the thought of it. It seems to me then to offer me the final and absolute freedom.'

At other times Willie treated the prospect of his demise with a deliberate flippancy. An utter stranger wrote a letter to him which began: 'Since I intend to communicate with you in the next world, perhaps I had better tell you something about myself in this one.'

Willie put down the letter and turned to me.

'Perhaps I should put an advertisement in the Personal Column of *The Times*,' he said. 'I could use words something to this effect: "Mr Somerset Maugham declines to communicate with, or receive communications from, *anyone* in the next world – with or without an introduction."'

*

I was the only guest at the Villa Mauresque for the week-end of Willie's ninetieth birthday. Telegrams and presents flowed in from all over the world. The villa was besieged by reporters and camera-men.

'I really don't know what they're making all this fuss about,' said Willie. 'They cer-can't seriously think it's important. It's all extremely tiresome.'

'Never mind,' Alan said cheerfully. 'Your next important birthday won't be until you're a hundred.'

'I don't suppose I shall live that long.'

'In Nice there's a pensioner who's a hundred and four,' Alan said. 'And they say he's quite spry.'

'A hundred and four!' Willie said. 'No! I definitely refuse to live to a hundred and four. I don't like the sound of it at all.'

Throughout that day a black fog seemed to envelop his mind, and his intelligence only shone out intermittently through the darkness like the beam of the lighthouse on Cap Ferrat which I could see that night flickering through the trees of the broad terrace outside the over-heated drawing-room.

The older Willie became the more he longed for death and the more he dreaded it. And the older he grew, the sadder he became as he looked

The garden at the Villa Mauresque

W. Somerset Maugham and Robin Maugham in the garden at the Villa Mauresque

back on his failures. But remorse for opportunities missed is not unique to Willie. The reality in life is never as fine as the original dream. All of us, if we are honest, know that our achievements are tawdry compared with our first untarnished ambitions. And this is a universal tragedy.

*

'If you believe in prayer,' Willie said to me when he was ninety, 'then pray that I don't wake up in the morning. That's the best thing that could possibly happen to me.'

This was the final cause of Willie's unhappiness. His life had not worked out according to his plans. In *The Summing Up*, at the age of sixty, he had written, 'For my own satisfaction, for my amusement and to gratify what feels to me like an organic need, I have shaped my life in accordance with a certain design, with a beginning, a middle, and an end . . .' He thought, then, that he was near to the end of his carefully shaped existence. And at seventy, 'ten years closer to death', he felt that the end had been reached. In *A Writer's Notebook* he wrote[2]:

> When I was forty I said to myself: 'That is the end of youth.' On my fiftieth birthday I said: 'It's no good fooling myself, this is middle age and I may just as well accept it.' At sixty I said: 'Now it's time to put my affairs in order, for this is the threshold of old age and I must settle my accounts.' I decided to withdraw from the theatre and I wrote *The Summing Up*, in which I tried to review for my own comfort what I had learnt of life and literature, what I had done and what satisfaction it had brought me. But of all anniversaries I think the seventieth is the most momentous. One has reached the three score years and ten which one is accustomed to accept as the allotted span of man, and one can but look upon such years as remain to one as uncertain contingencies stolen while old Time with his scythe has his head turned the other way.

'I have had enough,' he concluded. But his eightieth birthday came – and then his ninetieth. And still he lived on. But by then the whole shape of his life had been distorted, and in the intervals between the periods of occlusion Willie realised it. He was aware of the deterioration of his mind and body. He was acutely conscious of the squalor of old age and of its shames and defeats. But though part of him longed for what he believed would definitely be the complete and final oblivion, there was a relentless force in him that bound him to the wheel of life. At sixty he had spoken approvingly of suicide:

15

'I wonder why so many people turn with horror from the thought of suicide. To speak of it as cowardly is nonsense. I can only approve the man who makes an end of himself in his own will when life has nothing to offer him but pain and misfortune. Did not Pliny say that the power of dying when you please is the best thing that God has given to man amid all the sufferings of life?'

But in his eighties the obstinately persevering life force was present to halt his hand as it stretched towards the bottle of barbiturates next to the photograph of his mother on the bedside table.

*

After his ninetieth birthday Willie's moods grew more violent, and he seemed more tormented. He would sit muttering angrily to himself in a corner of the drawing-room, and he was apt to fly into a sudden rage with any one of the few guests who were invited to the house. Sometimes his face was contorted with malevolence and his small eyes glittered with hatred, and he would jabber obscenities. Then the fit would leave him, and he would bury his face in his hands, moaning that he was a horribly evil man. On such frightening occasions I would find an odd thought entering my head. I would wonder if in some way Willie's remorse sprang from a feeling that he had at some stage made a pact with the powers of evil. Perhaps he believed that the Devil had come to him in his youth and said, 'I will make you the most famous writer alive if you will give me your soul,' and Willie had answered, 'Done!' And now the Devil was coming to claim what belonged to him.

But I must try to forget Willie in his nineties. I must remember him as he was when I first got to know him well during the years before the war. I must think of excursions with him and Gerald Haxton on their yacht. I will remember long happy days with the deck gleaming in the sunshine of Villefranche Bay, and I will recall Willie's kindness to me then, and I will recall his wit.

His wit never altogether left him to the end.

'Dying', he said to me, 'is a very dull, dreary affair.' Suddenly he smiled. 'And my advice to you is to have nothing whatever to do with it,' he added.

*

Willie died on December 16, 1965. Looking back, I realise that though

I sometimes feared him, I was fond of him; but I am afraid I never understood him. Very few of his friends ever pierced the layers of morbid shyness caused by the misery of his youth; few ever caught a glimpse of his real character.

In the most brilliant of all his novels, *Cakes and Ale*, published in 1930, Willie writes this about the old and world-famous writer, 'Edward Driffield':

I had an impression that the real man, to his death unknown and lonely, was a wraith that went a silent way unseen between the writer of his books and the man who led his life, and smiled with an ironical detachment at the two puppets that the world took for Edward Driffield.

For 'Edward Driffield' in that quotation many people have substituted the name 'Thomas Hardy'. But I am convinced that it is a true description of William Somerset Maugham.

Notes

NOTES

Chapter 1   The Village Schoolmaster

1. Arthur Mee's *Lincolnshire* and W. F. Rawnsley's *Highways and Byways of Lincolnshire*.
2. *History of the Moulton Endowed Schools*, Rev. J. Russell Jackson (1890).
3. *The Victoria History of the County of Lincolnshire* (London, 1906), vol. ii.
4. The School was 'amalgamated' with Spalding Grammar School in 1939 and the buildings at Moulton were closed.
5. By the Rev. H. I. Longden (Archer & Goodman, Northampton, 16 vols., 1938–52).
6. The choice of Magdalene is interesting. Although William was no longer a boy, it is possible that he was given one of the valuable exhibitions, known as Holmes Scholarships, which are appropriated to Wisbech Grammar School. This is one of the many links in the long association between Wisbech and Cambridge which began in the sixth century when bands of Engles pushed their way up the Ouse and the Cam and made their settlements beside the river.
7. This was evident from the documents in my chintz-covered box and from the entry about William in Longden's *Northamptonshire and Rutland Clergy*, which reads: 'Rectory Pilton, Rutland, instituted 19th July 1762. Resigned 1764.'
8. William's arrival at St Martin's in 1759 was confirmed by an entry – a 'true copy' of a page from the register of baptisms – written in William's own hand, with the date April 23, 1759, and his bold signature, 'Wm. Maugham, Curate'.
9. I have never been able to discover precisely when or where the Reverend William Maugham married Susanna Reid, but their eldest child, also called Susanna, was baptised at St George's in Stamford on July 3, 1764.
10. *History of Stamford School*, B. L. Deed (1954), p. 34.
11. The date for this sermon can be fixed as November 29, 1759 – the day appointed by a proclamation by King George II some weeks earlier as 'a day of solemn thanksgiving ... through all the dominions of Great Britain'. The news of the great victory in this 'first world war', as Churchill calls it in his *History of the English Speaking Peoples*, had reached London on October 16. The dispatch from Wolfe two days earlier had caused despondency, and so the late news of victory was greeted with wild and public joy tempered only by the report that the

thirty-two-year-old General had died 'in the arms of victory' – as Nelson was to die at Trafalgar forty-six years later.

12. On August 1, 1798 – almost four months earlier than the sermon. In the spring of 1798 the French revolutionary executive had urged Napoleon to invade England, but he preferred instead to conquer Egypt in the hope of founding an Empire in the East. On May 19 he sailed from Toulon with his army and a large fleet, and on July 13 and 21 he defeated the Sultan's troops at the battles of the Pyramids. But Napoleon had not reckoned with Nelson, who sailed after him, found his fleet, and anchored in Aboukir Bay, east of Alexandria. The battle began before sunset. Napoleon's fleet was utterly destroyed. Only two of his ships of the line and two frigates escaped. Napoleon's army, now cut off from France, was defeated by Sir Ralph Abercromby nineteen months later, and the Mediterranean became once again a British sea.

13. The Reverend William preached his sermon more than six weeks after the battle (October 21, 1805) and more than a month after the news of Nelson's victory over Villeneuve's fleet had reached England.

14. In his sermon written 'for Nelson's Victory in the Nile' and delivered on November 29, 1798.

15. Sermon delivered on December 19, 1797.

16. *The Summing Up* (Penguin ed.), p. 176.

Chapter 2   The Captain of the Forecastle

1. Lord Bridport (Alexander Hood, the brother of Lord Hood) was then Commander-in-Chief of the Channel Fleet, which was preoccupied with blockading the French fleet in Brest.

2. It was on Bridport's flagship, the *Royal George*, that the naval mutiny had started at Spithead the year before.

3. This was in fact a 74-gun ship, the *Hoche*.

4. 'All (Governments of the day) were content to send out press-gangs to gather the men in promiscuously: if necessary, to knock them silly with a cudgel or the flat of a cutlass, and bundle them on board as mere prisoners: prisoners, moreover, without trial and with no time-limit set upon their sentence save only the duration of the War ... Authority often found them surly and recalcitrant ... Then it had to impose on them a very strict and sometimes brutal discipline, suitable rather for the gaol-bird than for the free man ... so it flogged them for all sorts of offences serious and trivial alike, often indiscriminately and sometimes ... with a brutality amounting to sadism.' *A Social History of the Navy, 1793–1815*, Michael Lewis (Allen and Unwin, 1960), p. 100.

5. *Ibid.*, p. 324.
6. The reverse of the cutting refers to the vacant throne of Greece.

Chapter 3   Gerald Haxton

1 & 2. The problem was also complicated by the fact that there had been several marriages between the villages of Moulton and Whaplode, for the two are separated by only a few fields. The Reverend William's eldest child, Susanna, had married Edward Smith of Whaplode in 1785, and one of his grand-children, Lucy Eleanor, a daughter of Thomas Marmaduke the cabinet-maker, married Emanuel Andrew of Whaplode in 1833.
3. It was an interesting letter, and I only wish I had time and space to go into the history of that particular branch of my family, one of whom – yet another Theophilus – emigrated to New Zealand in the 1870s.
4. Penguin ed., p. 135.
5. *A Writer's Notebook*, W. Somerset Maugham (William Heinemann, 1949). The book is dedicated: 'In Loving Memory of My Friend FREDERICK GERALD HAXTON, 1892–1944'.

Chapter 4   The Emigrants

1. Born March 25, 1834.
2. There was a second reason for the threat of war. During the Canadian rebellion against England two years previously in 1837, some Americans – without the approval of the United States government – were giving assistance to the rebels. In retaliation for this, on December 29, 1837, a Canadian force crossed into American territory and captured and set fire to the gun-running American paddle-steamer *Caroline* and sent her toppling over Niagara Falls. The dispute became more intense three years later in February 1841 when a Canadian, who had boasted on American soil that he had killed one of the crew of the *Caroline*, was convicted of murder. The prospect that the Canadian might be executed brought from Lord Palmerston, the British Foreign Secretary, a threat of 'war immediate and frightful in its character'.
3. The letter is undated, but it was most likely written in the late summer of 1839.

Chapter 5   Early Maughams

1. Quoted in one of three small ruled exercise-books which were lent to me by the headmaster of Appleby School.
2. Then known as Battleborow or Battleborough.

3. This is borne out by Robert Maugham's will, made in 1814, which describes him as 'of Battleborow in the parish of St Michael Bongate otherwise St Lawrence Appleby . . .'

4. The original 'Brough Stone' was bought and presented to the Fitzwilliam Museum, Cambridge, in 1884. I am grateful to Mr Richard Nicholls, the present Keeper of the Museum, for his free translation of the inscription which I have quoted.

5. I also told Lady Lowther that I had recently been in touch with Mr C. Roy Hudleston, the Society's Editor of Transactions. Many years ago and unknown to me, he had tried to establish our pedigree. Mr Hudleston had written that 'the number of Maughams in Westmorland, Cumberland, Durham and Northumberland proved unexpectedly large and the same Christian names kept cropping up'. He added, 'Unfortunately, I found that the more I knew, the less I knew!'

6. Routledge and Kegan Paul (London, 1958).

Chapter 6   The Breakthrough

1. The registers also mention his younger brother William and his sisters Catherine and Jane.

2. Census Returns for 1851.

3. I think that William Maugham the clerk, of Chancery Lane – Willie's great-grandfather – died before 1814, as there is no reference to him in the will of his father, Robert the glazier of Appleby; and if he had been alive then his father would almost certainly have mentioned him – if only to cut him off with a shilling. I think also that he married Catherine Harrison before he came to London, and that she too was born in Westmorland, for I saw several Harrison tombstones in Appleby. That she was the mother of Willie's grandfather is proved by his baptismal entry and by a 'certified true copy' among my papers of an entry in a family Bible, inscribed 'Catherine Maugham, The Gift of her affectionate son, R. Maugham'.

4. We found a reference to their son William, also baptised, like his cousins, at St Dunstan's in the West, in August 1789; and the church has an entry in its registers for the christening in 1785 of the daughter of Jonathan Maugham, an attorney – perhaps another cousin from Westmorland – who was living in Clifford's Inn, one of the legal seminaries which was once attached to the Inner Temple.

5. This was the letter in which Theophilus Maugham the sailor thanked his brother William for 'the things which You was kind enuff to Send me'. See p. 24.

6. There was another remark in this letter about Christmastide that puzzled me at first. William wrote: 'I wish you could get such another Goose as that which the Major sent last Xmas, or a fine Turkey. He promised to send me another. If you see him, jog his memory.' Several months later we discovered that the Major was Robert Tutt, a brother of 'Uncle Tutt'.

7. The third and last letter that I have from William the hatter is dated February 12, 1805. He wrote to his father in Moulton to express 'uneasiness' that the old gentleman was 'so very indifferent' in health, and hoping that he would regain his strength 'as the fine weather advances'. Then comes a reference to the Tutts: 'My Aunt and Uncle are both pretty well, he is quite free from the gout.' (But 'Uncle Tutt' was to die eighteen months later.) The letter ends with a reference to Hannah and their son, who was then five and a half years old. 'My wife desires to be kindly remembered to you, and Bill sends his Duty. Thank God they are both well.'

8. The Rate Books are kept in the archives at the Westminster Public Library.

9. To these four Inns of Court were later attached subordinate 'Inns of Chancery' such as Clifford's Inn and Staple Inn.

10. By William Albert Samuel Hewins, the political economist and historian.

11. The royalist Élie Decazes, favourite of Louis XVIII, lately raised to the rank of duke and sent into 'honourable exile' as Ambassador to Great Britain.

12. Robert Maugham records in his diary that 'Lord Ellenboro' & Mr Parke were among the passengers' on the *Lady Cockburn*. Lord Ellenborough had lately succeeded his father, the Lord Chief Justice of England, who had died two years before, and he was to make his own mark as a rather unusually pompous Governor-General of India; and 'Mr Parke' was almost certainly James Parke, later Baron Wensleydale, who had just appeared before the House of Lords as one of the junior counsel in support of the Bill of Pains and Penalties against Queen Caroline, the unhappy consort of King George IV. The King, who had succeeded to the throne on January 29, 1820, had made two previous attempts to rid himself of his German wife. This time he enlisted the help of the Government, who instituted proceedings in the House of Lords against her for adultery in an attempt to secure her divorce. But the popular feeling was so strong in her favour that the Bill of Pains and Penalties was eventually dropped. King George and his ministers were saved from further embarrassment when Queen Caroline died on August 7, 1821.

13. An Inn of Chancery attached to Lincoln's Inn.
14. I am indebted to the Law Society for permission to quote from the *History of the Law Society*, by Pretor W. Chandler, privately published in June 1925, to celebrate the centenary of the Society's work.
15. *The Summing Up* (Penguin ed.), p. 13.
16. By H. W. Pickersgill, R.A.
17. *Outlines of Character*, Robert Maugham (Longmans, 1823).
18. Mrs Foster wrote in her letter that her grandfather, Thomas Maugham, had been 'sometime secretary' to Frederick Gye the younger, the great impresario of Covent Garden, who was responsible for the success of the Italian and later the German opera in England, and who 'launched' such famous singers as Patti, Lucca, and Albani who married his son Ernest Gye. Thus Thomas Maugham met many of the stars and prima donnas of the day, and when he and his wife emigrated to Brisbane in the 1880s they took their love of music and the theatre with them. Their grand-daughter, Mrs Foster, was before her marriage a lecturer at the Conser-vatoire of Music in Sydney; her family possesses many old programmes, 'elaborately printed', of the operas the Maughams had enjoyed in Lon-don; and she remembers her grandmother talking of first nights of Gilbert and Sullivan at the Savoy, and hearing Albani and Giuseppe Mario – 'the divine Mario' – singing at Covent Garden. So here was another interest – an interest in music – that had somehow crept into the Maughams since they came south from the bleak fells and misty valleys of Westmorland.
19. It has now been removed to Surrey and is one of the most famous public schools in England.
20. Isabella Sarah Wilks was probably a godmother to Robert's and Mary's eldest daughter Isabella, and certainly a fairy godmother to all the Maugham family, whom she treated much more generously – to the tune of about £500 each – than she did her own children, one of whom became notorious as a swindler. This was John Wilks (died 1846), one-time Member of Parliament and journalist, but better known as the promoter of a number of fraudulent companies which earned him the nickname of 'Bubble Wilks'. Mrs Wilks may have been a satisfied client of Robert Maugham's, or she may have been related to his wife Mary. Her husband, who survived her, was an attorney in Finsbury Square, and his father was the celebrated nonconformist preacher Matthew Wilks. Whatever the connection may be, Mrs Wilks undoubtedly approved of the Maughams as deserving of her fortune.
21. His first mention in the archives of the General Register of Shipping and Seamen, at Cardiff, shows that Frederic Maugham had previously served

in the *Calcutta*, from December 1853 until July 1854, when he joined the *Prince* with the rank of 'Purser'.

22. *The Summing Up* (Penguin ed.), p. 162.

23. Barbara Sophia von Scheidlin was born in Nuremberg on August 6, 1827, and it appears that her life was in danger because she was baptized only thirteen days later, at home. Her parents had been married at the famous Protestant Lutheran church of St Sebald, on May 1, 1816. I wish to thank Mr Patrick Montague-Smith, editor of *Debrett*, Herr Walter von Hueck, archivist of the Deutsches Adelsarchiv in Marburg, and the archivist of the Landeskirchliches Archiv in Nuremberg, whose researches have enabled me to trace the von Scheidlin family through several generations of bankers and market managers (Marktvorsteher) in the city of Nuremberg, back to Barbara Sophia's great-great-grand-father, Johann Kaspar von Scheidlin (1701–1762). I understand that a complete genealogy of the family is given in *Genealogisches Taschenbuch der adeligen Häuser Österreichs*, edited by H. W. Höfflinger (Vienna, 1911), vol. iv, pp. 413–424.

24. St Thomas's Church stood on the north side of Breams Buildings, to the east of Chancery Lane. The church no longer exists and the parish is united with that of St Dunstan's-in-the-West.

25. This was only five days before old Robert Maugham died, but the event must have been unexpected, as it would hardly have been seemly for the family to celebrate a marriage if their father was known to be near to death.

26. It seems that the two families were on the most intimate terms. The friendship began with Henry James Dixon and his wife Jane and Willie's grandfather Robert and his wife Mary. H. J. Dixon was a freeman of the City of London and a member of the Painters Stainers Company, and one of his ten children, William, was of an age with Willie's father Robert Ormond Maugham. In his will, H. J. Dixon mentioned his 'most esteemed friend, Miss Julia Maugham'; and Julia was godmother to one of his grandchildren – Helen Julia, whose father was Frederick Dixon, a surgeon in Hove. Among the few papers we have been able to trace that relate to those days there is a facetious poem which old H. J. Dixon addressed to Julia Maugham in December 1865, when he was seventy-six and she was thirty-three. The poem is on the curious subject of 'Feet', and concludes:

> My rhymes seem halting in their measure,
> So take away or add a foot or two at pleasure,
> Your pretty little feet may make them go more steady;
> I fear that *I* have put my foot in it already.

27. I am greatly indebted to Mr A. D. Macleod Robinson, of Messrs. Dixon Ward & Co., of The Green, Richmond, Surrey, for information on the Dixon family. This firm, whose links with my family go back more than a century, passed from Albert Dixon, at his death in 1915, to two of his sons, Albert Henry ('Bertie') Dixon, who died in 1938, and his half-brother John Dixon, who died in 1958, with both of whom Mr Macleod Robinson was in partnership. They once acted both for my uncle Willie and his eldest brother, Charles Ormond Maugham, and the firm is still associated with the successors of 'Maugham et Dixon' in Paris.

Chapter 7   The Maughams in Paris

1. All we can discover of Charles Snell, Junior, is that when he was married at Vellore on January 11, 1840, he was described in the register as 'a native of Madras', and he was thirty-eight years old when he died and was buried at Cuttack on March 5, 1857. He then held the post of Senior Sub-Assistant Surveyor, and I think his death must have been due to cholera or jungle fever or some other endemic disease. The Indian Mutiny and the consequent slaughter of Europeans did not erupt until some weeks later.

2. The record of Charles Snell's service given in the Indian Index at the Society of Genealogists differs slightly from the information I have quoted, which was obtained from the Indian Records Section of the Commonwealth Relations Office, London.

3. The curious can read all about it in *The Genealogists' Magazine* for June 1952, in which, as I mentioned in Chapter 1, Mr Patrick Montague-Smith has traced the 'Two Royal Descents of Viscount Maugham, Lord Chancellor, and Mr W. Somerset Maugham'.

4. There appears to have been a close friendship between the Somerset and Todd families. In the *Commander-in-Chief's Papers* at the War Office there is an interesting personal letter, dated April 1, 1828, from Lord Charles Henry Somerset to his brother Lord Fitzroy Somerset (then Military Secretary to the Duke of Wellington), recommending the purchase of an ensigncy for young Francis Todd, then aged eighteen. The two families may also have been linked in marriage, as the name Lovell is common both to the family of Frances Heathcote, who married General Sir Henry Somerset in 1817, and to the Todds. A certain Lovell Todd, 'of a Durham family', was born in Falmouth in 1767, and it is an added coincidence that two of his own children were born at Pendennis – more than forty years before Francis Todd came to the Castle. Lovell

Todd was connected for some years with the Falmouth Mail Packet Station, in whose records he is shown as captain of the *Hanover*, in 1795, and of the *Prince of Wales*, in 1799; and he also bought several estates in Cornwall at the end of the eighteenth century.

5. There is a postscript to the Somerset story that is worth mentioning. Some time ago a gentleman in New Orleans wrote to Willie's publishers, Doubleday & Company, and the letter eventually came to me. The writer was Mr Earl L. Maugham, and he wished Willie to know of the birth of his son, in July 1962, whom he had given the second name of 'Somerset' after his 'famous cousin'. Unfortunately, I was not able to prove any close link – though a link obviously exists – between my branch of the family and this Mr Maugham, whose great-grandfather emigrated from England to America about 1813. But I was fascinated by the fact that a boy in New Orleans in the mid-twentieth century should inherit a name, all unsuspecting, from a bewhiskered old soldier who, in his own dashing youth, had fought on the field of Waterloo.

6. Among the Brereton papers in his possession, Mr Patrick Montague-Smith came on two transcriptions of extracts from letters written by Mrs Snell, concerning the early days of her marriage. The first shows that she and the major 'spent some months' in Exeter, at No. 3 Baring Place – 'such a pretty house & so comfortable'; and the second refers to the four-month-long voyage to India, which I suppose was in 1838. It was an unfortunate time to choose, for Mrs Snell was pregnant. Either she was innocently unaware of her state or she tried to conceal it until almost the last moment. When she endured terrible toothache she did not realise that the cause was probably due to the calcium deficiency associated with pregnancy. 'I suffered so much,' she wrote, 'that the ship's surgeon took them out on the voyage to India. Had it been known, I might have kept them, for I was in an *interesting* position and was confined two months later of a dear little baby who just breathed and died. They told me the Capt. baptized her Frances, but I was insensible at the time and of course knew nothing.'

7. From the Register of Baptism for 1840, at the Commonwealth Relations Office, London.

8. In the archives of the town hall of St Servan there is a record of a concession bought by Mrs Snell for Rose's grave, on March 13, 1869 – the day after her death. The plot was rented for fifteen years, and later renewed for a further fifteen years. The librarian in St Servan kindly searched for the site of the grave, in the hope of finding a headstone, but there was no trace of it. By 1899 Mrs Snell was herself old and ill, so perhaps she forgot to renew the concession; and so, as is the custom in

France, Rose's body would have been exhumed and her bones buried in a common grave.

9. *The Summing Up* (Penguin ed.), pp. 14–15.

10. The street has twice been renamed since 1880, and the house was demolished and rebuilt in 1930. The site is now 25 Avenue Franklin D. Roosevelt.

11. For this and subsequent quotations from my father's autobiography, see *At the End of the Day* (Heinemann, 1954), pp. 3–18.

12. His elder brother, William Dixon, had died on February 6, 1867.

13. *Show*, June 1962.

14. Isabella Frances Sophia, daughter of Herman Merivale, Permanent Under-Secretary of State for India.

15. William Peere Williams-Freeman. Born October 16, 1834; married, April 15, 1863; died September 18, 1884. According to the *Foreign Office List* for 1884, he held many junior posts in the Diplomatic Corps, at Stuttgart, Copenhagen, Dresden, The Hague, and Washington, before going to Paris in 1873. Apparently he was 'unemployed' from August 1878 until September 1881, when he 'resigned' – probably due to illness – but his family remained in Paris for several years. (His great-grandfather, Admiral of the Fleet William Peere Williams, adopted the additional surname of Freeman in 1822.)

16. *Somerset Maugham. A Biographical and Critical Study*, Richard Cordell (Heinemann, 1961), p. 3.

17. February 1, 1882.

18. February 6, 1882.

19. February 2, 1882.

20. These few quotations from French sources were traced after intensive searching by the Office de Documentation of the Société des Amis de la Bibliothèque Nationale, who examined no less than twenty-eight biographies of Mérimée, Doré, and others, and also several French journals and periodicals covering the period from 1863, when my grandparents were married, until 1882, when my grandmother died. My debt to the Office de Documentation is considerable, as their patient researches have enabled me to evaluate my grandmother's standing in Paris society, instead of glibly repeating the usual well-worn phrases that have found their way into countless biographies of my uncle Willie.

21. Willie himself, in *The Summing Up*, gave his mother's age at her death as thirty-eight, and this has been repeated by his many biographers. The explanation may be due to the fact that on the death certificate of her last child, Edward Alan Maugham, as entered in the *Minutes des Actes* of the Préfecture de la Seine (of which I have a copy), her age is also given as

thirty-eight. But it is clear from the Register of Baptism at the Commonwealth Relations Office, London, that she was born on May 10, 1840. So she died only three and a half months before her forty-second birthday.

22. The Hon. Alan Percy Harty Molyneux Herbert, son of the third Earl of Carnarvon. He was physician to the famous Hertford British Hospital in Paris, founded by Sir Richard Wallace in 1871; and he was decorated for his services to the English poor during the siege of Paris and afterwards. For some reason Mr Herbert later declined to act as an executor of my grandfather's will. He died in 1907, aged seventy.

23. The French death certificate, of which I have a copy, states that he died on June 24, at 5 p.m., and this is confirmed by the certificate I obtained from Somerset House.

Chapter 8   Willie's Schooldays

1. In the preface written for the Penguin edition published in 1963.
2. Pp. 13–21.
3. At Pluck's Gutter, about eight miles north-east of Canterbury, on a branch of the Stour river.
4. *Somerset Maugham, a Biographical and Critical Study* (Heinemann, 1961), p. 12.
5. Hugh Walpole's diary quoted by Rupert Hart-Davis in *Hugh Walpole, a Biography* (Macmillan, 1952), p. 316.
6. *Cakes and Ale* (Penguin ed.), pp. 10–15.
7. *The Fine Art of Literary Mayhem*, Myrick Land (Hamish Hamilton, 1963).
8. Charles Evans, Chairman of William Heinemann, Ltd., the publishers of *Cakes and Ale*.
9. *The Fine Art of Literary Mayhem*.
10. *W. Somerset Maugham, A Candid Portrait*, Karl G. Pfeiffer (W. W. Norton & Company, Inc., New York, 1959), p. 97.
11. Rupert Hart-Davis, pp. 21–22.
12. The foundation of the school is, of course, much earlier, and historians have traced its descent from the seminary established in Canterbury by St Augustine at the end of the sixth century.
13. The first sentence of *Catalina*, 1948.
14. The first sentence in English of *Then and Now*, 1946.
15. Published by Fisher Unwin in 1898.
16. *Classics and Commercials. A Literary Chronicle of the Forties*, Edmund Wilson (W. H. Allen, London, 1951).
17. Originally written for the *New Yorker* magazine, June 8, 1946.

16

18. In Mr Malcolm Cowley's review of *The Razor's Edge* in *The New Republic*, for instance.
19. *The Condemned Playground, Essays: 1927–1944*, Cyril Connolly, Routledge, pp. 253–254.
20. In his preface to a new edition of *Liza of Lambeth*, published in 1934.
21. Bishop Ernest Roland Wilberforce, d. 1907.

Chapter 9   Willie at the Vicarage

1. *Cakes and Ale* (Penguin ed.), p. 59.
2. A recent letter from Mrs Nesfield mentions this prize. 'Mr Smith has since given the book to Dr Nesfield. It has the Vicar's writing and commendation inside. We are vastly amused that this book – the adventures of a Muslim boy – was thought suitable for a divinity prize.'
3. The cause of death on his death-certificate is 'Hypertrophy of the Prostate Gland several years. Chronic Cystitis about 2 years.'
4. In Mr Richard Cordell's introduction to *Of Human Bondage*.
5. The first Mrs Maugham was Miss Charlotte Etheridge's godmother, and the Vicar was her brother John's godfather.
6. *A History of All Saints' Church, Whitstable*, by I. W. Green. (Elvy Bros., Whitstable.)
7. Archibald Campbell Tait.
8. She died at Bad Ems in Germany on August 26, 1892.
9. Penguin edition, p. 20 and pp. 554–555. It is very odd that Willie never corrected this mistake, which has persisted since the first edition of 1915.
10. In *The Summing Up* (Penguin ed.), p. 15, Willie wrote that his mother in her letter asked the Vicar to be godfather 'to one of her sons'. But in *Of Human Bondage* (Penguin ed.), p. 554, Philip says that the letter 'was about himself'.

Chapter 10   Family Ties

1. 'I give and bequeath to my nephew William Somerset Maugham my leasehold house of No. 20 Westbourne Street Hyde Park but subject to and charged in exoneration of my residuary estate with the payment of an annuity of ten pounds per annum to Mrs Ellen Maugham for her life being an obligation I have undertaken for the benefit of my said nephew . . .' (See also second footnote in Appendix V.)
2. I am indebted to Mr and Mrs Helmut Gernsheim, the distinguished photography historians, who put the date of the photograph 'in the early 'eighties' – when the Reverend Henry Macdonald Maugham was

aged about fifty-three. But when I was staying with Willie for his ninetieth birthday and showed him the photograph he did not recognise it.

3. Mr Cordell also states that Willie's brother went to Eton (*Somerset Maugham. A Biographical and Critical Study*, p. 6). But he was in fact educated at Dover College.

4. Cordell, p. 6.

5. Born in London on June 12, 1909, and christened Charles Ormond Beechey Maugham.

Chapter 11   The Lord Chancellor

1. For an account of my father's undoubted skill as a lawyer, see Appendix VIII.

2. 'The separate ownership of royalties had been found to be a deterrent to the proper working of the industry, and while the ownership of coal was to vest in an independent statutory body, it was proposed to buy out the royalty owners by distributing to them as compensation a global sum. The sum in question represented 15 years' purchase of the average annual income and amounted to £66,450,000.' *Lives of the Lord Chancellors: 1885–1940*, by R. F. V. Heuston (Clarendon Press, 1964).

3. *Ibid.*, pp. 554–555.

4. *At the End of the Day*, p. 396.

5. Towards the end of her life my much-beloved sister Kate Mary Bruce wrote the first draft of a short book mainly about the Romers and the Bruces – which she intended to revise. The provisional title was *Family Group*.

6. *At the End of the Day*, pp. 24–26.

7. Written in *The Times*, October, 1950, when Asquith was a Lord of Appeal in Ordinary.

8. A. A. Milne, in *The Times*, October 1950.

9. The whole article is reprinted in Appendix IX.

10. *At the End of the Day*, p. 22. This statement is in curious contradiction with my father's earlier remarks on Albert Dixon, one of his two guardians, and on the happy vacations he spent with his aunt and uncle at Paston, near Peterborough. See first footnote in Appendix V.

11. *Ibid.*, p. 59.

12. Three generations of Romers became Lord Justices. I think that all three of them in their day were offered the position of Master of the Rolls and declined it.

13. When I wrote *Nomad*, I had not included Churchill's crack about my father's loving the Germans because my father was still alive, and I thought it might have irritated him.
14. *The Truth about the Munich Crisis.*
15. *The Chequer Board*, by Kate Mary Bruce (Heinemann).

Chapter 12 Willie's Last Years

1. Penguin ed., p. 192.
2. P. 335.

Appendices

APPENDIX I

In September 1962 I wrote to Sir Anthony Wagner, Garter Principal King of Arms, asking him if he could arrange for me to be helped in my task of trying to discover some information about my family coat-of-arms and crest.

He replied as follows:

Since I see that the last edition of Burke's *Peerage* does not assign you any arms, it rather looks as though no right had been established at that date and that if there is one it must depend on carrying the line back to a very early armigerous ancestor. That being so, what is wanted in the first place is a general search in our records to see what light they throw on the situation and if you care to let me have the sum of £30 on account of the work, I will have this put in hand.

After further correspondence I received the following letter:

The search has now been made and the results I am afraid are disappointing. The Arms shown in your photograph are not on record at all, and it looks as if this is a piece of amateur invention done for some member of your family by somebody in the past. A faint glimmer of light is thrown on the situation by the fact that a notoriously unreliable book entitled Fairbairn's *Book of Crests* gives in its 1892 edition a crest for Maugham (not further identified), a lion's gamb erased holding the hilt of a brown sword in pale.

Now your example shows a lion rampant holding in the paw the hilt of a broken sword in pale, so that the same mind may have been at work on the two versions.

With this result before me I thought it best to carry the search a little further, and have established that no Arms of any kind are on record for any family of Maugham.

This, at all events, clears the air and makes it plain that your proper course is to apply for a Grant of Arms in the ordinary way, and for this purpose I enclose a form of Petition. The fee on the Grant including the Supporters appropriate to a Peer is £222. 10s. 0d. to which £12 has to be added if you wish to have an illuminated heading to the Patent rather than the less attractive printed heading. If you would like me to proceed I suggest that you sign the Petition and return it to me with a cheque for the fee, payable to the College of Arms, and a note of any views you may have in regard to the design. Failing any such views I shall be happy to make suggestions.

The 'form of Petition' is written in such splendid language that I cannot resist quoting it:

To His Grace
  The Duke of Norfolk, K.G.,
    Earl Marshal and Hereditary Marshal of England.

My Lord Duke,
  I have the honour to represent unto Your Grace that it being a privilege of the Peers of this Realm to bear Supporters to their Arms as well for their greater honour and dignity as to distinguish them from persons of inferior rank and His late Majesty King George VI having been graciously pleased to create my late father Frederic Herbert Maugham a Peer of the United Kingdom by the name style and title of VISCOUNT MAUGHAM I therefore have the honour to request that Your Grace will be pleased to issue your Warrant to Garter Principal King of Arms for his granting and assigning such Supporters as may be proper to be borne and used by me and such of my descendants as the said Dignity may hereafter devolve upon and also the Kings of Arms for their granting and assigning in the same Patent such Armorial Ensigns as may be proper to be borne and used by me and my descendants.

                    I have the honour to be,
                      My Lord Duke,
                        Your Grace's obedient Servant,

I never sent the Petition, and I never sent a cheque for £222. 10s. 0d. nor the extra £12 for 'an illuminated heading to the Patent', and so I am a Peer without a Coat-of-Arms and without Supporters.

APPENDIX II

Although I have never been able to prove the link between Mr Ralph S. Maugham's and my branch of the family, the physical resemblance, which must have endured through many generations, is so remarkable that I feel justified in including an account of our researches into the matter.

At the time of my uncle Willie's trolley-car ride up the Hudson in 1910, his American 'cousin', Ralph S. Maugham, senior, was half-way through his devoted career, which lasted forty-four years, as Tenafly's 'beloved schoolmaster'. This life-work was crowned in 1929 – three years before his death – when the town honoured him by naming its handsome new grade school, the 'Ralph S. Maugham School', which I am happy to say still flourishes.

The schoolmaster's father was Joseph Beaumont Maugham. Joseph was born about 1834 and lived with his family in London until they decided to emigrate to New Haven, Connecticut, where they had friends. Joseph and an elder sister, Alice, were sent on ahead, early in the 1850s, and arrived safely; but two younger brothers who followed both died at sea; and their parents, perhaps fearful of risking the voyage, decided to remain in England.

Ralph S. Maugham, junior, described his grandfather as 'a rare character – a soldier and a scholar'. 'In 1860,' he said, 'my grandfather was a married man with one son – who was my father. But he returned to England for about a year, and his voice and his pen were freely used against the Confederate States. And when the Civil War broke out he came back and joined the Union forces, as a private. He fought in several battles, was wounded twice, taken prisoner and then exchanged, and finally discharged with the rank of sergeant-major. After that he turned to teaching, became a professor, and was principal of several schools in New Jersey. He also founded a newspaper, the *Tuckerton Beacon*, and was its editor for many years; but he was no businessman and couldn't save a dime!'

Going back another generation we come to Joseph Beaumont Maugham's parents, Ralph and Charlotte. In the Census Returns for 1841 they were shown as living at 60 Lower Sloane Street, in the London district of South Chelsea; and this was confirmed by the birth certificates, in 1839 and 1842, of two of their six children, which we found at Somerset House. Each of these entries of birth gives Ralph Maugham's occupation as 'Merchant's Clerk'. Twenty years later, when the family had moved to No. 3 Oxford Street –

where his wife Charlotte died on January 30, 1862, at the age of sixty – Ralph is described as 'Paper Maker's Clerk'; and at his own death, on December 24, 1875, when he was living at 24 Winchester Street, in the district of Pimlico, his occupation was given as 'House Decorator's Clerk'. He was then seventy-five years old, so he must have been born in 1800.

Mr Ralph S. Maugham's comment on all this was, 'My sister and I were under the impression that our great-grandfather owned a decorating business at No. 3 Oxford Street. Maybe he did at one time.' But later we discovered in the London Directories that the property in Oxford Street was occupied in 1859 by John Trumble & Company, a firm of wall-paper manufacturers, and in 1863 by Henry Lyons, a clothier. So I had to tell Mr Maugham that his ancestors didn't appear to be any grander than mine; and that his great-grandfather had doubtless been Mr Trumble's clerk for a while, and been given accommodation above the workshop.

All Ralph and Charlotte Maugham's children mentioned in the 1841 Census are given as 'Born in County' – the county of Middlesex; but against the parents themselves are the unhelpful remarks 'Not born in County'. So, remembering that there was some link with Durham, I wrote to Ralph S. Maugham for more information. Back came the answer, 'My sister Elsie Adams recalls that Father said the family came from the village of Fence Houses, which is near the city of Durham. In 1956 she visited England and spent about an hour there. She saw many Maughan tombstones in the cemetery – all spelled with an *n*.'

When I looked at the map, I saw that Fence Houses is not so far from Whitburn, where, I remembered, Mrs Maturin had told me that her grandmother, Jane Maugham, was born about 1812, and I remembered that it is also quite near Newcastle-upon-Tyne in Northumberland where that fashionable Maugham doctor drove out with his carriage and pair and his dalmatians.

The plot thickened when Mr Ralph S. Maugham wrote again from America. His sister-in-law, the widow of his brother Monte, who stammered so badly, had come across a letter written to Professor Joseph Beaumont Maugham in 1910 – three years before his death. It was from the Parish Clerk and Verger of Hexham Abbey in Northumberland, who remarked, 'I noticed you still spell your name Maugha*m*', and continued, 'I find that your uncle, Mr Maughan, was School Master in what was then the Hexham Free School. The building is still standing, but is now used as stables; the house that he lived in . . . is about a hundred yards up the same road and still standing complete. The only position filled by your uncle in the church was that of Superintendent of the Sunday School. Mr Maughan died at Hexham on April 26th, 1852, aged 47 years . . .'

I handed all this information over to a member of the Society of Genealogists, who, after diligent searching, reported that although there was no trace of Ralph Maugham in the registers of Houghton-le-Spring – the parish in which lies the village of Fence Houses – evidence had been found of his schoolmaster brother, Thomas. He appeared in the 1851 census for Hexham as 'teacher in the National School'. And then, 'Born at Bishop Auckland' – which is only about nine miles south of the city of Durham and fifteen from Fence Houses. And in the registers of baptism at the old parish church of St Andrews in Bishop Auckland was the entry, under the year 1805, 'Thomas Maughan, born Sept. 11th, Baptised Dec. 22nd. 7th son of Thomas Maughan, of Bishop Auckland, Blacksmith, by his wife Jane Cheethamall of Witton-le-Wear'.

Thomas the blacksmith was as far back as we could go in our search for the direct ancestors of my American 'cousins'. But we had found that both Maughams and Maughans were numerous in Durham and Northumberland – spelled with either an 'm' or an 'n', almost at the whim, it seemed, of whoever was entering their names in the various records. And we had found that most of them – like my own proved ancestors – were of humble birth and occupation.

APPENDIX III

What became of Lucy Eleanor Andrew? And what became of her descendants?

I had the letters typed out and sent copies to two organisations in Ohio – the Peninsula Library and Historical Society, in Summit County, and the Western Reserve Historical Society, in Cleveland – asking for their help. After much patient research by Miss Harriet Scofield in Cleveland, by Mrs Carmen Jordan in Peninsula, and by other kind correspondents elsewhere in Ohio, this is the story that emerged.

In November 1848 – three and a half years after the death of her husband – Lucy married again. She married an English-born widower, William Bagley, who was also farming in the township of Boston in Summit County. By then her eldest son Manny was almost fifteen, but he must have grown up quickly during the years he had borne the responsibility for helping his mother during her widowhood. Her brother-in-law Robert Andrew, with his weakness for 'that damned infernal liquor', cannot have been much help to Lucy in her troubles. When her son Manny was twenty he married, in 1854, a Frances Gillingham, but I don't think she had any children by him, and she probably died young. Manny Andrew must have moved away from Boston to the village of Pennsville near Twinsburg, closer to Cleveland, for that was the address given by Manny at the time of the Civil War when he joined up together with a third of a million Ohio men and youths who flocked in to serve with the Union Army.

Manny enlisted on August 28, 1861, and he served as a private in Company 'K' of the 19th Ohio Volunteer Infantry. I have no record of his brief military career, but I know that his service took him deep into the Confederate South – as far as Nashville, Tennessee. It was there, on November 10, 1862, that he was honourably discharged because of 'heart trouble and rheumatism caused by exposure'.

When he returned to civilian life, Manny earned his living as a carpenter, and some years later – it must have been in the late 1870s – he married again. His second wife was Rachel Witla, and they had four children. He had returned to Boston, Summit County, by that time, though I presume that his mother was dead by then and his step-father as well.

I might never have known about Manny's military service or about his family had it not been for the lucky find of Mrs Carmen Jordan while she was searching through the records kept at Summit County Court House in Akron. There, under the entries for February 1885, she found the birth, in Boston, Ohio, of Lucy Eleanor Andrews with an *s*, and then in August 1905 her marriage to Edward S. Costello. Mrs Jordan told us that she then 'called the only Edward Costello listed in the Akron telephone directory and was answered by Mrs Costello'. Yes, said Mrs Costello, her Christian names were Lucy Eleanor, after her grandmother, her parents were Emanuel and Rachel Andrew (without an *s*), and her step-grandfather was named Bagley. So Mrs Costello, who lives with her two daughters, Kathryn and Mary, in Sand Run Road, Akron, is a great-great-granddaughter of the Reverend William Maugham of Moulton. Unfortunately she has little recollection of her father. Mrs Costello wrote to say that when her mother Rachel died in 1890, she and an elder brother, Fred – some of whose children now live in Alliance, Ohio – were placed in the Orphans' Home in Xenia, which is down in the south-west of the State. She knew that her father lived on for some years, and that he 'died at the State Soldiers' Home near Sandusky'. But from the day they entered the orphanage, 'the children never saw or heard from him again'.

A few weeks later, after exchanging several letters across the Atlantic, I heard from Major John W. Parker, the Commandant of the Ohio Soldiers' and Sailors' Home at Sandusky. He had taken great trouble to search his records and trace the end of Manny's story – which was unknown even to his children. Major Parker also sent me a brief history of the Home. The idea for it was first raised in 1886, when 'a very fine and patriotic group of people in Ohio' decided that their State needed a Home 'which would care for its Honorably Discharged Soldiers and Sailors who fought in the Civil War, and who were disabled to the extent that they needed some help'. A big site was eventually chosen close to the shore of Lake Erie, three miles south of Sandusky, and the first seventeen old soldiers and sailors were admitted when the Home was opened on November 19, 1888. Since that day, more than twenty thousand veterans have been admitted – the most recent being those disabled in the Korean War – and nearly three thousand of them are buried in the Home's Cemetery.

Like Mrs Costello, I had supposed that her father must have entered the Home soon after 1890, when Manny's wife died and he put his children into the orphanage at Xenia. I was surprised to learn that he was not admitted until January 30, 1906. One can only wonder how Manny fared during those sixteen lonely years. His admission papers show that he received a pension of twelve dollars a month and that he was troubled with 'Sciatica Rheumatis and Chronic Nephritis', and this was confirmed by the surgeon of the Home's Hospital, who added that 'he suffers from conditions of old age'.

Manny was then almost seventy-two. But despite the 'conditions of old age', he was evidently restless, because he walked out of the Home only a few months later and went to do farm work for a family named Libbey, in Bedford, a few miles outside Cleveland. Major Parker tells me that there is a letter in his files which was written by Nina B. Libbey on April 28, 1907, 'advising that Mr Emanuel R. Andrews was staying with them, doing farm work; that he would like leave or his discharge with the provision he could return at any time he wished'. So Manny was discharged from the Home at Sandusky on May 1, 1907.

Manny was certainly a tough old soldier, but by the time he reached the age of seventy-four, farm work had become a little too strenuous – even for him – and he returned to the Home and re-joined his former comrades at Sandusky in April 1908. Two years later, at half-past four in the afternoon of December 11, 1910, he died there of meningitis. He was buried in the Home's cemetery – a long way from the flat fields and woods with their snowdrops and daffodils and 'all sorts of tulips and crocuses – blue, white and yellow' that surrounded his native village in Lincolnshire.

APPENDIX IV

I owe a considerable debt of gratitude to Dr P. H. Reaney, the distinguished etymologist, for the patience and scholarship with which he examined each possible derivation of our family name, and for guiding us to what I think is the most likely source – Malham and Kirkby Malham in the West Riding of Yorkshire.

Dr Reaney began by demolishing the cherished belief of my American namesake, Ralph S. Maugham, that 'the first Maugham' was groom to William the Conqueror. He wrote sternly, 'There cannot be any truth in this claim. The groom's surname, if he had one – which is doubtful – is unknown and would certainly have been French, which Maugham cannot be.'

He then dealt with the two 'Maugham' place-names in Cumberland – *Pow Maughan* and *Maughonby* with their possible Old Welsh origins: 'In my opinion there can be no connection with Cumberland place-names. *Maughonby* is a very late spelling for a name originally spelled with the root *Merch-*, and one we should certainly not expect. We should need, too, evidence that the personal name involved remained in use in the 13th and 14th centuries and underwent the same peculiar changes as in the place-names.'

Then he mentioned the Irish theory. Dr Reaney thought that 'this might be a possible origin, but proof would require 12th–14th century examples, clearly derived from a personal name, with some evidence that the personal name was used in England.' He suggested a study of the name and its variants in Edward MacLysaght's *Irish Families*, a standard work published in 1957 by the former Chief Herald of Ireland.

Here, under the heading, 'MacMahon (Mahon, Vaughan)', we are told that this name comes from *MacMathghamba*, which is said to have derived from the Irish word for 'bear'. The name is borne by two distinct clans: one, chiefly associated with County Monaghan in Ulster, and the other, more important and more numerous, belonging to County Clare. They descend from Mahon, son of Murtagh Mor O'Brien, King of Ireland, who died in 1119, and their last chief fell at the battle of Kinsale in 1602. Here indeed is an origin I should love to claim, but I defy any Maughams to find the twelfth to fourteenth century evidences which are so necessary if we are to prove kinship with the Bear King of Ireland.

According to MacLysaght, the name *Mahon* – although sometimes an abbreviation of *MacMahon* – is also borne by two distinct clans, one in South Galway and the other in County Sligo. This surname – properly Ó *Mochdin* in Irish and *Mohan* in English – spread into Munster where it was anglicised into *Vaughan*. (This Vaughan is Irish of Gaelic stock and not of the same origin as the Celtic Vaughan of Welsh descent.) MacLysaght also mentions the variant *Maughan* as being found in County Mayo; but my hopes in this direction were curbed by Dr Reaney, who wrote, '*Maughan* as a name may be Irish, but to prove that the *Maugham* family is of Irish origin requires a specific Irish connection.'

Next, Dr Reaney considered a possible connection with Scotland, and suggested that we should look at families in Lanarkshire and particularly in the old parish of Machan, now called Dalserf. This was quite a new idea; but, undaunted, we consulted the best authority on Scottish origins – George Black's book *Surnames in Scotland* (published in New York in 1946). And there we found Machan, a very small estate in the Vale of Clyde, and we noticed several references to men who bore the name and variants of it as early as the thirteenth century – Adam *Machan* in 1203, Thomas *Machan* in 1262, Sir Adam de *Mauchan* in 1300, David de *Machane* in 1367, John *Mauchan* in 1548, and so on up to the end of the seventeenth century. The variant *Mauchan* seems very close to *Maugham*; but we had to limit our researches when we realised what a vast amount of time would be necessary to discover whether, and if so when, any of this Scottish family crossed the Border and settled in the northern counties of England.

I should mention, however, that Dr Reaney was inclined to think that this Scottish name might be linked with a single family found among the Free-men of York in the fifteenth and sixteenth centuries – Richard *Maghan* in 1476, Alexander *Mawghan* in 1519, John *Mawgham* in 1537, and Ralph *Magham*, son of Alexander *Magham*, in 1559. Now both entries for Alexander identify him as a locksmith, so within forty years we have a variation in spelling and also what Dr Reaney describes as the 'not uncommon change of final *n* to *m*'.

Finally Dr Reaney dealt with our most recent research which had been prompted by the finding of those names, de *Malgham* and de *Malghum*, in Yorkshire, which Dr Reaney considered 'must derive from Malham or Kirkby Malham in the West Riding'. He explained that though the 'usual pronunciation' is *Malham*, the name was 'sometimes pronounced *Mawm*'. He added that though he could not 'give a definite etymology for Maugham', a search of the local documents in Yorkshire might prove 'fruitful'.

We might of course have searched for years, and our search would have been complicated by the fact that there are many seventeenth, eighteenth, and nineteenth century examples of our family name in both the North and West

Ridings of Yorkshire as well as in Cumberland, Westmorland, Durham, and Northumberland. But this time we were lucky. In the Library of the Society of Genealogists we found a rare and valuable book, *The Parish of Kirkby Malhamdale*, written by John William Morkill, and published in 1933. The author is described on the title page as 'Lord of Calton and other Manors', and he must have had a very personal knowledge of this beautiful part of Yorkshire, with its famous wildfowl reservation, Malham Tarn. The book was printed after his death by George Bellows in Gloucester, and there is a preface by his widow showing that the book was the result of many years of interest and research. And it is from this book that I shall quote, with grateful admiration for the author's devotion to his task.

It seems that the greatest historical figure from the parish of Kirkby Malham was General Lambert, one of Cromwell's most valued supporters until he fell from favour. The manors in the parish were held by his family for more than two centuries. But much of these lands derived from the ancient estates of the *de Malham* family, or *de Malghum*, as their name was written in old Latin charters quoted by Mr Morkill. He wrote of the practice that began in the thirteenth century when landed families began to assume the name of the vill or lands which they held. This, he said, explained the fact that two or more brothers in the same family would adopt different surnames. Then, 'Malham, written in Domesday, Malgum, and in post-Domesday charters, Malghom or Malghum, is thought by Whitaker[1] to have been "so called from the monosyllabic name of its original possessor in Saxon times" (the "ham" or settlement of Malgh). He is, perhaps, correct, and I have found no alternative etymology suggested.' Then comes Mr Morkill's most interesting comment, which supports Dr Reaney, 'A local contraction of the name is "Mawm", but I have not met with this form in any document.'

It is not easy to extract the few facts we need out of a book that is, genealogically speaking, rather technical, and more than three hundred pages long. We must concern ourselves chiefly with the descendants of William de Malham, or de Malghum, who in the fourteenth century acquired through marriage the Manor of Calton – one of the eight townships within the parish of Kirkby Malhamdale – and also estates in Norfolk. Mr Morkill wrote, 'The forbears of William de Malgam . . . had long been seated in the neighbouring vill of Malham, from which their surname was obviously derived . . . They were a family of local importance to whose generosity the Abbey of Fountains owed no small share of its possessions in Malham . . . William and Alice Malham were the founders of a family which flourished at Calton for more than two hundred years, and during that period occupied a leading position in the dale.'

[1] In his *History of Craven*.

The Malhams might still be occupying 'a leading position in the dale' had it not been for those internecine quarrels that so often menace what are politely called the 'landed gentry'. The familiar pattern of deaths and claims and counter-claims so divided and weakened the family that by the end of the sixteenth century all their estates in Kirkby Malhamdale had been acquired by the Lamberts. (It is worth noting that one of these latter Malhams was christened Marmaduke, which may possibly explain why the Reverend William Maugham of Moulton chose this name for one of his sons.)

This sudden ending of their long association with this corner of the West Riding may account for the fact that the local parish registers, which have been printed by the Yorkshire Parish Register Society for the years 1597 to 1690, show practically no reference to the old landed family of Malham or Malghum. And as the later records have not been published, it would be necessary to search the original registers, or any surviving Bishops Transcripts at York, for any later traces of the family. But we do know – from Boyd's *Marriage Index for Yorkshire*, in the Library of the Society of Genealogists – that a William Maugham of Kirkby Malham married in 1698 an Elenor Hind. (I have sometimes wondered if this might be a very early marriage of William Maugham of Brough, for he had a daughter Elenor who was baptized in 1711. But the wife who was buried at Brough in 1717 bore the name of Ann.)

To carry one stage further this quite plausible theory that the Maughams may have originated in the West Riding of Yorkshire, we must move six miles east of Kirkby Malham to the village of Linton. Here, in the parish registers, which have been printed from as early as 1588 until 1812, the name *Mangham* occurs frequently; and there are at least three entries – obviously for the same family – where the name is written *Maugham* – in 1603, 1604, and 1607. Also, the Christian names have a familiar ring – Simon, Robert, William, John, and Christopher. We had found the marriage of a Simon Maugham in the registers of Brough for 1671. And my great-great-great-great-grandfather, William Maugham of Brough, had a son Christopher who was baptized in 1716.

In these Linton registers, the rector who transcribed them (the Rev. F. A. C. Share, M.A.) gave the variants of Mangham as *Manghan, Mangan, Mongam, Mongham* and *Moungham*; and as I have said, there are at least three entries under Maugham, though this variant is not in the index. (This change from *n* to *u*, between text and index, occurs elsewhere, and I noticed an instance of it when I searched some registers in the library at Penrith.)

Two facts clearly emerge from all these researches. The first that the Malham or Malghum family of Kirkby Malhamdale sometimes pronounced their name 'Mawm'. And the second is that *all names* have gone through certain changes in both spelling and pronunciation – even as late as the eighteenth century. At a time when few people could read or write, the parish clerk or the curate – the latter not always familiar with local families – wrote down the nearest equivalent to the sound of the name that he thought suitable. These entries were often made in rough note-books, and later transcribed on to sheets of parchment that were sent up to the Bishop at the end of the year. Thus more errors might creep in. Even in the calendars of a will, a name might be spelled one way in an index, another in the margin of the will, and still another in the will itself. Within my own family, William Farringdon Maugham, the hatter of Covent Garden, appears in some old London Directories as Maughan; his cousin, William Maugham, baptized at Appleby in 1759, was entered as Maughan in the registers; and even today, many of my friends still pronounce my name 'Maughan'.

In spite of this confusion between Maughan and Maugham in the northern counties of England, and in spite of the possibility that some Maughans – perhaps an entirely different family from my own – may claim kinship with the Mahons and MacMahons of Ireland, I feel sure that my forbears, for many generations before the birth of William Maugham of Brough, have their roots deep in the earth of Malhamdale. And beyond that, like most other English families, we are lost in the mists of antiquity.

APPENDIX V

Of the three surviving daughters of Robert Maugham of the Law Society the one that interests me most is Julia.[1] She remained a spinster till the end of her days, and I remember Willie telling me that there was 'something strange about great-aunt Julia'. When Robert Maugham died in 1862, his widow moved from Chancery Lane to 20 Westbourne Street in Paddington,[2] and for more than twenty years Julia looked after her elderly mother. When Mary Maugham died on September 18, 1874 – her death was caused by a carbuncle – Julia was forty-two years old. Her sudden independence must have released a long-stifled urge for adventure. She made several visits to Africa, and I believe that it was in equatorial climes that she met a young man named Reginald Charles Fulke Greville. We do not know how they met; nor do we know why they became friends. But we do know that some years later, in 1905, Fulke Greville changed his aristocratic-sounding name to Maugham. He was in fact young enough to be Julia's son; and perhaps I malign both of them if I impute any other motive in their relationship. No doubt he welcomed the companionship of a woman considerably older than himself. Certainly he cannot have enjoyed much maternal affection during his boyhood, for he was illegitimate.[3]

[1] The others were Catherine Louisa, a spinster, who died on February 5, 1884; and Isabella, the eldest, who in 1862 had married the Rev. William Andrew (born 1820), the first son of the Rev. James Andrew of Whitby, Yorkshire. William Andrew, who had been a Fellow and Tutor at Worcester College, Oxford, became rector of Paston in Northamptonshire and an honorary Canon of Peterborough. (Although Paston is only about thirteen miles from Moulton and Whaplode in Lincolnshire, I found no evidence to link this Andrew family with Emanuel Andrew, the husband of Lucy Eleanor Maugham – see Chapter 4.) My father in his autobiography, *At the End of the Day* (p. 20), recalled the happy holidays from school that he spent at the rectory with Isabella and William Andrew, who had no children of their own and gave him 'all their affection'. When Canon Andrew died in 1891, only a few months after his wife Isabella, he left five hundred pounds to my father whom, as he wrote in his will, 'we have regarded and loved as a son'.

[2] The lease of this house in Westbourne Street was eventually bequeathed by my great-aunt Julia to my uncle Willie. See footnote 1 to Chapter 10.

[3] We found the clue in the certificate of his first marriage, in 1884, where his father is given as 'Reginald James McCartney Greville (deceased)', formerly a captain in the

Reginald Charles Fulke Greville had a distinguished career in the Consular Service; he became well known *after 1905* as an author, and as a zoologist, and he lived to the ripe old age of ninety. But for the last fifty-one years of his life he went by the name of Reginald Charles Fulke Maugham. His entry in old issues of *Who's Who*[4] tells nothing of his parentage or his change of name; we are given only the date of his birth, August 19, 1866. By patient searching, however, we found a small paragraph in *The Times* for October 12, 1905, in which he gave notice that, by Deed Poll, he had assumed and intended 'henceforth on all occasions and at all times to sign and use and be called and known by the surname of "Maugham" only, in lieu of, and substitution for' his 'present surname "Greville".'

Julia Maugham's friend was twice married, first in 1894, when he was still Mr Greville and using two additional Christian names, Algernon and Cecil.

[4] The entry in *Who's Who* for 1954 reads: 'MAUGHAM, Reginald Charles Fulke, C.B.E. 1927; F.R.G.S.; F.Z.S.; *b.* 19 Aug. 1866; *m.* 1st, 1894, Alice Anne Jane, *d.* of late Dr T. Smith-Hewitt, Winkfield Lodge, Windsor (marriage dissolved 1905); 2nd, 1907, Hilda Wollaston, *y.d.* of late John Greene, of The Panels, Bury St Edmunds, Suffolk. *Educ.:* privately. Served in Inniskilling Dragoons; Secretary to the Nyasaland Administration, 1894; British Vice-Consul at Blantyre, 1896; at Chinde, 1897; at Quilimane, 1898; Consul at Beira, 1902; at Lourenço Marques, 1908; and at Antofagasta (Chile), 1912; Consul-General, Liberia, 1913–20; Consul-General, Dakar, Senegal, 1920–28; present at storming and capture of Chikala, 1894; took part in the Southern Angoni Expedition, 1896 (British Central African medal and clasp 1894–98, and Queen's South African war medal); Gold Medallist, Société d'Histoire Internationale, Paris. *Publications:* Portuguese East Africa, 1906; A Handbook of the Chi-Makua Language, 1909; Zambezia, 1910; Wild Game in Zambezia, 1913; The Republic of Liberia, 1920; Africa as I have Known It, 1929; Nyasaland in the Nineties, 1935; The Island of Jersey Today, 1939; Les Bêtes Sauvages de la Zambezie, 1939; Jersey under the Jack Boot, 1946.
Recreations: gardening, literature. *Address:* Spring Bank, Vallée des Vaux, Jersey, C.I. *T.* Central 815. Club: St James'.'

Brigade of Guards. He was thus a direct descendant of Fulke Greville, 5th Lord Brooke (died 1710), and a kinsman of the Earls of Brooke and Warwick. *Burke's Peerage* shows that Captain Greville was born on November 27, 1848, the fourth son of the first Baron Greville of Clonyn, County Westmeath (created 1869); that his only marriage was in 1871, to Louisa Maud, sister of John Lord Churston, and that he 'died without issue' in February 1878, at the age of twenty-nine. (He was noted as a trainer of horses and as a gentleman rider, known to his friends as 'Limb', and his death was caused by a fall in a steeplechase at Sandown Park.) No mention is made of the youthful indiscretion, when he was barely seventeen years old, that led to the birth of his illegitimate son in August 1866.

His marriage certificate then describes him as being in the service of the British South Africa Company; but at that time he was on leave in Brighton, at 20 Arundel Street, and his bride was living at the same address. She was Alice Hewitt, aged twenty-one, whose father, then dead, had been a doctor in Windsor. What is curious is that they were married without ceremony in the Register Office at Brighton; whereas thirteen years later – two years after they had been divorced and he had changed his name to Maugham – his second marriage was 'solemnised' with the full religious ceremony at a church in South Africa. This was at St Cyprian's, the Anglican church in Durban, in August 1907. The bride was Hilda Wollaston Greene, 'daughter of the late John Greene of The Panels, Bury St Edmunds', and the local paper[5] described it as a 'Fashionable Wedding', followed by luncheon to one hundred guests at the Marine Hotel, after which the couple left 'on a short tour through the South African Colonies to the Victoria Falls of the Zambezi', on their way to Beira in Mozambique, where Mr Maugham was then stationed as British Consul.

So there is the mystery – still unsolved. My great-aunt Julia died in 1910, but there was no mention of Reginald Charles Fulke Maugham in her will. Eventually R. C. F. Maugham and his second wife retired to St Helier in Jersey, where he wrote a book on the German occupation, *Jersey under the Jack Boot*, and he died there on December 10, 1956. Many people still living there remember him as Mr Maugham; but no one was able to shed any light on his change of name.

[5] *Bury Free Press*, September 28, 1907.

APPENDIX VI

Francis Todd – Willie's maternal great-grandfather – was described as 'a gentleman of high respectability'; he owned considerable family property in Yorkshire, and had business interests in both London and Manchester. He also had a special interest in metallurgy: the County Archivist at Truro told us that he came to Cornwall 'to work the Baldhu and other mines', and in 1840 he published a paper entitled *Improvements in obtaining Silver from Ores and the Matters containing it*.[1] Mrs Snell later recalled that her family came to Falmouth in 1835, though it is not exactly clear when they moved into Pendennis Castle; but we do know that Francis Todd was eventually allowed to lease Castle House, the Governor's residence, in order to oust a troublesome general who refused to leave when his appointment was terminated. At that time Pendennis was no longer regarded as an important military fortress, and Francis Todd took possession of the Castle House, together with the 'Castle Garden and Hospital Field', for an annual rental of only twenty-five pounds.[2] A few years later he foolishly invested his private fortune in a local tin mine that failed; and he retired to London, where he died, in Ebury Street, in 1851.

Francis Todd's family background was conventional enough, but that of his wife was quite exciting. She was Caroline Perceval Brereton, born in 1785 – a cousin of Spencer Perceval, the only Prime Minister of England ever to have been assassinated, who was shot as he entered the lobby of the House of Commons, on May 11, 1812. She was a niece of the 'tall, manly, and elegant' Major William Brereton, the intimate friend of Sheridan and Master of the Ceremonies at Bath between 1777 and 1780; and she was a descendant of a family as aristocratic and colourful as the Maughams had been humble and dull.

I was lucky to discover that Mr Patrick Montague-Smith, editor of

---

[1] Reprinted by Eyre and Spottiswoode, 1856.

[2] In the past, Pendennis Castle had boasted both a Governor and a Lieutenant-Governor, but by 1841, when Francis Todd and his family were shown in the Census as occupying the Castle House, the garrison had dwindled to the size of a platoon, under the command of a fifty-nine-year-old lieutenant who was designated the 'Barrack Master'.

Debrett, was not only a distant cousin of mine but that he was also writing a history of the Brereton family.[3] His researches have saved me endless trouble, and my gratitude to him is matched only by my admiration for his intimidating genealogical trees and copious notes, which helped me to follow the story back nine centuries, since the time when one Ralph, 'a near relative of Gilbert de Venables, who came over from Normandy with the Conqueror', was given lands in Cheshire, from which he took the name of Brereton, 'the settlement in the briars'. From then on, the Breretons have 'ever been warriors' – in the Crusades, the campaigns of Edward III, under Henry V at Agincourt, the siege of Harfleur, at the Battle of the Spurs in 1513; in Ireland, where some of them settled, during the reigns of Henry VIII and the first Elizabeth; in the Civil War – in which they fought on *both* sides – and in every other conflict up to the most recent times. One Brereton was beheaded in the Tower of London for 'consorting with Queen Anne Boleyn'; and another, during that turbulent age, murdered with his own hands two of the family of O'Neill, the rulers of Ulster, after they had been his unsuspecting guests at supper. Their story is one of feuding and fighting all the way. Even the elegant Brereton who succeeded in Bath to the 'vacant throne, once possessed by Beau Nash', was skilled in the use of the sword, and his younger brother Robert Brereton, a captain in the 49th Foot, served, at the Cape and in Jamaica, during the Seven Years War against France.

*

Caroline Perceval Brereton, Willie's maternal great-grandmother, was born in Jamaica. She was the youngest child of Robert Brereton's third wife, who was nearly forty years his junior and younger than her own stepson. Life in the colony then must have been pleasant enough for the Europeans, and Robert Brereton was fortunate in having chosen as his second wife the daughter of a wealthy landowner who had a great house and two thousand acres, 'abounding with slaves'. While she lived, he rose in esteem, as a politician and as a judge. He owned a town house in Kingston and a 'pen' in the country. But after she died he squandered her fortune, and after his own death in 1790 Caroline and her sisters were brought back to England by their young mother, who soon married again. And in 1808, at the age of eighteen, Caroline married Francis Todd.

[3] All the information in this appendix and in chapter 7 on the Brereton and Todd families, quoted or otherwise, is based on Mr Montague-Smith's manuscript.

APPENDIX VII

Mrs Snell's will led us to another discovery – a big pile of letters that she had sent to her niece Mabel Yarde, the daughter of Henry Somerset Todd.[1] The letters, written in purple ink on paper with wide black Victorian edges of mourning, cover the last years of Mrs Snell's life and they reveal her curious love for Mabel Yarde – the niece whom she had only seen once, as a baby, when she last visited England in the summer of 1865. Perhaps for this very reason they are also full of the inmost thoughts and confidences that are often easiest to tell to strangers. Few of the letters were dated, and most were difficult to decipher, but the picture that emerged was one of a sad old lady who could not pluck up the courage to come home to England and who was utterly neglected by her own grandchildren – with the possible exception of Charles Ormond Maugham, and even he seems to have acted towards her more from duty than devotion.

The letters begin about 1889, when Mrs Snell was living at 118 Rue Chanzy in Le Mans. She congratulates Mabel Todd on her 'engagement to Mr Yarde', and then writes 'Had you been a child of my own I could not have been more delighted . . . I am particularly glad you are marrying a clergyman as it is what I have always wished for you.' But there is a slight note of anxiety that Mabel, in her new happiness, should not forget her 'old Auntie who loves you so much'. Then comes the first mention of her unhappy old age. 'My hands are so swollen I have quite a difficulty to write tonight.'

There is a slight similarity between Mrs Snell's letters and those I have quoted earlier from Emanuel Andrew in Ohio, for both reveal their isolation from their families at home and their growing despair. Just as Emanuel struggled to keep his farm going, so Mrs Snell also tried to keep her hands and her mind lively, writing more children's novels and weaving pictures in tapestry. 'I still do large pieces of work and am now busy with the great picture of Pontius Pilate washing his hands,' she writes in one letter to her niece. 'My days are not half long enough. All the light hours from 12 to 4, I work at Pilate. At 5 I dine and then work and write till eleven and often later. I sleep very badly, and if every minute of the day were not so occupied so as to prevent my thinking, I should go mad.' She adds, 'Sometimes I can

[1] The letters were shown to the author by the late Miss Dorothy Yarde, grand-daughter of Henry Somerset Todd.

neither work nor write as my fingers swell up so, and also my hands.' And in another letter she writes, 'I am far from well and am suffering very greatly. The pains are fearful when they come on and make me scream with agony. It comes on so suddenly and goes away as suddenly as it comes. It has lasted 5 hours today. It is terrible to suffer as I do, but God knows best . . .'

Sometimes there are flashes of anger. 'So somebody has thought fit to write to me at last!' Sometimes, touches of humour. 'The people here think I am so stupid because I like boiled mutton and turnips.' Very rarely, there are expressions of pleasure, such as on October 22, 1900, when she mentions her eldest grandson, Charles Ormond Maugham: 'My Charlie, his wife and 3 little girls are all coming down to see me. I shall be so pleased . . .' And sometimes there is a comment on the war in South Africa, or a snippet of local news. 'There have been two dreadful murders,' she wrote one day, 'and I fear there will be two executions in Le Mans. My servant declares she will go & see them. The women here are really *brutal* in all their ideas. I do not know which is the worse – Guillotining them or tying them to a tree and shooting them *dead* like dogs. I think the head sergeant has to fire a revolver into the culprit's ear in case he is not dead. I'll never live in a garrison town again, for although I do not *see* these things, I hear so much about them and dream of them all night.' But such goings-on, gruesome or otherwise, did not hold Mrs Snell's attention for long, and the theme of illness and loneliness predominates in all her letters. I think the most pathetic of them all is the one in which she wrote, 'I never look out of the windows, and I hate seeing all the happy families on Sundays and holidays.'

The librarian at Le Mans discovered that Mrs Snell left her house at No. 118 Rue Chanzy in about 1900 and then moved into one of the ten apartments at No. 34 Rue Gastelier. There she died, on October 24, 1904, at the age of eighty-nine. Apparently her death had been expected for some time, because an English friend in Le Mans, Eliza Fowkes, had taken up the correspondence with the niece in England and was also in touch with Charles Ormond Maugham in Paris. Miss Fowkes described the last scenes on a postcard that she sent to Mabel Yarde on October 26. She wrote, 'I send you a card as I promised, to tell you we laid your dear Aunt to rest yesterday in the Public Cemetery here. Mr and Mrs Maugham came by early train from Paris . . . We met at the house – your Aunt's few friends, several co-religionnaires and many of the people living in the same house. Mr Farques, the pasteur, had a little service at the house – we then all walked to the Protestant Church for a service and then to the Cemetery. We had fine weather. We intend going very soon to arrange the grave . . . Mr and Mrs M. were obliged to return to Paris by 7 p.m. but they are coming again in about a fortnight to decide about things . . . The coffin was not closed down till after the grand-children's arrival. She looked sweet and calm to the last.'

*

Mrs Snell's life and her death pose several questions that have never been answered. For all her complaints of loneliness, she was constantly attended by a servant, Marie, by whom she was 'most carefully nursed' to the end. But she must have been sadly aware that her own family paid little attention to her. So far as I know, neither Willie nor my father nor their other brother Harry ever troubled to visit her – though she was their only surviving grand-parent – nor did any of the family bother to renew the concession on her grave, because in 1924 her body was exhumed and 'her ashes scattered to the wind'. The librarian at Le Mans informed me that 'the place where she was buried has since been used four times'.

The real mystery concerns her estate. I have seen several letters exchanged between her niece Mabel Yarde and Charles Ormond Maugham, and it seems that neither of them got their inheritance because poor old Mrs Snell – in Charles's words – was 'one of those people who can never make ends meet.' Several pawn tickets were found in her apartment; and she had borrowed a considerable sum of money against her insurance policies with the Caisse Générale des Familles – a firm which went bankrupt shortly before her death. The result was that Mrs Snell's executors were liable to pay back the full amount borrowed, plus interest, to the creditors of the insurance company; while the company itself was expected to pay a dividend of only fifty per cent. Charles Maugham wrote, 'Of course, everything will have to be sold and the proceeds paid to the creditors'; but as he doubted whether a sale would raise sufficient money, he advised Mabel Yarde that 'the best thing will be for you and me to leave the estate entirely alone'.

Mrs Snell's possessions did in fact raise the necessary money. The sale was arranged, in two auctions early in 1905, by 'les domaines' (the state organisa-tion responsible for the clearance of estates); and the proceeds – so Charles Maugham must have presumed – should have gone to the creditors of the bankrupt insurance company. But almost sixty years later I learned that the money had never been claimed. The librarian in Le Mans told me that it 'represented quite a capital . . . the equivalent of a very beautiful car'.

So that is the end of the story of Willie's grandmother, Anne Alicia Snell – the sad, rather embittered old lady living in a garrison town in France, whose death was not given even a line in the local press, whose grave is now occupied by a stranger, and whose estate has never been claimed. I pestered almost every second-hand bookseller in England and France, hoping to find some of her novels for children, but without success. Mégard, her publisher in Rouen, went out of business years ago; and no copies exist in the public libraries of either St Malo or Le Mans. Only in the Bibliothèque Nationale in Paris are there the twelve titles I mentioned earlier – and those archives are as sacrosanct as the British Museum or the Library of Congress. I secretly hoped that Willie had read some of Mrs Snell's stories as a boy, and that they had furnished him with plots for his own novels. I thought it would be amusing to discover that Willie had plagiarised his own grandmother. But since I could not spare the time to make a trip to Paris and spend hours there in the Bibliothèque Nationale, I had to abandon the search.

Then, as so often happened during the writing of this book, I had a piece of luck. Mrs Snell's great-niece, Miss Dorothy Yarde, found a few of the books that had once belonged to her mother. Some of them are in English – tiny little paper-backs published at fourpence by Thomas Richardson and Son of 26 Paternoster Row. But most of them are in French. Half a dozen of her books were reprinted by Mégard et Cie of Rouen in a uniform edition for their Bibliothèque Morale de la Jeunesse in the 1890s – with such titles as *Les Deux Chaumières*, *Les Filles du Capitaine*, *Le Château des Neiges*, and *La Chaumière Suisse*. I have read a few of them, and I can understand why they were successful as children's books in those days, for they are a mixture of tender piety and romantic heroism, and the engravings are delightful. Willie may have read some of the volumes as a child – but no one can suggest that his own works were influenced either by the style of his grandmother's works, or by their moral content.

APPENDIX VIII

I am grateful to Mr Heuston, author of *Lives of the Lord Chancellors, 1885–1940*, for permission to quote the following account of my father's handling of the famous 'Northcliffe Will' case.

Maugham was also concerned with the lengthy proceedings which followed the death of Lord Northcliffe and the struggle for the acquisition of his shares in *The Times*. On the one hand there was Northcliffe's brother Rothermere, and on the other hand there was the family of John Walter which had printed and published *The Times* for several generations, and was now anxious to regain control in order to conduct the newspaper on traditional lines. Rothermere possessed the advantage of having a large sum in ready money wherewith to purchase the shares, but Walter had the advantage of having an option under the will of Northcliffe. The option itself, however, was of somewhat dubious value, because the will could or might have been contested on several grounds. In addition time was running against Walter because the break-up of the coalition Government, a few months after Northcliffe's death, had vastly increased the value of the shares and, in consequence, the sum to be found by him. It so happened that the fate of *The Times* was decided on the same day as the fate of the coalition Government itself, Thursday, 19 October 1922. By lunch-time it was known throughout London that the Government was out of office as a result of the vote at the Carlton Club meeting that morning. At 2 p.m. all parties appeared in court before Sir Henry Duke, the President of the Probate, Admiralty and Divorce Division. Maugham appeared for Sir George Sutton, the administrator of Northcliffe's estate. It was known that Rothermere was prepared to offer an exceedingly high sum for the shares. After a lengthy argument Maugham rose to say that it had occurred to Sutton and his advisers that Walter's option might be recognised in this sense, that instead of having three months in which to make up his mind, he should be obliged to decide within a very short period.

'Of course, if it is asked why he should do that, the answer is, because it is not certain that he has any rights at all. If there is to be any dealing with this interest at all, it is a case where, it seems to me, both sides may very well be advised to make something in the nature of a concession to the other. If, by reason of any opposition, the thing should not go through, it may be that Mr Walter will lose all his rights. That is, to some extent, a matter of gamble, of which I know nothing.

'What I was going to propose was this: if Lord Rothermere exchanges with the administrator, subject to your Lordship thinking that it is a proper course, a contract conditional to the sanction of your Lordship of the contract for the purchase of the whole of the shares at the price in question – there is no objection to my stating the figure.'

A breathless moment then ensued in court; no objection was stated, and Maugham proceeded with, according to the official historian of *The Times*, 'a sentence that astounded the Court': 'The figure suggested is £1,350,000 payable according to the terms of the document before me, as to £500,000 within fourteen days of the Order approving this agreement, and the balance at certain other dates.' This was indeed a stupendous sum and the time stipulated for finding the money was short in the extreme. Nevertheless, with the assistance of the Astor family, the money was found by John Walter and the shares of *The Times* passed out of the control of the Northcliffe interest. A great national institution had been saved.

APPENDIX IX

From *The Granta*, March 1, 1889.

THOSE IN AUTHORITY

At the Union

MR FREDERICK HERBERT MAUGHAM is one of the best specimens of the all-round man that Cambridge can show at the present time. He honoured Paris by choosing it as the scene of his entrance into the world nearly twenty-three years ago, and ever since that memorable event there has clung to him a certain aroma of Parisian delicacy and lightness which he is accustomed to renew and increase by frequent visits to his birthplace. None of the large public schools can claim him as a pupil, but in spite of this (or shall we say in consequence of it), he obtained a scholarship at Trinity Hall, in 1885, and faring onward on his Academical voyage, eventually came to anchor in the second class of the Mathematical Tripos of last year. So much for Mr Maugham's scholastic achievements. As a rowing man, he has climbed to an even dizzier pinnacle of excellence. It would be tedious to recount all his aquatic performances from the moment that he first took his seat in a Fresh-man's tub, to the present time. Suffice it to say that he helped the Hall second boat to win the 'Ladies' at Henley, in 1887, by occupying what sporting reporters are wont to term the sixth thwart, that he has twice rowed in the Head of the River Crew, once at No. 3, and once at No. 7, and that he steered the Hall Four to victory in the Cambridge Fours last year in the fastest time on record, having previously won the Stewards at Henley. But, of course, his greatest watery triumph is his performance in the University crew of last year. Cambridge clamoured for a No. 7. Several had been tried and found wanting, when suddenly Mr Maugham appeared, and in his quiet and deli-cate fashion effected an entrance into the crew. Rowing men at first mis-trusted, but soon they marvelled, and finally grew enthusiastic, and in the meantime the small gentleman who had so much moved them continued to row with the length of a giant and the regularity of a pendulum. His swing was as steady as the gait of an Esquire Bedell, and as slow as the mental process of an Essex peasant, whilst his work was as vigorous, and his endur-ance as inexhaustible as the port-consuming capacities of his College Combination Room. This year he is once more at his old place, and again he is one of the mainstays of the crew. We have considered Mr Maugham as a scholar and an oar. Let us now turn to another side of his versatile character. Not satisfied with reading and rowing, he determined to speak as well. The members of the Union appreciated the grace of his mellifluous accents, they were charmed with his silvery periods, and applauded to the echo the burning passages in which he descanted on the virtues of the Conservative Party. There are some who assert that Mr Maugham deals in sentences as long as his swing, there are others who accuse him of primness in his elocution; but these, we may be sure, are but the forgeries of jealousy. Be that as it may, his fellow members have installed him in one Union Office after another, until, at the end of last term, they elected him to a permanent place on the beadroll. of fame, and a temporary occupation of the Presidential Chair. He has since filled it with a dignity and decorum eminently satisfactory to his admirers, and to all who have striven to catch his eye.

Moreover, Mr Maugham is a supporter of music. He sings a good song, in which he proves conclusively that whatever sobriety his friends may have observed in his habits, drinking is the only occupation suited to an Undergraduate and a human being. He can play the piano, and has frequently been known by the aid of this instrument to soften the manners of his friend and fellow lodger, Mr Orde, and prevent them from becoming fierce. He is also a member of the 'Ermine', which he hopes some day to wear. He has often been epigrammatic, and sometimes sarcastic, but he has never said an unkind word, or done an unkind action. His good sense is as strong as his manners are gentle, and his friendship as valuable as his presence in a crew. He is a universal favourite, in spite of his universal success. He has a supple body, but unbending principles, and is an emphatic exception to the general rule, which has defined a *charmant garçon* as one *qui avait tous les vices*. Cambridge admires him. He returns the compliment by admiring THE GRANTA. He is mostly called 'Freddie'.

INDEX